Francophone African Women Writers

UNIVERSITY PRESS OF FLORIDA

Gainesville   Tallahassee   Tampa   Boca Raton

Pensacola   Orlando   Miami   Jacksonville

**IRÈNE
ASSIBA D'ALMEIDA**

FRANCOPHONE

 AFRICAN

WOMEN WRITERS

DESTROYING

THE EMPTINESS

OF SILENCE

Copyright 1994 by the Board of Regents of the State of Florida
Printed in the United States of America on acid-free paper

99   98   97   96   95   6   5   4   3   2

Library of Congress Cataloging-in-Publication Data
Almeida, Irène Assiba d'.
Francophone African women writers: destroying the emptiness of
silence / Irène Assiba d'Almeida.
p.   cm.
Includes bibliographical references and index.
ISBN 0–8130–1302–X
1. African literature (French)—Women authors—History and
criticism.   2. Feminism and literature—Africa—History.   3. Women
and literature—Africa—History.   4. Women—Africa—Intellectual
life.   I. Title.
PQ3980.5.A46   1994
840.9'9287'096—dc20   94–26083

The University Press of Florida is the scholarly publishing
agency for the State University System of Florida, comprised
of Florida A & M University, Florida Atlantic University,
Florida International University, Florida State University,
University of Central Florida, University of Florida,
University of North Florida, University of South Florida,
and University of West Florida.

University Press of Florida
15 Northwest 15th Street, Gainesville, FL 32611

A l'affectueux souvenir de Thérèse Tossivi Kpénou
et de Philippe Tossou d'Almeida, ma mère et mon père
et qui ont trop tôt rejoints les Ancêtres et qui sont
pourtant si près, si près de moi.

A ma grande Sênami, ma fille, rayon de soleil
dans mon coin de ciel.

A toutes les femmes d'Afrique qui ont levé la voix,
tracé la voie et continuent de lutter pour
"tuer le vide du silence."

*To the fond memory of Thérèse Tossivi Kpénou
and Philippe Tossou d'Almeida, my mother and father
who, too soon, returned to the Ancestors and
yet are so close, so close to me.*

*For Sênami, my daughter, a ray of sunshine
in my corner of the sky.*

*For all the women of Africa who have paved the
way, raised their voices and are still struggling to
"destroy the emptiness of silence."*

CONTENTS

Contents

PREFACE

The earliest impulse to write this book came from a paper I delivered at the annual African Literature Association Conference at Madison, Wisconsin, in 1991. The paper was entitled "La Prise d'écriture des femmes africaines francophones" [The 'taking of writing' by Francophone African women writers]. This "taking of writing" in the sense of a militant appropriation of the written word began, I believe, with Kuoh-Moukouri, who published *Rencontres essentielles* in 1969. (See note 1 in the introduction for documentation regarding this matter.) That first book was an opening for the new literature by women, which became a prominent part of Francophone African writing during the 1980s and has grown tremendously in quantity and in quality since then.

Working on that first paper was a real blessing, for I became enthused and inspired by the women's writing, which constitutes one of the most significant recent developments in the history of African literature. My renewed interest in this body of writing in turn caused me to probe the conditions of women's appropriation of the written word and the female authors' own awareness of their new roles as writers, as women, as Africans. I also became aware that there was, in English, very little criticism of this work, no extensive study, and certainly no book entirely devoted to Francophone African women from Africa south of the Sahara. This critical silence, coupled with the lack of translation of their literary production, meant that women's work was still invisible, still immersed in silence for a considerable part of the world, even including the African world. I strongly felt this critical void needed to be filled, and that need became a primary reason for writing this book.

The new literature of African women represents all literary genres but in this book I have chosen to concentrate on autobiography and on the novel, though even this limitation of the subject left me with a complicated task of selection and organization.

Francophone African women writers from different parts of the continent have different intellectual, social, and religious backgrounds; they hold various ideological stances; they are endowed with different writing skills. Yet they also have much in common: they share a history of colonialism, they generally live in highly patriarchal societies, and their life experience is informed by the fact that they are women. Because of the complexity of these related situations, I have had to problematize inclusive terms such as *African, feminism, Francophone*. I had to discuss feminism, for example, as it is perceived and used in contemporary Africa, showing for instance how a writer like Werewere Liking offers means of reconceptualizing feminism in African terms.

I have concentrated on a few novels representing a spectrum of women writers. I approach these novels through three social categories, beginning with a representation of the self, moving to women's position in the family, and concluding with the writers' concerns for society as a whole. The complicated nature of this deceptively "simple" model is explored in my concluding remarks. As for my remarks on methodology, I have been careful to point out that any criticism of African fiction must take into consideration not only the "written page" and the literary theory it requires, but also the "unwritten" background to be found in the intersection of culture, history, and politics. I also reflect, in closing, on my own position as a critic, born and raised in Africa, now living in North America, often finding myself at crossroads, in an "insider-outsider" position.

Yet, above and beyond the diverse problematics posed in this book, I wanted to "destroy the emptiness of silence" in the same way that Francophone African women writers do. That is why, though I have written this book with my colleagues and students in mind, it is my hope that it will go beyond the confines of the academic world and reach a more general public. It is indeed important that as many people as possible know that African women have "taken writing" and used this new medium as a liberating force to champion the cause of women and of a new African society. A self-definition and a reconstruction of the African woman, new perspectives in articulating difference, an inventive way of using language, a strong sociopolitical commitment within a femino-centric perspective: these are some of the striking elements that the writings of Francophone African women eloquently offer.

I would like to thank the women's studies program at the University of Arizona, which offered me a Rockefeller Summer Fellowship in 1991. This fellowship was invaluable in the early stages of this work. Among my colleagues and friends, I would like to thank first and foremost Jonathan Beck, who as department chair agreed to release me for the fall semester of 1991 to concentrate on my writing. His interest in my work and his encouragement have been unfaltering all along. I would also like to thank Carole Boyce Davies, Sonia Lee, and Janis Mayes for their readings, suggestions, and sisterly support. My thanks also go to Olabiyi Yai for reading parts of the manuscript and giving me severe but extremely valuable feedback. To Karen Smith, Angene Wilson, and Tina Morton, who read the entire manuscript, I am particularly indebted. This book would not have been possible without the help and support of such good friends as Philip Massey, who saw the difficult beginnings, Poovi Abaglo, who was always there, Sion Hamou, who was the inspiration for the conceptualizing diagrams in the introductory chapter, and Mary Ababio, who kindly offered her expertise in making the diagrams. My deepest gratitude goes to Lee Van Demarr, my editor then, my friend now, for the hard work, the stimulating discussions, the unrelenting encouragement, and the genuine interest in my project. My graduate students I must also thank, in particular Bridgett Longust, who was an extremely helpful assistant to me. I would also like to thank the members of my family on both sides of the Atlantic, especially my sister and dearest friend, Grâce d'Almeida Adamon, for her unconditional emotional support. My thanks also go to my lovely niece, Lucie Viakinnou Brinson, who listened to my frequent gripes and encouraged me all the way. My very special thanks to my loving daughter Sênami, who witnessed the ups and downs, found it hard to be around a writing mother, but who understood.

INTRODUCTION

The subtitle of this book—*Destroying the Emptiness of Silence*—comes from Calixthe Beyala, a Cameroonian writer who, through one of her characters in *Tu t'appelleras Tanga* [Your name will be Tanga], affirms that women must come to voice in order to "tuer le vide du silence" [destroy (literally, kill) the emptiness of silence] (17). The metaphor of silence figured in the title of this book recurs frequently in feminist discourse. Silence represents the historical muting of women under the formidable institution known as patriarchy, that form of social organization in which males assume power and create for females an inferior status.[1]

Prise d'écriture

Reiterating the concern with women's silence acknowledges the fact that if women have made significant social advances by challenge and accommodation, by opposition, resistance, and subversion, their enforced silence—in particular the denial or limitation of their literate expression—remains nonetheless a common and painful reality. This is especially the case in more traditional patriarchal societies, where women's expression has been limited to specific artistic forms. "Destroying the emptiness of silence" is therefore an appropriate metaphor to describe the *writing* of women in Africa. The strength of the verb "to destroy" (or "to kill") recalls a similar figure used by Nawal Al Saadawi, albeit in a different context: "Writing is like killing, because it takes a lot of courage, the same courage as when you kill, because you are killing ideas, you are killing injustices, you are killing systems that op-

1

press you. Sometimes it is better to kill the outside world and not kill yourself."[2] Al Saadawi sees writing as annihilation of silence, as a weapon to destroy the ideas that perpetuate subjugation and inequity. For Beyala, however, silence creates an emptiness generated by the knowledge of one's potential and the impossibility within patriarchal society of fully developing that potential. Women's social possibilities are linked with their ability to articulate their experience, understanding, and desire, an articulation that cannot be realized unless the silence imposed upon these women is destroyed.

I emphasize the *writing* to indicate my particular concern in this book: the void of written literary expression by African women. That void is not evident in orature, in which African women, both as custodians of cultural lore and educators of children, have been the choice storytellers, a role that has been much emphasized, especially by female critics such as Carole Boyce Davies, Mildred Hill-Lubin, and Madeleine Borgomano.[3] Yet women were not only transmitters of orature; many among them were *griottes*,[4] producers and composers of lyrics in the various genres that were open to them. Karin Barber shows the broad scope of women's involvement in the production and performance of *oriki*—a genre of Yoruba poetry—and the title she chose for her book, *I Could Speak Until Tomorrow*, evokes the power of the word that women possess within oral traditions and the limitlessness of expression that accompanies it.[5] Of course, there is a continuum between the artistic modes of speaking and writing. It is significant that in their autobiographies, African writers such as Nafissatou Diallo, Aoua Keita, and Kesso Barry emphasize the role played by their mothers and grandmothers as transmitters of orature.[6] Moreover, in their written work, women such as Mariama Bâ and Aminata Maïga Ka cast *griottes* as characters and thus introduce a new element in African fiction, in which the *griot* was formerly almost exclusively a male character.[7] In orature, even though they could not fully participate in all genres, women's discursive position has been important, a situation almost totally antithetical to that which has long prevailed in literature.

The dynamics of speech and silence are far from being simple and clear-cut. For African female writers, speech and silence are not always antithetical; silence is not necessarily a negative attribute. For instance,

Véronique Tadjo in the context of ritual shows that silence and voice complement and balance each other to form a *parole complète* (total speech) that is at once "silence et verbe, action et inertie" [silence and speech, action and inertia] (*A Vol d'oiseau*, 67). Also, Colette Houéto affirms: "Le silence, chez nous, fait partie de la parole. . . . Le silence parle" [Silence, for us, is part and parcel of speech. . . . Silence speaks] (57). Obviously this is an oxymoron that makes perfect sense when, used as a strategic ploy, silence becomes eloquent.[8] As we will see further on, Werewere Liking advocates silence as a way of finding an inner voice that initiates creativity. This silence has positive connotations because of what it achieves and because it is self-imposed; it involves a personal choice and makes a crucial distinction between the two propositions, "to be silent" and "to be silenced." Whereas the first is voluntary, the second is coercive. It is to the second sense, and in the realm of literature, that the title of this book refers. Here, the emptiness of silence that needs to be deconstructed and destroyed is what has been called "silence in print" (C. Miller, 257).

Beyala's plea to destroy the silence has been uttered by predecessors both within and outside the literary world. One of the most daring voices not only inviting but also aggressively urging women to speak up was that of Awa Thiam. Her 1978 book, *La Parole aux négresses* (translated as *Speak Out, Black Sisters* in 1986), which shocked African women and became the subject of heated debates, opens with the following statement: "Black women have been silent for too long. Are they now beginning to find their voices? Are they claiming the right to speak for themselves? Is it not high time that they discovered their own voices, that—even if they are unused to speaking for themselves—they now take the floor, if only to say that they exist, that they are human beings—something that is not always immediately obvious—and that, as such they have a right to liberty, respect and dignity?" (11).

Women from the French-speaking sub-Saharan areas of Africa have at last responded to Awa Thiam's challenge and are increasingly producing poetry and theoretical and fictional writings; their response, however, is long overdue. Indeed, if modern African literature written in European languages took shape as a corpus in the 1930s,[9] it was not until the late 1960s that Francophone African women began to write.[10] It is, however, only within the last two decades that African women have succeeded in making their voices heard, finding a wide audience among men and women alike, within and outside Africa.[11] Placing women writers among what he calls the "novelists of the second generation," Séwanou Dabla acknowledges the importance of women's entry into the literary world: "Se fait entendre par exemple, et de plus en plus, le témoignage vivant et original des 'paroles de femmes,' qui viennent, de la part des intéressées elles-mêmes, contrebalancer la vision unilatérale que la littérature donnait de la femme africaine" [We hear increasingly, for instance, the original and spirited testimony of 'women's words,' which, coming from women themselves, counterbalances the one-sided view of the African woman hitherto portrayed in literature] (18).

To understand how far women's writing has progressed in the past decades, one might examine the place allotted to women in a few landmark anthologies of earlier Francophone African writing. In 1948, Léopold Sédar Senghor compiled his *Anthologie de la nouvelle poésie nègre et malgache de langue française* [Anthology of the new black and Malagasy poetry of French expression]. This anthology included no female poets because, at the time, there were none in print. Nor would a male writer of Senghor's generation have imagined there should be a place for female poets or novelists. In 1972, more than two decades later, *Who's Who in African Literature: Biographies, Works, Commentaries* (which includes African writers in various European languages) mentioned seven female writers, though only one of them, Annette M'Baye d'Erneville of Senegal, was from the Francophone world. Another decade later, Ambroise Kom edited a *Dictionnaire des oeuvres littéraires négro-africaines de langue française; des origines à nos jours* [Dictionary of black African literary works of French expression; from the beginnings to the present day] (1983), an anthology that included twelve women.[12] Although the number of female poets and novelists was still insignificant, at least quite a number of the critics who contributed to this dictionary were women.

While even a cursory look at these few anthologies demonstrates that women have been lagging behind in literary production—a clear indication of women's intellectual oppression—it does not explain why that lag exists. Several studies, including Mineke Schipper's *Unheard Words:*

Women and Literature in Africa, the Arab World, Asia, the Caribbean and Latin America (1984), Carole Boyce Davies's introduction to *Ngambika: Studies of Women in African Literature* (1986), and Christopher Miller's chapter on Senegalese women in *Theories of Africans: Francophone Literature and Anthropology* (1990), have looked for the explanation. They have suggested two general reasons: colonial ideology and African traditions. Colonial schools were opened to men first, ostensibly in the name of the vaunted *mission civilisatrice,* but actually to suit a specific male-oriented colonial agenda. There were also, within African societies, rigorously defined gender roles that first denied and later only grudgingly allowed women's access to Western education. Thus, when women started to go to school, their education was intended to turn out good wives and mothers, and they were never expected or trained to produce literary works.[13] Even when education became more varied and more sophisticated for women (I am thinking in particular of the convent schools in which the female elite was trained), the writer's gap was not closed.[14] But if it is true that during colonization, women were automatically excluded from the arena of letters by historical, political, and cultural factors, including education and training, certain important questions still remain unanswered: What were the social conditions that made women so vocal in orature and yet so silent in literature? And then, what factors explain the sudden burgeoning of women's writing in the 1970s? These questions and their answers lie outside the scope of my study, though I shall hazard a few suggestions regarding them.

To begin with, although it is appropriate to link orature with women's presence and literature with their absence, the orature / presence proposition must be qualified in the spirit of Eileen Julien, who, in *African Novels and the Question of Orality* (1992), warns against an overromanticization of the oral traditions. As mentioned above, women were vocal in orature, but only in certain genres—poetry, for instance. And even within these genres, only specific forms, such as praise or satirical poetry, were allotted to women. The forms that were canonized, such as epic or divination poetry, were the preserve of men, and Julien is right when she argues that "this hierarchic form [the epic] is tied to nationalistic agendas and military might, which have been and continue to be, for the most part, provinces of patriarchy" (47).[15] The gen-

res reserved for men no doubt required a much longer training, a training which would have removed women from their primary functions:
economic production and procreation. Women did not have the leisure
to indulge in protracted training.

In *Journeys through the French African Novel* (1990), Mildred Mortimer suggests that it was possible for women to begin writing in the
1970s because of changes that occurred in the literary canon, which became more open, more receptive to new writers, new ideas, new literatures. This insight is not really an answer to my question, but a different
way of posing it. The canon does not open voluntarily; it must be made
to open. That is why I term what women writers have achieved in the
world of letters a *prise d'écriture*, a "taking of writing," in the sense of
a militant appropriation or seizing. Indeed, the term prise d'écriture connotes another term, *prise d'armes* (taking up arms), and though I find the
military metaphor unsavory, here to rise up in arms implies a necessary
battle for liberation. It is only by waging such a battle that a break-
through is possible, not depending on the generosity of the dominant
group, but on the deliberate action of those who take up arms to seize
power. For women, then, writing becomes a symbolic weapon, as
Mariama Bâ points out: "Books are a weapon, a peaceful weapon perhaps, but *they are* a weapon" ("Mariama Bâ," 214).

Another important factor in the emergence of women writers might
be the increased presence on African soil of publishing houses. It is striking to see that the largest number of female writers come from Senegal
and Cameroon, two countries having long-established local presses.
These presses are crucial for literary initiative as writers know they will
have opportunities for the publication and distribution of their work.
The emergence of an educated readership that has the means and leisure
to read and values education and literature is also a factor, tied, of course,
to the others. All of these factors have probably contributed to making
the prise d'écriture possible in Francophone Africa, indeed, possible to
such an extent that there exists today a profusion of texts by women.

In 1985, Christine H. Guyonneau compiled a comprehensive, anno-
tated bibliography entitled "Francophone Women Writers from Sub-
Saharan Africa," which included 367 entries for women writers and critics. The increase from earlier anthologies and compilations is remark-

able. This is partly due, no doubt, to Guyonneau's extreme thoroughness; she succeeded in uncovering numerous books and articles that had been published but remained virtually hidden because they had not appeared in any anthology. Also, although the bibliography subject headings list only works by women, some of the critical works, including reviews, essays, and dissertations, are written by men. Nevertheless this numerical increase is a clear indication that today there are more female writers in all genres, and also that women have emerged as a significant group of literary critics. Brenda Berrian's various bibliographies attest to the productivity and vitality of women's writing, one of the most significant recent developments in the history of African literature.[16]

There is no doubt that for the last two decades female voices have sprung up to revive the role women have traditionally played as producers of orature, but that these voices now tell their "modern stories" through the medium of the written word and have, to paraphrase Audre Lorde, transformed silence into language and action.[17] As we have seen, this radical change is due in part to contextual factors.[18] Yet these factors cannot in themselves fully explain the essence of the concept of prise d'écriture, which implies a *volonté de pouvoir*. This determination to take power lies in the women writers themselves, irrespective of contextual contingencies.

Having made a place for themselves in the literary world, women have also begun to express their conception of writing and to demonstrate a new awareness of their role as writers. This represents a crucial step in women's identification as public voices and actors, and in breaking through the wall of silence that has frequently closed off women's experience from general public discussion. For that reason it is useful to examine what some of the writers of this era have said about their new roles. Interestingly, the interview has been the forum through which women have been able to articulate what writing means to them and what they would like to achieve through this new-found medium; interesting, as the interview seems an obvious bridge between oral and written forms of expression. Women writers have given frequent interviews in scholarly journals, but even more frequently in popular magazines such as *Jeune Afrique* and *Amina*, a widely read women's publication. These interviews illustrate the strides made by women not only by becoming writers but also by expressing their conception of their role as writers.

For Calixthe Beyala, writing is a means of finding, of defining one's place in the world. It is an inner probing for self-knowledge. It also constitutes a privileged tool for communication: "Je crois que dans l'écriture, on cherche avant tout à se connaître, à communiquer quelque chose qu'on a découvert et qu'on ne peut garder pour soi. C'est à la fois un accomplissement, une remise en cause permanente de soi et des autres" [I think that in writing, one seeks above all to know oneself, to communicate something that one has discovered and cannot keep to oneself. It is at the same time an achievement and a permanent questioning of self and of others] ("Un nouveau roman," 85).

This quest for self-knowledge has led African women to begin representing themselves in fiction, and to gradually call into question the male view of themselves as mythical and symbolic figures. In reference to this desired transformation, women have emphasized the necessity of abandoning the idealization of women. Indeed, in the fiction written by most males, especially those of the negritude era, women were often idealized, primarily as mothers and also as symbols of Africa. Mariama Bâ forcefully challenged that vision: "Les chants nostalgiques dédiés à la mère africaine confondue dans les angoisses d'hommes à la Mère Afrique ne nous suffisent plus" [We can no longer be satisfied with the nostalgic songs dedicated to the African mother, and confused by men in their anxieties with Mother Africa] ("Fonction des littératures," 7).[19] This challenge was motivated by the fact that when women were not flat, secondary characters, they were placed on a pedestal and idealized to such an extreme as to neutralize their existence as real people. With the prise d'écriture, women were at last, through fiction, able to represent themselves fully and earn recognition as full-fledged human beings.

One way in which women established their new identities as writers was by speaking as *writers* about their craft; for writing is also an aesthetic endeavor, one whose stringent demands Werewere Liking, for instance, may expatiate on: "Je n'ai pas une écriture conventionnelle. Elle est difficile à faire accepter, parce qu'elle travaille sur elle-même en tant que forme d'art. . . . Les écrivains africains se souciaient plus, jusqu'à présent, du fond que de la forme alors que la littérature est un art. Du grand art. Le texte doit atteindre une certaine sensibilité des fibres, plus importante que la soif d'anecdotes" [I do not have a conventional writing style. It is difficult for my writing to find acceptance because it is a work of art that works on itself. . . . Up to now, African writers were more preoccupied with content than they were with form, whereas literature is art—one of the great arts. A text must attain a certain sensitivity of feeling, more important than merely quenching a thirst for anecdotes] ("La femme," 70).

Catherine N'Diaye has reinforced the idea of literature as work *and* as art—a work of art in the complete sense of the word. Asserting that "les professions de foi et les recueils d'anecdotes ne sont pas de la littérature" [professions of faith and collections of anecdotes are not literature] (160), she situates the act of writing in terms that may seem elitist but that, in reality, are concerned with the rigor necessary for writers to succeed in their craft: "En quête d'identité, nos écrivains croyaient souffrir d'un manque. Ils ont cru qu'ils avaient le devoir de répondre à un besoin—de boucher un creux. En fait, ils voulaient inconsciemment, naïvement, oblitérer la littérature. Oublieux qu'ils étaient de ce que le désir d'écrire ne peut jamais naître du simple besoin—de ce que l'art ne saurait surgir d'un manque trivial. Il y a une condition *sine qua non* à l'effet esthétique, c'est cette conversion du besoin en désir. C'est à cette condition qu'on invente une autre beauté" [In the quest for an identity, our writers believed they were suffering from a lack. They believed that they had the duty to respond to a need, to fill a void. In fact, they wanted unconsciously, naïvely, to obliterate literature. They forgot that the desire to write is never born from a simple need—that art can never arise from a trivial lack. The aesthetic effect entails a sine qua non condition, the conversion of need into desire. Only by fulfilling this condition does one reinvent beauty] (159–60).[20]

Aminata Maïga Ka also conceives of writing as a response to a need, as she has testified: "A mon avis, toute personne qui décide d'écrire, et c'est mon cas, le fait uniquement parce qu'elle éprouve le besoin, et c'est comme un appel, comme une piqûre de guêpe, qui l'oblige à se libérer de ce qu'elle ressent en son for intérieur. Cet appel crée un besoin, une nécessité d'*ex*tirper de soi ce que l'on éprouve, d'*ex*poser ses tripes au regard du public. Ecrire, pour moi, c'est *ex*orciser un mal qui est en soi, c'est partager ce que l'on ressent" [In my opinion, every person who decides to write, as in my case, does so solely to respond to a need, and it is like a call, like a sting of a wasp that compels the release of what is felt deep inside. This calling creates a need, a necessity to *ex*tirpate from within what one feels, to *ex*pose one's guts to the gaze of the public. To write, for me, is to *ex*orcise an ill that is within the self, it is to share what one feels] ("L'écriture qui libère," 123; emphasis added).

Like Calixthe Beyala, Maïga Ka stresses the role of writing as communication and sharing. Both Ka and N'Diaye reflect on "need," though they view it differently. Ka's position is illustrated by the metaphor she uses to explain the origin of her need to write; it is motivated by "the sting of a wasp." Thus, Ka is at the stage of the primal need of the writer to express herself, and her choice of words is significant: extirpate, expose, exorcise. The recurrence of the prefix *ex* emphasizes the writer's desire to go out of herself. The movement here is clearly one of *ex*pectoration, whereas N'Diaye's movement is one of elaboration, an indication that in her case, "need" has been at least partially transcended.

Even though I have chosen the preceding quotations to emphasize different topics in women's pronouncements on writing—to show the diversity of concerns, how all these writers are preoccupied with self-knowledge, the questioning of self and other, as well as the aesthetic dimension of writing—they also at least imply the importance of their social context. Focusing on the concept of sociopolitical commitment, Aminata Sow Fall emphasized the social context and function of writing that must accompany aesthetics to create a work of art:

L'envie d'écrire m'est venue petit à petit. . . . Pendant mes études à Paris, j'écrivais des poèmes, des petites choses, mais sans jamais penser que l'écriture serait un jour mon outil de travail. Quand je suis rentrée au Sénégal, j'ai trouvé la société très changée, l'argent était devenu la valeur primordiale, surtout dans les grands centres urbains. Ce que je voyais et que je ressentais m'a poussée à écrire. J'ai voulu exprimer ce que je ressentais, examiner ce que je voyais. . . . Pour moi, l'écriture est un témoignage, un moyen de filtrer la réalité à un moment donné. Ce n'est pas pour dire que l'esthétique n'a aucune place dans la création littéraire; après tout écrire un roman c'est inventer une histoire à partir d'une réalité. Ce n'est pas du reportage. Quant à l'art pour l'art, ce n'est pas mon propos, ce en quoi je me sens en harmonie avec l'esthétique africaine. ("Entretiens," 24)

[The desire to write came to me slowly. . . . When I was a student in Paris, I wrote poems and little things, but I never thought that writing would someday become my stock in trade. When I came back to Senegal, I found the society very much changed; money had become what was most valued, especially in the large urban centers. What I saw and felt drove me to write. I wanted to express what I felt, to examine what I saw. . . . For me, writing is a testimony, a means of filtering reality at a given moment. This does not mean that aesthetics has no place in literary creation; after all, to write a novel is to invent a story based on reality. It is not reporting. But art for art's sake is not my concern and, in that, I feel in harmony with the African aesthetic.]

In sociological essays dealing with women's "place" in society, mention is often made of a dichotomy between private space and public space. Yet beginning with Michelle Zimbelist Rosaldo's landmark article "Women, Culture and Society: A Theoretical Overview" (1974), many Africans and Africanists have shown that women, at least in West Africa, have always worked in the public sphere, though certain restrictions were imposed on them. They fully participated in matters involving religion, politics, and the economy. West African women, for instance, had always worked both inside and outside the home, and their involvement in trade and agriculture afforded them relative financial autonomy.[21] Nevertheless, West African society *is* strongly patriarchal, and so, for contemporary women writers, writing becomes a crucial step in challenging those patriarchal restrictions. Thus, writing becomes an extraordinarily liberating force because *what you cannot do or say, you can write.* Writing makes it possible to *dire l'interdit*—speak the forbidden. And language in the writing of African women is necessarily both an aesthetic expression and a powerful weapon, able to convey a committed message while destroying the emptiness of silence.

Feminist / *Misovire* Consciousness

As this brief survey of the situation of African women writers perhaps suggests, an all-important issue for these writers is "feminism," and how it is perceived in contemporary Africa. Some critics believe that African women were feminist before the fact: "African women have always been feminists in the sense that they have always been concerned with women's rights in society, their rights as people. They also knew that they were members of a community and they always insisted on their rights, so there were indigenous feminisms. . . . They [women] always recognized that they were women and they had their own women's world and they did not want that world shattered" (Ogundipe-Leslie, "African Literature," 12). Filomina C. Steady contends that "the black woman is to a large extent the original feminist" (*Black Woman*, 36).

This belief in an early feminism in Africa also exists because, as I have suggested, in traditional Africa women played full economic, social, and, occasionally, political roles in society. More generally, African women, although recognizing the need to address the issues of exclusion, exploitation, and the multiple colonizations faced by women, nevertheless have been suspicious of Western feminism (Emecheta 1988), and at the extreme, have rejected it altogether. Aminata Sow Fall's well-known exclamation, "Féministe? Moi?" [A feminist? Me?] is a pointed example. In her insightful introduction to *Third World Women and the Politics of Feminism* (1991), Chandra Talpade Mohanty articulated the complexity of the problem: "The term *feminism* is itself questioned by many third world women. Feminist movements have been challenged on the grounds of cultural imperialism, and of shortsightedness in defining the meaning of gender in terms of middle-class, white experiences, and in terms of internal racism, classism, and homophobia. All of these factors, as well as the falsely homogeneous representation of the movement by the media, have led to a very real suspicion of 'feminism' as a productive ground for struggle" (Mohanty et al., 7).[22]

It is true that at the outset of the movement, feminist theoretical analyses and practice tended to reflect the viewpoints of white, middle-class women of the Western world, and thus played into racist, dominant ideologies. Today, with the input of "women of color" and with the recognition of all kinds of complexity, there have been attempts to pluralize the word *feminism* and refer to feminism*s*, which might account for a diversity of classes, races, backgrounds, and concerns within feminist theory and practice. Even within Western feminism, there is an increasing need to make room for the diversity and multiplicity of approaches (see for instance Warhol and Herndl, *Feminisms*). Thus the problem of diversity has led women to qualify the word feminism and speak of *black feminism, African feminism,* or *"Third-World feminism."* Still other attempts have involved morphological invention, as in Alice Walker's use of the word *womanist* to describe a black feminist or feminist of color, a term also used as a concept and organizing principle by Chikwenye Okonjo Ogunyemi.[23] Of course, it is not only a question of semantics that is at stake here, for Walker explains how womanism is different from feminism for historical, racial, and political reasons. It is in view of these differences that other African-American women coined new terms. Cleonora Hudson-Weems has invented the term *Africana Womanism,* and Freida High W. Tesfagiorgis speaks of *Afrofemcentrism.*[24] Whatever the designation, however, "Third World women have always engaged with feminism, even if the label has been rejected in a number of instances" (Mohanty et al., 7). Critics such as Molara Ogundipe-Leslie and Carole Boyce Davies, who have examined the ambivalence generally felt by African women in relation to feminism, have pointed out that such ambivalence in fact does not preclude the relevance of feminism in Africa.

As a pioneer in articulating African feminist thought, Molara Ogundipe-Leslie provided a model exploring the problems of feminism as they relate to class, African traditions, men's behavior, and the conditioning of women, and also as it pertains to literary-critical endeavors.[25] She specifically points out the obstacles or metaphorical mountains standing in women's paths, and urges women to rid themselves of these six "mountains on their backs," which impede the advent of a contemporary African feminism. And in her groundbreaking introduction to *Ngambika,* Carole Boyce Davies elucidated Ogundipe-Leslie's six mountains as being: (1) woman's oppression by colonial interventions, (2) the heritage of African tradition, (3) her educational deprivations, (4) her men, (5) her race, and (6) herself. She then describes in seven insightful points the forms that feminism may take in Africa: (1) Recognizing a common struggle with African men against foreign domination, this brand of feminism is not antagonistic to men; (2) it acknowledges affinities with international feminism while insisting on its own specificity;²⁶ (3) it looks back into history to account for indigenous feminisms; (4) it respects women's status as mothers while questioning compulsory motherhood and the valorization of male offspring—it sees the positive aspects of polygamy, especially as it relates to child care, while condemning the privileges that men have in marital relationships; (5) it respects African women's self-reliance, social organizations, and cooperative working practices while rejecting the exploitation of women's work; (6) it takes into consideration the peculiar situation of women in societies undergoing war, national liberation, and socialist construction; and (7) it looks at traditional and contemporary avenues of choice for women (7–10). Boyce Davies develops her argument further to include African feminist understanding of the interconnectedness of race, class, and sexual oppression, and its leanings toward a socialist orientation, before laying the groundwork for an African feminist critical approach to literature.

I agree with Boyce Davies's points in general, but must take exception to inserting the so-called advantages of polygamy in a feminist agenda: "It [African feminism] sees the positive aspects of the extended family and polygamy with respect to child care and the sharing of household responsibility, traditions which are compatible with modern working women's lives and the problems of child care but which were distorted with colonialism and continue to be distorted in the urban environment" (9). Boyce Davies mentions that Buchi Emecheta supports that position, and in fact, Emecheta has remarked that "in many cases polygamy can be liberating to the woman, rather than inhibiting her, especially if she is educated. The husband has no reason for stopping her from attending international conferences . . . from going back to University and updating her career or even getting another degree. Polygamy encourages her to value herself as a person and look outside her family for friends" ("Feminism," 178).²⁷ Emecheta goes on to recount the story of a little boy who, in a polygamous household, "enjoys being loved and looked after by two women, his mother and the senior wife," and she adds, "what a good way to start one's life" ("Feminism," 179).

I am afraid both Boyce Davies's and Emecheta's positions are those of intellectual academics who—like most of us—do not have to confront the problems of polygamy in their own lives. While the loving situation described by Emecheta might occur, the opposite may also often occur, and the child be rejected by a jealous co-wife. So that what we are witnessing here is a certain idealization of polygamy, in ways that do not necessarily coincide with the *experience* of women who endure that institution. It is also rather different from most female writers' fictional description of the difficulties associated with polygamous marriages. In her own works, Emecheta hardly draws a glowing picture of polygamy, nor do other female writers, such as Mariama Bâ or Aminata Maïga Ka.

This disagreement notwithstanding, Boyce Davies and Ogundipe-Leslie—two writers who complement each other—have been very influential in my own thinking about the issue of feminism. If Ogundipe-Leslie's spare definition of feminism, "the recognition of a woman as a human being," sounds, as she says, "like a trivial statement or like a truism" (11–12) to someone versed in the intricacies of Western feminism, it nonetheless remains a central concern for an African woman. Beyond ideological definition lies the fact that African societies are immensely different from those of the West, different in their political struggles, different in their social formations, and different within details of life. Ogundipe-Leslie's terms are those reflecting the ideals of universal humanism, because the recognition of a woman as a human being should be the foundation of any discussion of gender relations anywhere. Yet its application is culture-specific and varies immensely, as an examination of Carole Boyce Davies's seven points readily shows.

One country in Francophone Africa that has taken the lead in feminist consciousness is certainly Senegal. In the very first issue (July 1987) of *Fippu* (Wolof for "rebellion"), the magazine of the Senegalese feminist movement called *Yewwu Yewwi* (a Wolof expression meaning "wake up and then wake someone else up"), Marie-Angélique Savané spells out the fifteen goals of the movement:

Nos objectifs seront

1. de prendre en charge et de traduire dans nos actes les justes aspirations des femmes: ouvrières, paysannes, ménagères, intellectuelles, prostituées, domestiques, etc. . . .

2. d'élever notre niveau de conscience et de renforcer notre engagement multiforme dans une lutte pour la liberté, la démocratie, le progrès et la justice sociale.

15

3. de réfléchir et d'agir sur la situation des femmes, aux plans économique, social, politique, culturel et psychologique dans le passé, le présent et l'avenir.

4. de renforcer notre compréhension des mécanismes de l'oppression dont nous sommes victimes.

5. de développer une nouvelle conscience féministe faite de résistance et de lutte contre toutes les idéologies qui oppriment et secondarisent les femmes.

6. de lutter contre toutes les formes d'oppression des femmes, dans la vie privée comme dans la vie publique.

7. de revendiquer et de faire respecter et appliquer nos droits: droit au travail et à un salaire décent, droit à un salaire égal pour un travail égal, à la formation, à la santé, droit à contrôler notre fécondité notamment par la contraception et l'avortement.

8. d'exiger la participation des femmes à toutes les instances et les institutions politiques, économiques, sociales et culturelles.

9. de faire introduire la composante femme à tous les projets de développement économique et social.

10. de faire exercer le droit à la fonction maternelle.

11. d'aider les femmes à acquérir par des mesures spécifiques en matière d'éducation et de formation, un savoir et un savoir-faire qui leur permettent d'améliorer leur existence.

12. d'initier en rapport avec les femmes, des projets socio-économiques qui les aident à renforcer leur autonomie.

13. de susciter et d'entretenir la solidarité entre les membres.

14. de nous solidariser avec toutes les femmes sénégalaises (à l'intérieur comme à l'extérieur du pays) victimes de l'exploitation et de l'oppression.

15. de nous solidariser avec toutes les autres femmes opprimées particulièrement celles victimes de l'apartheid. ("Appel," 7)

[Our goals will be

1. To attend to and translate into action the just aspirations of all women: workers, peasants, housewives, intellectuals, prostitutes, domestic workers, etc. . . .

2. to raise our level of consciousness and to reinforce our multiple commitments to struggles for freedom, democracy, progress, and social justice.

3. to reflect and act on the economic, social, political, cultural, and psychological situation of women in the past, present, and future.

4. to strengthen our understanding of the mechanisms of the oppression that subjugates us.

5. to develop a new feminist consciousness made of resistance and of struggle against all ideologies that oppress women and relegate them to a secondary position.

6. to fight against all forms of oppression of women in private as well as public life.

7. to claim our rights and demand that they be respected and implemented: right to work and make decent wages, right to equal pay for equal work, right to education, to health and to reproductive control, in particular by contraception and abortion.

8. to demand the participation of women at all levels in political, economic, social, and cultural institutions.

9. to make sure that women are represented in all projects involving economic and social development.

10. to ensure the right to motherhood.

11. to help women acquire, through specific educational and training programs, knowledge and know-how that will enable them to improve their living conditions.

12. to take with other women the initiative for socioeconomic projects that will help them consolidate their autonomy.

13. to foster and maintain solidarity among its members.

14. to foster solidarity among all Senegalese women who, within and outside the country, are subject to exploitation and oppression.

15. to foster solidarity with all other oppressed women, especially those who are victims of apartheid.]

My reason for including this lengthy document in its entirety is that I find the feminist agenda of a specific country such as Senegal useful, indeed necessary, to complement Ogundipe-Leslie's and Boyce Davies's pronouncements. This agenda is in fact a program of action that begins with a commitment to all Senegalese women, whatever their socioeconomic backgrounds. This inclusive approach is extremely important to dispel the notion that feminism is only of interest to bourgeois, educated, and Westernized African women. Feminism envisaged here involves a recognition that women, regardless of their class (and even if some classes *are* privileged), are all subject to patriarchal law based only on their gender. As such the "female condition" becomes a rallying point where a strongly advocated solidarity among women is imperative.

Another striking point in this agenda is the insistence on the necessity for women to educate themselves in order to better understand the mechanisms of oppression and be better equipped to combat them in public and private life. This feminism demands more than a basic right to be considered a human being. It fights for more equitable laws and rights for women's work, health (including reproductive control), and education, rights that are indispensable if women are to improve their living conditions and "consolidate their autonomy." The demands are further pressed to include women in development projects as well as to give them a genuine presence within social, political, economic, and cultural institutions, all these requirements to be obtained in a context of freedom and democracy. This political dimension of the struggle is important to women in Senegal and also sensitizes them to the plight of women's oppression under regimes such as apartheid.

Feminism here is a real struggle, framed and determined by Senegalese women themselves. That they are able to articulate their position, their demands, and their line of action in a country where Islam is a vital determinant is a clear indication that Senegalese women have found creative ways of responding to their specific situation. The Senegalese model shows that the women of the Yewwu Yewwi movement do place their struggle in a historical, political, and ideological frame, but they are not overly interested in theoretical issues. They are engaged in what I would term a *practical* African feminism. Indeed, their agenda is clearly one that sees feminism as a practical tool that must serve to empower women, working by themselves to better their lives here and now: "Notre combat doit être mené par *nous-mêmes*. Aucun peuple, aucune catégorie sociale ne s'est libérée en déléguant la responsabilité de sa destinée à d'autres instances qu'aux siennes propres: il n'existe pas de libération par procuration" [We must wage our battle *ourselves*. No people, no social class, has ever freed itself by delegating the responsibility

of its destiny to any agency other than its own; there can be no liberation by proxy] (Savané, "Appel," 7).[28]

The Senegalese model constitutes another reason that I strongly believe that feminism as a concept, a theory, a practice, a movement, a
mode of being and of beholding the world, and an instrument of struggle has a place in contemporary African society and scholarship.
Therefore, like Cheryl Johnson-Odim (1991) I have retained the term
feminism, while recognizing that its *meaning* must be modified. I can
give the term *feminism* a wide definition and see it both as a woman's
consciousness of being oppressed because of her gender and as her willingness to find ways, either individually or collectively, to put an end to
that oppression. But even when it is so defined, feminism has to be re-
cast in an African mold to fit the contours of issues faced by women on
the African continent and within specific countries. This reconceptualization can be accomplished through literature and theory as well as
through direct action.

Perhaps I might best demonstrate my position by discussing Werewere
Liking's means of reconceptualizing feminism in African terms. Her
reconceptualization gives the African woman the option of being a *misovire*, a term found in Liking's *Elle sera de jaspe et de corail* [It will be
of jasper and coral], a work she classified as a *chant-roman* (novel-song)
and subtitled *Journal d'une misovire* [Journal of a misovire].

Misovire is a word that Werewere Liking invented much in the way
that Alice Walker invented *womanist*, with the difference, however,
that Walker's term has positive connotations; it is a celebration of womanhood. *Misovire*, by contrast, is a word invented *against* men, though, as
we will see, it is not intended to convey a totally negative meaning. The
very act of invention is in itself of primal importance as Liking engen-
ders a new language, more adept at describing her reality, more attuned
to her sensitivity, more consonant with her ideological stance. The act
of invention both reinforces and goes beyond the concept of women
coming to voice. It is the genesis of a language fashioned by women to
bring into being that which is not. It is also intended to fill a void. The
French language includes the words *misanthrope* and *misogyne*. *Misanthrope* denotes a person who does not like human beings in general,

19

misogyne a person who does not like women; but no word exists to refer to a person who does not like men. Werewere Liking's invention is critical in that it shows how gender ideology pervades all spheres of human endeavor, including linguistic constructions.[29] It is precisely to counter these forms of dominant patriarchal ideologies that Liking, who is an expert at mixing categories, combines Greek and Latin components to invent *misovire*.[30]

Her invention is all the more important as the creation of the word also creates the function, and the possibility of another reality. Yet, disregarding the literal etymological meaning of *misovire* as "man-hater," Liking offers a very different definition for her neologism: "Une femme qui n'arrive pas à trouver un homme admirable" [A woman who cannot find an admirable man] ("A la rencontre de," 21). For those—especially if they have a Western world view—who may ask whether it is necessary for a woman to find an admirable man, Liking's answer is unequivocally yes. Yet Liking's definition is deliciously ambiguous. In saying that a misovire is "a woman who cannot find an admirable man," Liking ingeniously offers two possible readings. The phrase could either mean "I cannot believe that an admirable man exists" or "an admirable man does exist, but I have not yet found him." Despite the ambiguous nature of her definition, what remains clear is that Liking does not advocate separation by gender, and it is perhaps appropriate to use a linguistics metaphor and say that Liking would rather see women and men in a syntagmatic relationship.

Indeed, Liking's stance does not limit itself to an antimale rhetoric, but stresses instead a balance between demand and persuasion.[31] So she exerts force by the act of inventing the term *misovire*, and yet moderates that force with a certain subtlety through the special definition she gives the word. This is the balancing act that remains at the heart of how women negotiate their demands, indeed their positions, within African societies. With the redefinition of woman as misovire, Liking emphasizes men's shortcomings in contemporary society, reminding them of a lack of dignity, of a lost sense of values that cause women to move away from them: "Elle (la femme) se sent entourée par des 'larves' uniquement préoccupées par leurs panses et leurs bas-ventres et incapables d'une aspiration plus haute que leur tête, incapable de lui inspirer

des grands sentiments qui agrandissent, alors, elle devient misovire"
[She (the woman) feels that she is surrounded by "larvae" solely preoccupied with their bellies and their loins and unable to aspire to something that reaches higher than their heads, unable to inspire her with
feelings that can uplift her, so, she becomes a misovire] ("A la rencontre de," 21).

Liking's remarks are not intended to alienate men from women, but
to make men think about gender relationships.[32] Thus despite the problems they face vis-à-vis feminism, despite their hesitancies, their steps
forward and back, while African women struggle to articulate and theo-
rize their own conception of feminism, at the same time they put pressure on men to make them active agents in achieving the goal of social
transformation. It is therefore important to restate that the invention of
misovire does not constitute a gratuitous act; it is done for a redressive
purpose, for besides filling a linguistic void, the word aims at destabi-
lizing the status quo, and it shows the extent to which social reality and
literary expression are inextricably intertwined. Misovire has a double
function, as a concept that is both a social construct and as a device used
to construct a poetics. It would be inaccurate, however, to contend that
Liking's perspective is shared by all African women. For instance, an
analysis of Beyala's first novel, *C'est le Soleil qui m'a brûlée* [It is the
sun that burnt me], clearly indicates her belief that man must be killed—
one would hope symbolically—in order for woman to be born.

Liking's stance is both appealing and inspiring, for I interpret her redefinition of misovire as a willingness to make a decisive departure from
conventional meaning, yet also a willingness to both distance and differentiate African feminism from Western feminism. In this context,
Werewere Liking's position reveals an interest not so much in feminism
as in a new form of humanism—not a humanism that was distorted by
the West at a certain point in history and served as a tool to exclude the
"other," but a humanism that tolerates no exclusion, a humanism capable of transforming society as a whole.[33] It is in that sense that she
dreams of a new race that will be "of jasper and coral" and can only be
born:

Quand l'homme ne jouera plus au porc
Quand la femme ne sera plus chienne en chaleur

21

Quand je ne serai plus misovire et qu'il n'y aura plus de misogynes. . . .
(153)

[When man will no longer be a pig

When woman will no longer be a bitch in heat

When I will no longer be a misovire and when men will no longer be
misogynists. . . .]

The acts of rethinking, recasting, reconceptualizing, and redefining by the writers I've been looking at lead to a formulation of the concept of self-representation. Because of the hegemony of dominant discourses and sociopolitical structures within and outside Africa, African women have mainly been represented as "other" and also as marginal, silent, absent from the public sphere, confined to private spaces.[34] No doubt these women *are* marginalized, not only as women but also as blacks, Africans, and members of the so-called Third World.[35] Yet as they demonstrate, writing means empowerment and can serve to undermine the marginalizing project and move from margin to center.[36] Becoming their own *créatrices*, women use a poetics to reject representation by others that they view as mere construction, an invention of the African woman in the same way as Valentin Mudimbe speaks of "the invention of Africa."

As they express themselves in their own words, in their own terms, the meaning of self-representation becomes perceptible. It is an act that, because it is mediated by the creative process, does not reproduce reality but nevertheless does produce through fiction a kind of social reality, one having the power to expose, to modify, and even to subvert preexisting reality. Self-representation is also the very fact of writing the self, of restructuring experience to make room for a new self-definition. It results in self-constructed identity contextualized within politics and history. Thus, having achieved their prise d'écriture—"taken" writing, laid hold of it—women are capitalizing on this new medium to see and represent themselves in a femino-centric perspective. They portray themselves as actors instead of spectators. They are at the core instead of the periphery. They explore, deplore, subvert, and redress the status quo within their fiction. They contend with the problems arising from sex, race, and class even as these exist within patriarchal, "postcolonial" societies.

Remarks on Methodology

The title of this book, *Francophone African Women Writers: Destroying the Emptiness of Silence,* although generally descriptive of my subject, uses two terms I must qualify. I am very much aware of the reductionism that occurs if one lumps diverse African countries under the general cover of "Africa" or "African." This tends to obscure, and sometimes deny, the specificity of individual countries. Africa is a mosaic of diverse peoples and cultures, and even within individual countries differences abound. Marie-Angélique Savané beautifully illustrates this with the metaphor of clothing: "Senegalese women are famous for their elegance. It is true that the *grand boubou,* the national *costume,* gives Senegalese women a certain majestic presence. But this seeming uniformity of dress and mannerism, owing to strong influence by the Wolof culture and Islam, must not mask the diversity of their behavior, based on their respective environments and specific cultures" ("Elegance," 593).

In the same way, the writers I am studying here represent a wide range of geographical and cultural diversity. They are from black Africa, but specifically from Cameroon, the Central African Republic, Côte d'Ivoire (Ivory Coast), Gabon, and Senegal, and so in using the term *African* my intent is not one of totalization. A *Pan*-African perspective, such as echoes through the title that Andrée Blouin gives her autobiography: *My Country, Africa,* is what I have tried to adopt.[37]

My second taxonomic uneasiness relates to the term *Francophone.* The writers whose work I examine all come from French-speaking Africa and use the French language as the medium of their art. This is a reality that is, at this point in history, inescapable. Yet *Francophone,* which simply means "French-*speaking,*" is not exactly appropriate to describe writing. In addition, the word cannot be dissociated from the term *Francophonie* and, as such, must be problematized in terms of its peculiar history. The word *Francophonie* was coined at the turn of the century by the French geographer Onésime Reclus, to designate "l'ensemble des territoires où l'on parlait français" [the ensemble of ter-ritories where French was spoken] (Deniau, 8).[38] Ironically, however, the concept of Francophonie as we know it today was conceived by three African leaders of newly independent states, Léopold Sédar Senghor of Senegal, Hamani Diori of Niger, and Habib Bourguiba of Tunisia, who wished to create a community that would be an enlarged, extended fam-ily based on a common language. Intended as a *grand rassemblement* under the banner of the French language, the concept has, over the years, come to be ideologically charged, and more and more Africans have grown uncomfortable with, and even suspicious of, Francophonie.[39]

Indeed, Francophonie can be used, and has been used, to suit linguis-tic and culturally hegemonic purposes. Most importantly, to call a per-son Francophone veils the fact that the person does have another language, in this case a first language, an African language. This lan-guage question as it relates to African fiction has been discussed by nu-merous writers and critics,[40] but it is important to note that women do not seem overly preoccupied with the problem, either ideologically or in regard to the uneasiness expressed by many of their male counterparts about trying to express an African reality with a foreign language. As their pronouncements on writing have shown, women's chief concern has been to express themselves, no matter what language they use in or-der to do so: their primary objective remains to destroy the emptiness of silence. But even if women seem to have sidestepped the problem of lan-guage in fiction as a group or as individuals, there is no doubt that the use of French as an "official" language and as a vehicle of letters in Africa still remains a problem with serious political ramifications.

Though the literature of Francophone African women is new, it of course has a history, demonstrable influences, and a pattern of develop-ment that I have made use of to help organize my study. To clarify that organization, I provide two diagrams, each representing a possible clas-sification of the works I will be examining.[41] The concentric circles of diagram 1 illustrate what I designate as three stages in the development of women's literary production. The first stage, "The Self: Autobiogra-phy as *dé/couverte*," is an exploration of autobiographical writing in which the self is at the center. I start with *De Tilène au Plateau: une enfance dakaroise* (1975), [*A Dakar Childhood*] (1982), by Nafissatou

Diallo, a novelist from Senegal. It is appropriate that *De Tilène au Plateau* open this study because of the book's historical importance. It is one of the first autobiographies, and indeed one of the very first books, written by a Francophone African woman. The second autobiography is by another woman from Senegal who writes under the pseudonym of Ken Bugul. Her book, *Le Baobab fou* (1983), [*The Abandoned Baobab: The Autobiography of a Senegalese Woman*] (1991), has notably broken the silence surrounding a number of taboos, especially those pertaining to women's sexuality. The final book of this section, *My Country, Africa: Autobiography of the Black Pasionaria,* was written by Andrée Blouin, a woman raised in the Belgian Congo, born of a French father and of a mother from the Central African Republic. *My Country, Africa,* whose author was an active participant in African liberation movements, is an example of how the definition of autobiography as concerned with the self can expand to encompass historical, social, and political issues.

The second stage, "Speaking Up, Disclosing Family Life," is symbolized by the family circle and concentrates on novels that are representative of family relationships and how women negotiate and redefine their role in that context. *Tu t'appelleras Tanga* by Calixthe Beyala deals with the notion of womanhood, and *Fureurs et cris de femmes* (1989) [Cries and fury of women] by Angèle Rawiri, a novelist from Gabon, addresses problems related to "compulsory" motherhood. *Un Chant écarlate* (1981), [*Scarlet Song*] (1986), by Mariama Bâ from Senegal, interna-

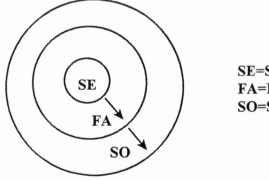

SE=Self
FA=Family
SO=Society

Diagram 1. Concentric circles.

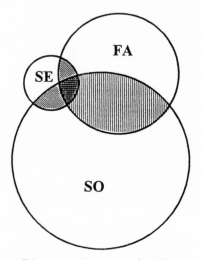

Diagram 2. Intersected circles.

tionalizes all the issues of women's social definition by including female characters from different nationalities within its narrative.

Finally, the chapter entitled "W/Riting Change: Women as Social Critics" enters the third circle and discusses how female novelists link problems that affect women's lives to those affecting society at large. Representative of this approach are Werewere Liking from Cameroon who, in *Orphée-Dafric* (1982), uses rituals of individual initiation as a way of organizing her narrative, and, by implication, as suggestions for the larger reformation of society. Aminata Sow Fall, yet another novelist from Senegal, foregrounds political responsibility in *L'Ex-père de la nation* [The ex-father of the nation] (1987), but in a way that calls attention to patriarchal assumptions underlying national institutions. The final book I discuss is *A Vol d'oiseau* [As the crow flies] (1986) by Véronique Tadjo from Côte d'Ivoire. Her book convincingly demonstrates that there is no necessary conflict between poetic expression and social themes.

Diagram 2 represents pictorially the subject of my concluding chapter, and the intersected circles, which show tensions as well as structural, thematic, and ideological connections among texts, represent a kind of critique of the necessary but deceptive simplification of diagram 1. Imaginative works always overflow the categories we invent to contain them, and we can learn from the overflowing as well as from our categories. The conclusion also emphasizes the quality, depth, and sensitivity that women bring to the corpus of African literature, and attempts to demonstrate how female writers have used the medium of the written word in order to become, as they were in the oral traditions, real producers of literary culture.

I would like to conclude with some general remarks about method. Any method one adopts implies choices with respect to theory. In writing about the works under consideration here, I cannot separate theory from the corpus of the literature I am examining. This corpus has two important determinants: it is *African* literature, and it is written by *women*. Moreover, I cannot dissociate theory from who I am: an African woman raised within an African culture and still closely connected to it, who yet happens to be trained in, influenced by, and appreciative of Western theories of criticism.[42] The implied conflict in this situation is familiar, I think, and closely related to the matter of an African feminism, which I discussed in the preceding section. We must recognize that any application of Western theory, however balanced and careful, involves the imposition of a Eurocentric point of view. A writer from an African background must have reservations about the appropriateness of critical methods born of societies that are—if I may generalize—inward-looking and inner-directed, framed in terms of the individual and the abstract.

Although I recognize the danger inherent in such generalizations, I believe that for me to have rigorously imposed a set of techniques imported from the contemporary Western language of literary criticism might have done violence to the subject matter I am dealing with. This is not to say that Western approaches cannot yield productive results for readers whose cultural frame of reference is the European / American academic context. But it must be understood that this is not the context in which African women's books were written or intended to be read. Readers should not, therefore, expect to find Derridian or Lacanian readings in this study.

My analysis of Aminata Sow Fall's *L'Ex-père de la nation* might serve as an example of the kind of critical reading I favor, one that emerges from within the text and also derives from particular, local circumstances. The title and themes of the novel connect the concepts of nationhood and fatherhood, both seen as instruments for the enforcement of patriarchal rule. I have, therefore, centered my analysis on the genealogy of the "fathers," an approach that makes it possible to show how Aminata Sow Fall presents the patriarchal institution at two levels, the family and the state, and dismantles that order by discrediting the notion of fatherhood at both levels. Thus the novel demonstrates the failure of the patriarchal institution to fashion a nation. One then can pose the question of whether or not the "mothers" of the text are able to take over and make the advent of nationhood possible. A family tree of "the mothers," parallel to that of "the fathers," is helpful in answering that question, and the contrast between the two sets of genealogy provides an essential understanding of how Fall joins the gender politics of family life to those of national politics.

Because the historical and sociopolitical dimensions of African women's writing are too salient to be overlooked, I have, as have all of the writers examined here, given equal value to text and context. In the only essay Mariama Bâ published, "Fonction politique des littératures africaines écrites" [The political function of written African literatures],[43] she reflects on the interrelationship of politics and art in Africa. Taking a historical perspective, and in the tradition of the most renowned African novelists, she strongly makes the point that in traditional Africa, not only was art deeply rooted in society but it was also made to serve a purpose; it was functional. Contemporary African writers, she contends, have not broken this continuum, and place fiction at the service of society. She goes on to explain how politics had to go hand-in-hand with creativity during the period of colonization, and how it is still a necessity today in spite of the difficulties of the task and the intolerance of some political regimes:

> Dans l'oeuvre d'édification d'une société africaine démocratique libérée de toute contrainte, l'écrivain a un rôle important d'éveilleur de conscience et de guide. Il se doit de répercuter les aspirations de toutes les couches sociales, surtout des couches sociales les plus défavorisées. Dénoncer les maux et fléaux qui gangrènent notre société et retardent son plein épanouissement, fustiger les pratiques, coutumes et moeurs archaïques

qui n'ont rien à voir avec notre précieux patrimoine culturel, lui revien-
nent, comme une mission sacrée à accomplir, contre vents et marées, avec
foi, avec ténacité. ("Fonction politique," 5)

[In the task of building up a democratic African society, freed from all
forms of constraint, the writer has an important role to play in awakening
consciousness and as guide. His (her) duty is to reflect the aspirations of all
social classes, especially the most disadvantaged. To denounce the ills that
plague our society and delay its full development, to denounce archaic
practices, customs and mores that have nothing to do with our cultural
heritage, this is the sacred mission that the writer must carry out, come
hell or high water, with faith and perseverance.]

Thus Bâ's position comes close to that of Aminata Sow Fall cited in an
earlier quotation: "Art for art's sake is not my concern and, in that, I feel
in harmony with the African aesthetic" ("Entretiens," 24).

The view that text cannot be separated from context, that a work of
art has no real autonomy and is dependant on external determinants of
history, politics, and culture, is a point of convergence of male and female writers in Africa.[44] They meet at this point because they are bound
by the same historical past, are victims of the same colonial and neocolonial maneuvers, and are living, in turmoil, the same political present. Yet beyond these common preoccupations, women have an additional role, again delineated by Bâ. The female writer, she affirms, "doit,
plus que ses pairs masculins, dresser un tableau de la condition de la
femme africaine" [must, more than her male counterparts, exhaustively
depict the condition of African women] ("Fonction politique," 6–7). In
the face of injustices, inequalities, social and institutional obstacles,
"c'est à nous, femmes, de prendre notre destin en mains pour bouleverser
l'ordre établi à notre détriment et de ne point le subir. Nous devons user
comme les hommes de cette arme, pacificique certes, mais sûre, qu'est
l'écriture" [it is incumbent on us women to take our destiny in our own
hands, to subvert, and not be subverted by, an order established to our
detriment. We must, as men do, use this peaceful but effective weapon
that writing is] ("Fonction politique," 7). Bâ concludes her essay with
these powerful words: "Il faut donner dans la littérature africaine à la
femme noire une dimension à la mesure de son engagement prouvé à côté

de l'homme dans les batailles de libération, une dimension à la mesure de ses capacités démontrées dans le développement économique de notre pays" [In African literature, we must give the black woman a dimension, commensurate with her proven participation, alongside men, in liberation struggles, a dimension commensurate with her demonstrated abilities in the economic development of our country] (7).

If the writers themselves position their work at the intersection of text and context, at the intersection of art and sociopolitical issues, the critic cannot escape that reality and must show that imaginary representations here help women make sense of their social experiences, make present what is absent, give voice to what is voiceless. This a measure of women's commitment and part and parcel of the poetics they are evolving in their prise d'écriture.

If I have deliberately privileged consideration of historical context and adopted my method to suit each text discussed, I have also supplemented these approaches with Western critical methods consonant with my work. For instance, basic tenets that run through various forms of feminist theory, such as recognizing the oppression of women and the tyranny of patriarchy, permeate my critical stance. In addition to feminist theory, I have found useful categories and techniques in narratology.[45] Thus, for example, my discussion of Mariama Bâ's *Chant écarlate* draws on the notion of focalization, and contrasts the position of narrators and focalizers to show how the interplay of various voices and shifting points of view constitutes an essential device that informs the structure, content, and message of the novel.

In addition to the sociopolitical and gender-based forms of marginalization experienced and fought by African women, their writings have also been excluded from the corpus of African literature, from that of women's literature, from the corridors of publishing and translation, and from the formation of the literary canon. Because of these exclusions, I have made three decisions. The first involves the choice of writers, so important in canon formation, which, by definition, privileges certain texts to the detriment of others.[46] I have elected to include books by lesser known writers as well as relatively well-established "classics." Also, because many of these texts are not widely available or not yet translated, I have found it necessary to provide plot summaries that specialist readers may find perhaps overly generous. It is my hope, however, that this book will make its way to a general readership as well as to specialist readers.

Second, as this introductory chapter demonstrates, this kind of study is by nature comparatist. After all, African women's writing defines itself by opposing and correcting the way in which African women have been represented in fiction, in particular by African male writers. Women's prise d'écriture is an innovation, and innovations can only be realized from what preceded them. It took Mariama Bâ's *Une si longue lettre* [So long a letter] to express, from within, and with extraordinary compassion and sensitivity, a woman's reaction to polygamy. She offered, of course, a picture extremely different from most male writers' portrayal of this institution. To be fair, however, and to place women's writing in its proper historical perspective, one must recognize that female writers have followed and benefitted from the groundbreaking anticolonial battles and perspectives of male writers. In this regard we must also keep in mind that some of the political issues pertaining to gender can be related to political responses to other kinds of oppression. I have nonetheless limited the emphasis on comparison in my text as much as possible. This book is not a comparative study in the sense that I do not wish to compare, at least in a systematic fashion, Francophone female writers with their male counterparts or with female writers from different literary traditions. The goal of this book is to analyze African women's works, as much as possible, on their own terms, to locate their special values, and to show how their literature may stand on its own.

Finally, to avoid presenting African women's writings in a synoptic manner, quotations have been used with a deliberate generosity. Some of the texts are not available in published translations, and where this is the case, I provide my own translation, always in tandem with the original. Along with performing their conventional function, quotations here are also a means of letting African women writers express for themselves what it is that they wish to communicate. In this way, in a work of literary criticism as well as in literature itself, the emptiness of silence may be destroyed.

CHAPTER ONE

THE SELF:

AUTOBIOGRAPHY

AS DÉ/COUVERTE

◎

The terms by which African Francophone women began to write inevitably included measures of compromise and mediation. Thus, when I began this study I suspected that these women's initial writings, especially the early autobiographies, would be marked by a cautious presentation of their experience as women. Francophone African women have been attracted by the genre of autobiography, more so than their Anglophone counterparts, and I wondered if they chose this form because it provided a "safe" entry into the world of letters, a way to begin writing that was "authenticated" by the genre itself, and that might by their selection of incident allow these writers to avoid contentious subject matter. Unlike most novels, an autobiography might succeed without a central pattern of social conflicts and could have served as a medium for women to speak in a whisper before finding the confidence to raise their voices in the process of destroying the emptiness of silence. Instead of such "safe" writing, however, I found works that were already deeply concerned with women's issues, and my initial expectations were largely contradicted by the close analysis of three autobiographies published between 1975 and 1983: *De Tilène au Plateau: une enfance dakaroise* [A Dakar childhood] by Nafissatou Diallo, *Le Baobab fou* [The abandoned baobab] by Ken Bugul, and *My Country, Africa: Autobiography of the Black Pasionaria* by Andrée Blouin.[1] What these three works showed me were different ways for revealing conflicts within the lives they depict, an approach I would generally characterize as *dé/couverte*.

I speak of autobiography as dé/couverte because the strategies that women devise to write their life stories fit particularly well the richness and plurality of meaning that this French word offers: *découvrir* is used to mean "to discover" or "to uncover"; in both senses the common element is "cover." At a conceptual level, this double endeavor can be seen as a form of diglossia, a double language, the one that covers *and* the one that uncovers. Pursuing an expansion of the semantic field, we find in these works, interestingly enough, that the dialectic of covering and uncovering results in a third movement, which is (though etymologically unrelated) that of "recovering." This act of recovering goes beyond simple discovery. It involves reappropriating for oneself something that was hidden or lost.

What some of these women cover is the very importance of their act of writing. They not only give the impression of discounting the talent involved in the creative process, they may even seem to imply that their life stories are hardly worth recounting.[2] In the paratext of her autobiography, Nafissatou Diallo warns the reader: "I am not the heroine of a novel but an ordinary woman of this country, Senegal: a mother and a working woman—a midwife and child-welfare nurse—whose home and career leave very little free time. . . . For the last few weeks I have started to write. What would a woman write about who has no claim for exceptional imagination or outstanding literary talent? She could only write about herself, of course" (*A Dakar Childhood*, ix).

Her foreword suggests that autobiography is the resort of a deficient imagination and prepares the reader to expect a mediocre talent that can only give birth to second-rate writing. Seen in this light, autobiography becomes a diminution, and the "I" is turned into a trivial, ordinary residual, as it were. It isn't only African women writers who speak this way of themselves, some female critics do also. Annette M'baye d'Erneville says of Nafissatou Diallo: "A mon avis, elle a mené une vie de femme exemplaire, discrète, efficace, plus mère de famille et épouse que femme publique" [I think that she led the life of an exemplary woman, discreet, efficient, more of a mother and wife than of a woman in the public eye].[3] The self-effacement and self-deprecation observed in Diallo's foreword—which has been characteristic of female writers irrespective of their cultural background—is here reinforced by d'Erneville's apologetic remark. Behind this form of apology lies the fear of social ostracism in general and of male ostracism in particular. Sidonie Smith makes this point about the social pressures of patriarchy when she speaks of women's effort to break a silence that is often self-imposed:

> Male distrust and consequent repression of female speech have either condemned her to public silence or profoundly contaminated her relationship to pen as an instrument of power. If she presumes to claim a fully human identity by seeking a place in the public arena, therefore, she transgresses patriarchal definitions of female nature by enacting the scenario of male selfhood. As she does so, she challenges cultural conceptions of the nature of woman and thereby invites public censure for her efforts. If she bows to the discursive pressure of anonymity, however, she denies her desire for a voice of her own. (7–8)

Those are the kinds of pressure that explain why Annette M'baye d'Erneville may say that writing is unimportant, or at least secondary to the "true" duties of a woman—"more of a mother and wife than a woman in the public eye." Yet a mere perfunctory look at African women's autobiographies contradicts d'Erneville's notion. The women un-cover their artistic talent and the centrality of their lives *as women*. With writing they find a new liberating force that enables them to "speak" openly concerning matters that once they could not have discussed in public. Through the very act of writing, Nafissatou Diallo has positioned herself, as have all women writers, in the middle of the public arena.

If women try to cover the importance of writing, they still *do* write and, in this prise d'écriture process, discover a self, or at least an authorial persona expressed by the "I," which is the hallmark of most autobiographies. The "I" is truly the defining characteristic of the autodiegetic narrative, in which author and narrator are one and the same person. Whether the "I" of the author / narrator is also the "self" of this author / narrator, however, has constituted a perennial puzzle for the scholars of autobiography.[4] In the final analysis, I accept that an autobiography *is* a fiction because, at the structural level, the necessarily structural level of textualization, it is a construction, a construction of one's life, of one's self. The past, which is the very essence of autobiography, is also by necessity a fiction, because it is reconstructed. The autobiography thus becomes an auto-fiction in which the subject "I" is the object of a narrative discourse that allows at once a means of distancing, but also a means of selection of the particles that will form the "I." In this way the narrator has with the "self" a relationship that is at once very close and very distant, and a relationship of complicity in a process of covering and un-covering.

Although Andrée Blouin wrote *My Country, Africa* in collaboration with an American woman, Jean Mackellar, both *A Dakar Childhood* and *The Abandoned Baobab* were written by their authors themselves in what would fit, to a degree, Philippe Lejeune's definition of the autobiography as "retrospective prose narrative written by a real person concerning his own existence, where the focus is his individual life, in particular the story of his personality" (*On Autobiography*, 4).[5] This definition has been criticized by theorists of feminism for its masculinist assumptions, which disregard the fact that women may view chronology and individuality differently.[6] The definition also needs to be modified to fit different cultural grounds. In the African context, auto-fiction is generally turned into socio-fiction, and within African societies, recounting the story of an individual life is often a pretext for reviving a historical moment and depicting a whole society. Despite these reservations, I concur with Lejeune's essential definition of what makes an autobiography. He states: "In order for there to be autobiography (and personal literature in general), the *author*, the *narrator*, and the *protagonist* must be identical" (5).

Although I treat these autobiographies as exemplars of the genre among Francophone women, that does not mean they are works similar in every way. The women who wrote them came from various backgrounds and led widely diverse lives, and so it is important to locate these women in time and space as well as in the political, social, and religious environments that shaped their lives.[7] Nafissatou Diallo was a Muslim woman, born in Senegal in the early 1940s, whereas Ken Bugul, also a Muslim woman from Senegal, was born a generation later. Andrée Blouin, the oldest of the three, was born in the former Oubangui-Chari in 1921. Their autobiographies, although different in many ways, have points of intersection and make for interesting contrastive analysis. Nafissatou Diallo and Ken Bugul are both from Senegal but belong to different generations, a difference crucial to how each views her society; both Senegalese women are Muslim, whereas Andrée Blouin is Catholic, which gives them disparate world views; Nafissatou Diallo and Ken Bugul are "fully" African, whereas Andrée Blouin is a *métisse.* All three women were born during the colonial era but have different responses to that history. They all converge, however, in the fact they experience life *as women,* and that is why the inscription of gender is so strong throughout their autobiographies. This is certainly the case in Nafissatou Diallo's work.

Nafissatou Diallo: A Legacy for the Future

Nafissatou Diallo, born in 1941 in Senegal, witnessed the rapid mutations that her nation went through in its passage from colony to nation-state, and she gave her autobiography, *A Dakar Childhood,* a specific goal: "Senegal has changed in a generation. Perhaps it is worth reminding today's youngsters what we were like when we were their age" (ix). Thus *A Dakar Childhood* can be viewed as a bridge between what once was and what is now. It is a legacy for the future. In defining her work this way, Nafissatou Diallo places herself in the traditional role of the storyteller whose duty it is to pass down the history of her people from one generation to the next. This role also allows her to carry out the uncovering process within a nonthreatening, familiar framework.

Nafissatou Diallo (who is called Safi in the autobiography) was a professional woman, the first girl in a long family line to attend the French school. Her grandfather allowed her to do so not only because he was getting old and more accommodating but also because Mame, Diallo's grandmother, was an efficient facilitator who backed her granddaughter's wish to go to school. That education served as a gateway to Diallo's future career as a nurse specializing in pediatrics.

In *A Dakar Childhood,* Diallo sets out to recount what it was like to live in Senegal in the 1940s as a young female growing up in a Muslim household. The autobiography follows a natural chronology, beginning with Safi's childhood, moving to her adolescent years, then to her maturation into a career woman, wife, mother, and, finally, a writer. Diallo unfolds the events in her life with effective sincerity; her story is relatively simple, the tone unassuming, and this is perhaps what has led critics to view *A Dakar Childhood* as an idyllic portrait of a changing society. Susan Stringer, for instance, says that Diallo depicts "a gentle world in which society is an extension of the family and social harmony the norm" (202). Charlotte Bruner describes Diallo's approach in the same vein: "She does not pretend to criticize her cultural milieu or to interpret the events of her own life as significant beyond personal narrative" (326). But although it is true that Diallo makes clear that she shares the values of Senegalese culture, which include commitment to family and respect for traditions, the world she portrays is deceptively harmonious, her attitude toward it deceptively uncritical. Thus, trained by her family and by the Koranic school system to be a good Muslim, she acknowledges the importance of Islam and embraces it; however, she does so as would an "iconoclast," a Muslim defined by Mbye Cham as one who professes belief in Islam but criticizes its interpretation and practice.[8] She remains closely attached to the "traditional" world of her origin, even as she suggests how that world is unfair or inadequate. In Diallo we see most subtly the pattern of give and take reflecting the "balancing act" discussed earlier.

Diallo uses such subtle procedures to unmask the dynamics of gender in her story, particularly a strategy I term the *in-passing discourse.* It is a strategy by which the writer describes in passing, that is, by what seem like innocent, benign observations, difficult issues women are confronted with in their daily lives. The in-passing discourse appears even in the foreword of *A Dakar Childhood,* in which, as self-effacing as Diallo sounds, she nonetheless mentions, in passing, the double burden she has to carry as a woman who works both within and outside of the home. Her double profession curtails the leisure time she could use to write and makes her a woman "whose home and career leave her very little free-time" (ix). It is in this oblique mode that the autobiographer un-covers the position of women, the way they are perceived and treated, and their roles within family and society.

Diallo's in-passing discourse reveals not only the exclusion of women from full societal participation but also the practices that restrict and control their private behavior in patriarchal and Islamic culture. She describes her grandfather's cultural legacy in these terms: "He had obeyed the stringent Islamic principles of his generation, bringing his children up strictly according to the old standards: men to the forefront and women kept at home, in the background" (36). These words pretend not to be overly critical; to certain readers they might even sound like praise. Yet given the cultural context and the time frame in which Diallo is writing, words like "stringent," "strictly," and "old" are hardly likely to be read as neutral, let alone as laudatory. The description of her grandfather's standards introduces a major subtext of her book: the secondary status given to women in the context of "old" Islamic culture.

The practice of female exclusion is most powerfully demonstrated in the scene in which Diallo is barred from her own wedding, according to the custom in Muslim society: "The wedding ceremony took place at home. . . . From my closed window I tried to peer through the blinds to see what was happening at the religious ceremony from which women were excluded. I could not see a thing" (117). Though this incident is related in a very matter-of-fact manner, it nonetheless presents a painfully absurd picture—a woman trying to steal glimpses of her own wedding—which, in its suggestion of absence and denial, reflects on the public situation of Muslim women generally. And of course, because this position appears absurd in the perspective of a "modern" woman, the absurdity is exaggerated by Diallo's understated presentation of it.

The narrator uses the celebration of another wedding, that of her cousin Ami, to un-cover the sexual ideology that demands female virginity. Ami was still a virgin when she married, a source of pride for Aunt Safi, the director of the ceremony: "You could not fail to do us honour; you could not do otherwise, seeing the noble blood that flows in your veins. . . . You have all the more merit in managing to keep yourself pure these days when young people no longer respect this tradition and sacrifice it for money, clothes, jewels! Yesterday I spent the whole day full of apprehension. I wondered what the final result would be. You have not disappointed me . . . I shall be able to look my enemies in the face, head high, and sing your praises!" (66–67).

Aunt Safi stresses the idea that Ami did not remain a virgin for her own sake, but proved she came from a noble family by keeping her honor intact. She did not allow herself to be lured from the adherence to and respect of traditional values, which are contrasted with the materialistic view of a society that seduces young girls into "selling" their bodies. This conflict of modern and traditional values, here reduced to the basic equation for women of virginity versus money, engages each writer I will discuss. One of their achievements as a group is to escape that reduction by describing the many possible meanings *modern* and *traditional* may have.

All the aunts in the family not only subscribe to Aunt Safi's belief but also want to make sure that their belief is passed on to the younger generations of women. That is why they join in the praise of Ami and urge other young girls to tread the same path: "Try to follow Ami's example; she has kept herself pure in spite of all the hazards of existence, and has given satisfaction to her husband and her family" (67). Young women who have committed the "sin of impurity," like one of Ami's friends, who is an unmarried mother, must suffer insults and unpleasant innuendos that irritate the young Safi: "I felt sorry for her. I thought these old women were horrible for viciously attacking a girl who was neither their daughter or any relation at all and who did not have to account to them for her behaviour" (66). This outburst of anger expresses Diallo's disapproval not only of the aunts' behavior, of course, but also of the social significance of this behavior in general.

Indeed, Diallo's whole depiction of marriage reveals the manipulation of women through their adherence to cultural norms, for, by a paradoxical and clever twist, the patriarchal system is channelled through and by women, acting as custodians of tradition. In a different work, reflecting on her father's reaction to excision, Kesso Barry, another autobiographer from Guinea-Conakry, makes this point more directly: "Mon père n'approuvait pas, mais il se taisait, car c'était là une affaire de femme dans laquelle il ne voulait pas intervenir. Reste à savoir s'il ne s'agit vraiment que des femmes. . . . Il me faudra des années pour me rendre compte que l'excision est une mutilation, et que, si sa pratique est un domaine strictement réservé aux femmes, ce sont bien les hommes qui, par en dessous, veillent au grain, au nom de leurs sacro-saints principes de mâles" [My father disapproved but he kept quiet because that was women's business and he did not want to interfere. The question is: Is it really women's business? It took me years to realize that excision is a mutilation, and that even if this rite is solely conducted by women, it is still the men who, indirectly, in the name of their sacrosanct male principles make sure that it is done].[9]

Diallo's mother died when she was very young. Her grandmother played a pivotal role in her life, providing her love, nourishment, and the richness of the Senegalese oral traditions through exciting storytelling. The adult Diallo remembers these stories vividly and uses them intertextually in her narrative, as most African writers do. Indeed, whether male or female, African writers are generally influenced by their oral heritage and incorporate several oral forms in their writing, so much so that Mohamadou Kane could say: "On ne peut analyser de dessein narratif sans référence au discours traditionnel" [It is not possible to analyze (written) narrative design without referring to traditional (oral) discourse] (29). Nafissatou transposes orality in her text by introducing the opening formulas to folk stories, and she does this directly in Wolof, her native tongue, to mark further the specificity of orature:

> There, we listened, touched or excited, to the tales and legends my grandmother told us.
>
> "*Léebón*—once upon a time" she would begin.
>
> "*Lippón*—yes, yes!" we chorused.
>
> "*Amon na fi*—there was a . . . " she continued.
>
> "*Dana am*—go on," we replied.
>
> " . . . little girl called Kumba who had no mother and no father." (2)

In addition to the transmission of this oral tradition, the grandmother closely directs Safi as she grows, being "both strict and loving" (6), and the bond between them is so strong, and the complicity so moving, that one can imagine the impact of Mame's words as she tells Safi on commencement of menstruation: "Keep clear of the boys . . . Avoid them like the plague. Even the smell of a boy could make you pregnant. *The shame and dishonor of that would kill me*" (74; emphasis added). The insistence on virginity puts unusual pressure on young girls, because they are made to understand that the reputation of their entire family is at stake. Given the importance of family and of "face saving" within Africa, virginity as a cultural value becomes an efficient means of controlling women's sexuality, while also maintaining patriarchy.

Family ties are again used to induce "good" behavior when Safi's father provides her with words of wisdom just after her wedding:

> Marriage is not a game. It is difficult to live together; clashes will occur, for as you know the tongue and the teeth cohabit but it sometimes happens that the teeth accidentally bite the tongue. It is the same in the life of a couple. Be understanding, be tolerant. . . . Be flexible with your husband, overcome your pride; admit when you are wrong. There is no shame in giving in to your husband. In spite of your "Westernisation" you will never wear the trousers and your husband will never wear the *pagne.* Be gentle, patient and generous like your mother . . . If you follow my counsel you will have no cause for regret and your children will benefit. (118–19)

As far as form is concerned, Safi's father uses the figurative language of oral traditions, but the content of his remarks suggests that submissive and proper behavior will ensure the continuation of tradition, as well as the blessing of children—a woman's most valuable asset. Indeed, women are made to believe that as custodians of traditions, they must pass on these traditions not only by way of words but also by example, by proper, honorable action. One way of ensuring that women—who are usually also mothers—maintain proper behavior is by having them believe that if they falter, their children will be cursed by divine wrath.

Safi had a loving relationship with both her grandmother and her father. The dedication of *A Dakar Childhood* reads: "To my grandmother and my father, without whom neither my life nor this work would have had any meaning" (x). But in her book, Diallo reveals a more complex view of her relationship with her father, admitting to both adoring and fearing him. The father is loving and caring but also a disciplinarian, the sole ruler of the household, the unquestioned master. Safi at one point describes the difference that his presence or absence makes in the compound, though even when he is away the idea of what he represents, the ultimate authority, reigns supreme. He is jealous and overprotective of his daughter, particularly in matters relating to Safi's love choices. The young woman recalls why her father gave her a thorough beating the day he caught her kissing a boy in the street: "In those days honour was very important: the honour of the family, of the clan. And this was no imported virtue, something learned from books: it was an inherent part of our traditional past. Our tales and legends were full of chaste girls, heroic warriors, mothers whose nobility endured to their dying day" (86–87). The in-passing discourse is at work again, here demonstrating the role of orature in shaping young girls' behavior. In "The African Woman Writer," Lauretta Ngcobo makes the same point more forcefully, contrasting the different expectations for boys and girls: "In our male dominated societies our oral traditions extolled the virtues of humility, silent endurance and self-effacing patterns of behaviour for our girls, while young boys received all the encouragement to go out there and triumph and survive" (81).

If Diallo's statement is complimentary, she is nonetheless rebellious when she measures the distance that separates her father's way of thinking from hers: "I wanted to live and I found my path barred with restrictions. I had fallen in love and he [my father] wanted to drown my love in what he called honour" (89). In the end, Safi falls in love and does not hesitate to break her engagement with another young man in order to marry the one she loves. When her flabbergasted sister asks her what family the man she loves is from, an all-important question in a highly stratified society, she retorts: "I do not know, I don't know! I love him. I don't care if he's a sorcerer, a griot or a jeweller. For him I'm prepared to flout all your traditions!" (110).

Safi's emotional resistance appears more forceful because she chooses her times and her issues; her outbursts occur at key moments, as a means of disapproving well-seated traditions that in principle cannot be questioned. The first outburst is triggered by what Safi considers reprehensible behavior on the part of her aunts, who insult an unwed mother for her lack of "virtue," thus humiliating her and imposing on her their own moral values. The second, quoted above, has to do with the origins of the man Safi loves. When she proclaims that she does not care whether he is a jeweller, a sorcerer or a griot, Nafissatou Diallo critically alludes to the caste system that still prevails in Senegal and creates a hierarchical divide based on hereditary class structures.[10]

Safi speaks angrily on two other occasions, once when she becomes indignant about certain funeral rituals, and again when she reacts against having to repress her emotions: "To show affection was considered ill-bred, westernized. In my heart of hearts I cursed the way we were brought up with this strictness, all these scruples and taboos" (58). All of these outbursts have a special significance, marking Diallo's underlying rebellion, which has been implicit in the in-passing discourse; more generally they function as social aporias that break down the harmonious surface of cultural wholeness otherwise idyllically described throughout the autobiography. Safi's position, then, is one that praises tradition while denouncing and opposing certain negative elements of that same tradition, a position reminiscent of the ambivalence in which African women often find themselves, and which Lauretta Ngcobo describes: "Our women are caught up in a hybrid world of the old and the new; the African and the alien locked in the struggle to integrate contradictions into a meaningful new whole. Women whose concern has always had to do with customs and traditions have the task to salvage what they can of our way of life, while dissenting strongly from those customs that they feel we have outgrown or ought to outgrow" (82). Ngcobo makes her remark in a book, *A Double Colonization*, which, as its title suggests, focuses on women's position in colonial history. Oddly, there is almost no political commentary in Diallo's autobiography, even though the writer grew up during colonial times. Susan Stringer rightly points out that Diallo's work "reveal[s] none of the ravages of cultural conflict so often referred to by African writers, nor [does it] express any hostility to colonization" (200).

Diallo, however, is preoccupied with the local cultural and religious traditions that surround her life, and it is in this domain that she goes beyond "dissenting" to un-cover the mechanisms of patriarchal society and "treats themes which subsequent writers will amplify" (Bruner, 326). Although she does this always within the parameters of her strong family ties, emphasizing the centrality of her relationship with her grandmother on the one hand and with her father on the other, at the close of the autobiography she expresses the hope that she has achieved more than just recording her feelings for her loved ones: " 'Write a book to say that you've loved your father and your grandmother? What's so new about that?' I hope that I have done a little more than that; perhaps I have lifted the taboos of silence that reign over our emotions" (133). Indeed, in her subdued and indirect manner, trying to find a balance, Diallo negotiates between the love of these two people and the tyranny they represent culturally and ideologically for the gendered self. Even though contained, her personal rebellion is always just below the surface, and it is in this submerged rebellion that the personal becomes political in a larger sense; this is the political dimension of *A Dakar Childhood.* In this way the in-passing discourse, even as oblique as it is, bears the seeds of power as it metamorphoses itself into quietly subversive utterance, revealing the cultural ideology grounded in a patriarchal system that, ironically, women are made to espouse and transmit.

Ken Bugul: The Process of Self-Discovery

Ken Bugul's *Le Baobab fou* is, according to Dorothy Blair, "the most striking piece of autobiography from Senegal so far" (*African Literature,* 121), and in my view, Blair's praise even understates the power and originality of the work. In it Bugul recreates her life in Gouye, the village where she was raised, depicting a lonely childhood marked by an early separation from her mother, a virtual absence of a father and the lack of emotional support from her larger family. She attends the French school, which becomes a refuge, and she does so well that she wins a scholarship to continue her studies in Belgium. Europe, however, only serves to focus her disillusionment: there she realizes the full implications of being black, colonized, and female, and so begins the search for an identity that will eventually take her back to Gouye, where the abandoned baobab, symbol of her cultural roots, finally signifies a possibility of rebirth.

The summary of the pattern of Bugul's book, of course, reveals little of its power, particularly the effect of her lucid analysis of the impact race and gender have on her life. In the process of self-discovery that she goes through she un-covers things that are too potent, too serious, too enormous, too sharply against the grain, too taboo; they are not things meant to be disclosed. That is why, although *The Abandoned Baobab* is an autobiography included in their series "Vies Africaines" [African lives], Bugul's publishers demanded that she abandon her real name, Mariétou M'Baye, and choose a pseudonym. M'Baye at first resisted this form of silencing, but without success; she then decided to take the name Ken Bugul, which in literal translation from the Wolof means "nobody wants." The phrase anticipates rejection, and because "nobody wants" is incomplete without an object, it is possible to complete the sentence by adding the object "me" (indicating the narrator), "her" (indicating the protagonist), or "this" (indicating what is happening). In other words, "nobody wants me," "nobody wants her," "nobody wants this." Beyond these possible semantics, however, the writer explained in a later interview the particular cultural meaning of her adopted name: "En Wolof, Ken Bugul veut dire 'personne n'en veut.' Lorsqu'une femme qui a eu beaucoup d'enfants morts-nés, a un nouvel enfant, elle l'appelle Ken Bugul pour le faire échapper à ce sort-là. Ce sont des noms symboliques que l'on donne ici, en Afrique. Si l'on dit 'personne n'en veut,' Dieu lui-même n'en voudra pas donc il ne le tuera pas; les esprits n'en voudront pas donc ils ne le voleront pas; les humains n'en voudront pas donc ils ne lui feront pas de mal. Et ceci permettra à l'enfant de vivre" [In Wolof, Ken Bugul means "nobody wants it." When a woman who has had several stillborn babies has a new child, she calls it Ken Bugul to prevent the child from suffering the same fate. It is one of those symbolic names given to children here, in Africa. If you say "nobody wants it," even God will not want it, therefore he will not kill it; the spirits will not want it, therefore they will not steal it; human beings will not want it, therefore they will not harm it. And this will allow the child to live] ("Ken Bugul," 153).

What is clear from this explanation is M'Baye's brilliant response to the silence imposed on her, the denial of her name. She finds in her culture a means to symbolically escape that silencing, for by naming herself Ken Bugul she ensures her survival as a writer born into a new name, in the same way that the child nobody wants is paradoxically more likely to live. And, of course, beyond destroying the emptiness of silence by the very act of writing and by the choice of a pseudonym that protects that writing, Ken Bugul continues to unmask the working of sexual politics in revealing through an interview—the perfect instrument for coming to voice—that the demand she take a pseudonym was predicated on her being a Muslim woman whose autobiographical revelations might constitute a scandal.

Nafissatou Diallo's *A Dakar Childhood* is narrated in a linear, chronological manner, with its ordered sequence giving equal weight to events as they occur. The nonchronological structure of *The Abandoned Baobab* has a very different effect. The book is divided into two parts. The first part, entitled "Ken's Prehistory," covers only fifteen pages, and, like a mythical tale of origin, is designed to place Gouye and its inhabitants in a spatial and temporal framework. It also serves to establish two important tropes of the text, the baobab tree and the amber bead that a child left to itself pushes into its ear. That child turns out to be Ken (hence it is her prehistory), who, abandoned at an early age by her mother, imitates women's gestures. She, however, puts the amber bead inside her ear instead of using it to adorn the ear, and the acute pain that results causes her to shriek aloud. This archetypal cry prefigures the series of painful events that will shape her life, for the events of Ken's short prehistory mark her existence in very profound ways.

The second part of the book, entitled "Histoire de Ken" (here again we have the polysemy of the French word *histoire,* which means "history," "story," or "tale"), is introduced by two pages set in a different font, in italics. This introduction serves as a preamble whose function is to link Ken's prehistory with her history, and lead the reader into Ken's story. "Histoire de Ken" is much closer—in structure and content—to the typical autobiographical genre, though in terms of chronology the narrative is both linear and nonlinear. With flashbacks—some as long as a whole chapter—and flashforwards Bugul manipulates time, constantly alternating past and present to create an elaborate narrative structure that, according to Elisabeth Mudimbe-Boyi, has a "progressive-regressive" movement.[11]

This structural complexity in which form itself is used to create meaning reflects the complication of Ken Bugul's life, a life rendered more complicated due to Bugul's female condition. The autobiography functions as self-analysis, and the narrative in *The Abandoned Baobab* is an instance of what has come to be called the inscription of the gendered self. Bugul's whole experience and quest are informed by the fact that she is a woman and, as a result, her identification with other women is very strong. From the first chapter, "Ken Bugul se souvient" [Ken Bugul remembers] (23), she documents the painful ramifications of womanhood: disillusion about sexual intercourse, pregnancy within months of her arrival in the West, abortion, prostitution. She recognizes that men are attracted to the woman in her. She is very conscious of her power, and vulnerability. Therefore, her political analyses center on the impact of both colonization and of sexual exploitation on women. Many of the events and situations that deeply affect her life are lived through her very body, the female body literally and figuratively bruised, marked physically and emotionally. Thus, it becomes impossible to dissociate Ken Bugul's self-consciousness from her female consciousness.

The events that mark her body have more than a private meaning. Indeed, it is in a dingy doctor's office that Bugul first understands her solidarity with the women standing in line with her. They are all waiting for abortions, for the care and mercy of a man who as a doctor is supposed to help them, heal them, save them. Instead he looks and behaves like an obnoxious quack. Describing the women of all colors and nationalities around her, she says: "We were there together without being together. We were looking at each other without seeing each other. We were women and surely we had the same nightmares, those that only women know" (43). Despite the sense of isolation she feels in every woman in that line, Bugul realizes that in some way women do have the same fate, and growing out of that realization she subsequently develops meaningful, long-lasting friendships with other women. Her friendship with Leonora fertilizes the birth of her "feminist consciousness" (50), but that consciousness is a conclusion she reaches only by way of a nearly total alienation from self, from family, and from society. Ultimately, in order to make sense of her life, Bugul must address the roots of her alienation, which can be found in the significance of the mother and in the impact of the French school and its colonial ideology.

In *The Abandoned Baobab*, the quest for the mother is a primary motif. Throughout her life Bugul dreams of having a close relationship with her mother, yet she calls her "the" mother, as though she represents a generic symbol of mother as biological function: "The eternal mother, the spring that never dries, the indispensable woman without whom life would not be" (12). Clearly, there is a paradox here in that, no doubt as a response to her mother's distance, Bugul sets apart what she wants to be close. Indeed Bugul wants the opposite of a function that distances from the mother; she seeks a *relationship* that would transform "the" mother into "her" mother.

There are only three instances in the book when Bugul refers to her mother as "my mother." The first occurs when, at the age of five, Ken Bugul sees a train taking her mother away: "All my life, I shall curse the day that carried my mother off," she exclaims (66). The refrain "Why did the mother leave?" becomes a recurrent question functioning as a leit-motif throughout the autobiography, and the question is rendered more poignant because it is never answered. The mother's departure becomes central to the structure of the book, the essential mystery for her daughter who cannot understand or accept the separation. And the loss of the mother is in fact a complicated loss, because for Bugul not only did the nefarious train take her mother away, it also erased her childhood, which, as she puts it, was shattered, stolen, not-lived.

The second time Bugul says "my mother" is when she speaks of being "replaced" by a niece. Bugul returned to her mother after a two-year separation, but in the meantime a child who was born to one of Bugul's sisters had taken her place in the mother's affection. The sister was only fifteen, so Bugul's mother looked after the baby, and Bugul experienced that event as a "substitution": "That is why, when I arrived, *my* mother was no longer. All that was left was the mother. All was silence" (112). That silence is so dominant in Bugul's life, and so unbearable, that she develops as her defense against it an inner world filled with interior monologues of all kinds, which balances the outer world's muteness. She navigates between dream, the realm of all possibilities, and an unchangeable reality. She has, in effect, two personalities: the first is internal and reflective, the second an external facade that is flashy, provocative, and carefree. The initial silence neither mother nor daughter could break grows into a wall of unspoken words, making it impossible to establish any connection. This silence confirms and deepens Bugul's initial experience of separation; what she wants from the mother is a display of affection and the comfort of being loved. She misses intimacy with the mother, for instance, when she realizes that her mother has never seen her cry (28), and her desire for the mother's warmth is rendered by physical images involving parts of the body: the mother's womb, her thighs, her breast. More than the comfort zone that a mother's body represents for everyone, it is for Bugul a paradise lost twice and constantly longed for.

The final use of "my mother" occurs when Bugul is dreaming of what she would have liked to have in life: "I dreamed of a brother, a father, a sister, of my mother" (129). Here, the other family members are "functions," whereas her mother is specified, "my," and yet listed among the daughter's absences. Having a mother, or not, takes on an emotional dimension of primary and primal importance. Bugul could not substitute a relationship with her father for her mother's absence; he is busy being a man of God and neglects his daughter's emotional needs. Bugul expresses her feelings about him best in explaining her emotions at his death: "What made me weep was the fact I was now called a fatherless child, I who'd never felt I'd had a father. Losing a father I had not had. That is what made me weep" (77). Already deprived of her parents, neither does Bugul have a close relationship with her brothers and sisters. During her childhood and adolescence she is moved about, living with family friends who do not care for her, or family with whom she has no real ties. She recalls feeling immense loneliness, and coldness toward others, feelings generated by neglect as she is shipped from house to house.

Bugul is isolated, alone in her "void of emotional life" (28), and to fill that void she embraces the French school, unwittingly creating for herself a different kind of alienation. The school represents what is different from her normal environment and therefore appealing. It is a refuge where her imagination can run wild, an escape from her dreary life, and a privileged space where she can dream of what she does not have and conceive of finding it. The school gives her a sense of purpose, and she works hard to accumulate knowledge, though it is knowledge of things that are foreign, and so her studies intensify a process of acculturation. She absorbs French culture so willingly and with such devotion that her single most important dream becomes traveling to Europe, the land of her "ancestors the Gauls," the "Promised Land." In her mind Europe becomes the ideal locus where all dreams can be fulfilled, where love can be found, where happiness will be guaranteed and loneliness liquidated.

In Europe, and specifically in Belgium, however, Bugul discovers the depth of her alienation. Her process of self-discovery proceeds through the painful mediation of alcohol, drugs, and prostitution, which she plunges into as a means of *divertissement*—not "entertainment," but Pascalian "diversion," here with no religious connotation. Bugul centers her life in a giddy round of "pleasures" that render her existence even more empty. What she finally discovers in Europe is "this supplementary being, useless, displaced, incoherent" (85).

Bugul's crisis of identity in Belgium is a matter of race as well as gender. She identifies not only with a Western culture that she sees as a dominant power but also with the white race that exercises that power. She has been nourished on colonial books that debased the black race: "In every school text I'd ever had, the Black person was ridiculed, vilified, crushed. . . . They'd be represented in the darkest of India inks, ugly and lightless. All stupidity, all foolishness, all awkwardness was theirs . . . " (90). Given this vision of blacks, there is a kind of mad logic in her desire to dissociate herself from her own race. This logic is forcefully dramatized in an episode in which, during a drug-induced hallucination, she visualizes tearing off her own skin to rid herself of her blackness (96). Frantz Fanon, in *Peau noire, masques blancs* [Black skin, white masks], analyzed the psychological implications of just such a terrible fantasy in the context of the Antilles. In the context of most African countries, however, the desire to escape one's blackness is an extremely rare phenomenon, either in real life or in literature. The rarity of her action adds to the force of an already powerful image: "I was tearing at my skin until it bled. Its blackness was smothering me . . . " (96); she even asks her friend Laure to help her: "I was clinging to her and asking her to rip my skin off. I did not want to have a black skin any longer" (96).

Obviously wanting to tear off one's own skin is an act of great desperation, an act that goes far beyond self-silencing; it inevitably leads to self-destruction. Why would Ken Bugul want to make such a hopeless choice? I think it is not the self-hatred so much emphasized in the literature of the blacks of the diaspora that is at stake here. It is important that this action takes place in Europe and not in Africa, or more precisely in Senegal, where the color of one's skin would not be an issue.[12] In the European context the color of the skin, the very first visual element of identification, becomes a sign, part of a signifying system that generates prejudice, discrimination, debasement, or insulting curiosity. The skin, neutrally, physiologically, is a necessary envelope that provides the body with a barrier against the physical environment. But in Europe, Ken Bugul's skin of course loses its physiological neutrality; it becomes a huge social stigma. That stigma makes it necessary to distinguish between her desire to escape her blackness and a desire to be white. What she wants to destroy is not the *fact* of having a black skin but the *significance* of having a black skin, which so conspicuously marks one's difference in a racist environment.

Ultimately, her confusion over gender and race meet in her ambition to be "a Black woman who appeals to the white man" (82), for her relations with white men are very ambivalent. She seeks them out, yet she is both attracted and repelled by the whiteness of their skin, and she begins to realize that she has been attracted by the most pathological aspects of Western culture. Her confession explaining why she became involved in prostitution—"They desired me, I pleased them; prostitution provided me with a moment of attention" (106)—shows the depth of Bugul's isolation. The condition that set her on the road to Europe is not healed there but exacerbated, and the racism that began in her French school texts reduces her own worth to "a moment of attention."

When Bugul sums up what she has to contend with: "To be a woman . . . to be a child without any notion of parents, to be Black, and to be colonized" (93), she recognizes her alienation as something imposed by specific social conflicts. When she analyzes her own defenselessness in these conflicts, she returns to her lack of what she calls *le repère*, a word that is used frequently in the narrative. *Le repère* has a double meaning: literally it means "landmark," but used figuratively it means "a point of reference." At times, she substitutes *référence* or *attaches* (links) for repère, and occasionally she qualifies those terms and admits that she has no "solid" or no "emotional" repère, no "essential reference."

The repère that Bugul lacks is represented by both people and place. For instance, Bugul sees its embodiment in grandparents: "With its grandparents, the child was never hungry, never thirsty. Grandmother and grandfather embodied the reassuring landmark . . . " (133–34). In the village, Bugul explains, people always make sure that children spend considerable time with their grandparents, the grandmother in particular, so they can acquire a strong sense of reference. But, as with the mother, Bugul is dispossessed of her grandmother, who does not wish a granddaughter to be the first woman in the family to break the chain of tradition by attending the French school. Although the loss of attachment to her mother seems almost accidental, estrangement from the grandmother arises out of a generational gap; unlike Diallo, Ken Bugul lacks family support for her educational plans—in fact, a crucial difference between the two writers' experience seems to be the attitude of their grandmothers toward attending a French school. This common factor suggests, of course, how strong the traditional family relationships are in Senegal, but also how much power women may discreetly exert within that setting.

In Bugul's history the failure of her family to provide an emotional foundation to her life means that the most important representation of repère becomes the baobab tree, which is so central to the narrative structure that it becomes a character in itself, omnipresent, playing a variety of roles. From the outset the French title, *Le Baobab fou* (literally, "the crazy baobab"), suggests a personification, the tree being seen as deprived of reason. This personification continues through the autobiography, for the baobab is given human attributes and feelings. The tree can speak, sing, laugh, cry, sleep, and dream. It can have facial expressions. It can give comfort. This tree is the longest living "person" in Gouye, the only witness, probably, to the three major events of Bugul's narrative that occurred in her small village in the Doucomane region of Senegal. It witnessed the formation of the village; it witnessed the departure of Bugul's mother; it witnessed the gradual removal of the village's children, who were taken away to French schools and so torn from their own traditions.

Ken Bugul chose the baobab as a central metaphor no doubt because it has a multiplicity of virtues and functions in traditional life. It is commonly regarded as a majestic tree, the monarch of the savannah, as it were, which lives to an old, old age. It is a solid tree with an unusually wide and thick trunk, its majesty enhanced by beautiful foliage and flowers of purple and white. The fruit, called monkey bread, dangles from the tree like a lantern from a long rope stem and holds seeds buried in a mealy pulp, which can be eaten or with which *ndiambâne*, a sweet drink, can be made. Unsweetened, it is used in various dishes. The tree's leaves are used in cooking; also, from the fibers of its bark paper, cloth and rope are made. In Doucomane country, the rope serves to weave hammocks. In addition, the baobab is useful as a medicinal plant to cure measles and diarrhea, and finally, in many African cultures, it plays an important role in mythical stories.

In *The Abandoned Baobab*, the baobab is a symbol of continuity and endurance. A new village is constructed where the old one, deserted by its inhabitants after a fire during Ken's "Pre-history," used to stand. In addition, it is the symbol for rebirth as the patriarch, the founder of the new village, chooses a space around the baobab to make a fresh start, to be reborn. The baobab is also a repère, not only as reference but also as landmark: "To show where the house was, one had only to point to the giant baobab tree" (17). In using the baobab as defining symbol, Ken Bugul subscribes to a well-established African tradition in which the symbolism surrounding trees is potent.[13] Further, the baobab can be viewed as a representation of Bugul herself—both are survivors. The baobab survived against all odds—the torrential rains did not wash its seed away, the fire that destroyed the village spared it. In the same way, Bugul is spared by her own process of self-discovery, and she implicitly compares herself to the symbolic tree. A tree, and a baobab in particular, stands for deep-rootedness, whereas Ken Bugul feels uprooted, alienated socially, culturally, spiritually. In examining her life, she is puzzled by the very possibility of such an alienation: "I, who had no frame of reference, how could I be alienated?" (105).

The question is pertinent because if indeed Bugul had no repère, her acquired Western culture could simply have filled a void; there would have been no conflict between Senegal and Europe. But the conflict developed because Bugul did have a cultural repère; she was not a tabula rasa. Her life in the village of Gouye had structured a cultural personality that she only pushed into the recesses of her consciousness, a situation illustrated by the way she repeatedly refers to the village, now seen in a nostalgic manner as an idyllic place, each time she is in trouble in Europe. Despite her alienation, her struggles of identity with gender and race, Gouye is indeed her point of reference.

In search of recognition and love, Bugul constructs in Belgium an identity that does not allow for the depth and complexity of her own self.

Her autobiography is a record of her coming to this awareness, and it moves with the fits and starts, the reconsiderations and ambivalences of self-discovery. What she discovers is both the multiplicity of selves and the depth of her cultural roots. The autobiography functions as a form of public confession and as exorcism. It is, in the writer's own words, "therapeutic writing," and the catharsis that results enables her to go on with her life. As I have indicated, the choice of the tree as the repère is significant. If the tree, symbol of absolute strength, represents Bugul, it means that she can find in herself the strength that would make her life worthwhile. This is the ultimate lesson in self-reliance.

Bugul's narrative conceals how and why the baobab went mad until the end of the book, when the meaning of the title is made explicit. There was a pact between the tree and Ken, but she did not keep her part of the bargain: "I had made a date with the baobab tree, I hadn't shown up and couldn't let it know, I didn't dare. The missed date had caused it deep sorrow. It went mad and died shortly thereafter" (158).

Is Bugul, then, responsible for the baobab's death? The death of the baobab tree hides an ambiguity that can be interpreted in at least two different ways. If the baobab becomes crazy and dies in the end, it means there is no hope for what the tree stood for, or for Ken Bugul's life, which has been dominated by the quest, for mother, father, family, for a link, a reference, a landmark. Yet it is stated that even if the tree is dead, it is still radiantly upright with all its branches. This could be construed as a sign of hope. The greatest cause for hope by far is the fact that Bugul is back in the village to pronounce the baobab's funeral oration. As Mildred Mortimer observes: "Returning to the point of departure, in order to recapture the promise of stability represented by the sturdy tree, Bugul is now ready to assume the identity that she first sought to escape. Hence, the protagonist's outer and inner journeys have led to self-knowledge and perception; writing has resulted in self-affirmation and healing" (176–177).

In a sense, Ken Bugul has observed the "autobiographical pact" proposed by Philippe Lejeune, which is "a form of contract between author and reader in which the autobiographer explicitly commits himself or herself . . . to the sincere effort to come to terms with and to understand his or her own life" (ix). Self-discovery, self-affirmation and healing all come about because Bugul has the courage to un-cover, to put in writing what is usually not-expressed, either by choice or because of social constraint.[14] In uncovering the emotional break between her mother and herself, Ken Bugul explodes the African image of the mother in symbiosis with the family, and particularly with her daughters. She shatters several concepts central and sacred to the African ethos—the family itself, the place of children within the family, the way they are treated and raised, the discourse about sexual matters, and even the intimate disclosure of self. She unequivocally shows how traditional values are garbled, a critique that will also be seen in writers such as Werewere Liking and Calixthe Beyala. In that sense, these female authors all take their readers beyond what Hans-Robert Jauss calls the "horizon of expectations" that had formerly been traced for readers of African fiction.

Andrée Blouin: Growing Up as a *Métisse* in Colonial Africa

In the autobiographies by Nafissatou Diallo and Ken Bugul, author, narrator, and protagonist are presented as a single person, and this approach, as I have suggested, fits Lejeune's definition of the genre rather well. The case of Andrée Blouin's *My Country, Africa: Autobiography of the Black Pasionaria,* however, presents different problems of definition and different questions about the circumstances within which African women may un-cover their lives. A young woman of mixed blood, a métisse (her father was French and her mother African), born in Oubangui-Chari, now the Central African Republic, Blouin grew up in the Congo. She is therefore French-speaking, but, surprisingly, her autobiography is written in English, "with the collaboration of Jean MacKellar." Blouin's autobiography is "auto" and "bio," but the "graphy" has been at least partly mediated by someone other than herself. It may have been fortuitous that the book is written in English, but the choice of language also may disclose a different form of covering than that used by Diallo or Bugul.

My Country, Africa is divided into two parts. In the first part, describing her childhood, adolescence, and early adult life, Blouin concentrates on the matter of what it meant to grow up as a métisse in Africa. The second part, which ends with an epilogue written by her collaborator Jean Mackellar, is a fascinating account of the political activities Blouin was involved in, in West Africa and in the Belgian Congo, during the years that immediately preceded that latter country's independence. Blouin discusses the political situation and the political leaders of the time in such an open way that writing her autobiography in English might be seen as a kind of self-protection. Indeed, she expresses sensitive political opinions and discusses political figures still living and active in such a way that writing this book in French, where it would have been more readily available to Francophone audiences, could have put Blouin's life in jeopardy. In an Africa, where freedom of speech is still, in many places and many ways, a privilege rather than a right, she had reason to be cautious. Writing in English, then, is a political covering, a concealment that in some ways resembles Marietou M'Baye's forced adoption of the pseudonym Ken Bugul.

The title of this section, "Growing Up as a *Métisse* in Colonial Africa," encompasses the two fundamental circumstances of Andrée Blouin's life. Her whole existence was marked by the fact that she was a métisse and that, born in 1921, she was to live through a time when the colonization of Africa was blatant and ruthless. The opening words of the autobiography attest to the special nature of Blouin's condition: "As punishment for the crime of being born of a white father and a black mother I spent my early years in a prison for children. This prison was the orphanage for girls of mixed blood at Brazzaville in the French Congo. The time was the dark years of colonialism in Africa" (3).

The physical and psychological space in which the métisse is confined and the system that makes confinement possible are suggested by her use of the words "orphanage," "crime," "punishment," and "prison," all key to understanding the psychological and emotional patterns that shaped the narrator's life. Even though its children have parents who are alive, the school is called an orphanage because, metaphorically, that name is a way of killing the parents, "fallen" fathers and "primitive" mothers, who have committed the "sin" of transgressing the unwritten laws of sexual behavior between the races. As Blouin came to understand: "The children of mixed blood were a shameful stigma to this society in which the lines for blacks and whites were so clear-cut. That we existed at all was evidence of error in the ways of the infallible colonials. We therefore had to be separated from this society" (33).[15]

Ironically, a symbolic "killing" of the innocent offspring occurs as well, when the children are raised in the "institution of purification," as the white Catholic nuns call their school. This killing, however, is mainly moral and intellectual. The métisses are taught to be ashamed of their mixed origins, of their "illegitimate" status, and this becomes the basic factor that shapes their sense of morality and affects their emotional lives. This status reflects the position of the African woman in mixed liaisons, for the children she might have are considered to be only hers, and not those of the white father. They are also considered illegitimate, even when the parents are married under the laws of the land, as were Pierre Gerbillat and Josephine Wouassimba, Blouin's parents; although these laws are valid for Africans, they are not binding for white males, who, under French law, may also marry a white woman. The position this arrangement leaves for the African "wife" is that of the eternal "concubine," making her children de facto illegitimate, a standing that is hammered into the métisses' consciousness in the orphanage. Consequently, the children grow up with no notion of self-worth, with an incommensurable guilt, and with the theological threat of burning in hell as punishment for their parents' sin. This moral assassination is reinforced by punishment of the body (the ultimate object of sin) that takes the most vicious forms: beatings, deliberate starvation (at one point Blouin resorts to eating the wet clay of the wall after the rains), and other privations.

It is not by chance that the narrator describes her living space as a "prison," for the orphanage is designed like a prison, with high walls separating the girls from the world outside and insuring that people on the outside do not see them. The métisses are indeed prisoners of the colonial social ideal, kept in seclusion as if they were eyesores, as if the mere act of seeing them would lead to widespread, instant miscegenation. This isolation is part of the intellectual "killing" of the girls, for it is intended to regulate their mental development, to allow them no models or ideas apart from those the nuns provide. What the nuns promote is a nearly total ignorance, giving the métisses less than a veneer of education.

Despite these conditions, the young girls are expected to be grateful for being provided a place where the sin of which they are the embodiment can be expiated. As Blouin observes: "That girls such as I were given opportunity to atone for our existence was considered one more proof of the white man's charity as he scourged the black man's land" (3). Her statement uncovers the hypocrisy of a system that hides reality and debases individuals, while purporting to be charitable. The system's intention, after all, is primarily racist: the nuns, and the priests who run a similar institution for boys, arrange marriages between métisse children, keeping them together to avoid spreading the "damage." They even create a special village (for métisse couples only) known as the village of Saint Firmin, for Monsignor Firmin Guichard, who conceived of the idea.

After fourteen years, Blouin can no longer bear the living conditions in the orphanage and runs away to the village of Poto-Poto. Escaped, she discovers the joys of freedom; however, she also discovers she cannot run away from her métisse status, the single most important determinant of her life. It is a condition that places her in a constant state of liminality, making it difficult to relate to blacks or whites, or even to other métisse women; like other métisse women, her "psychology is extremely complex" (85) and she is reserved about human contact. Occasionally, she suffers slights from blacks too. She recalls how hurtful their insults were, and how epithets such as "white of Africa," "badly bleached," or "café au lait" profoundly "touched a métisse's self esteem" (87). The whites' reactions to the métisse usually depended on the viewer's gender. "Most European women hated and feared the métisse" (88) because they often were their rivals. Indeed, for their "forbidden" sexual gratification, white men preferred the métisse to a black woman because "she was closer to his special level" (88). And this double standard, conveying conflicting messages, confuses Blouin: "The contradictions between what we métisses were taught to believe and what we experienced, as women, in our treatment by white men could, if one dwelt upon them too long, drive us mad" (88).

Part of the métisse condition, then, is a psychological inability to escape that "prison" of others' definition. The prison, which opens the book as a powerfully literal reality, becomes its dominant motif figuratively as well. It represents the social means of control, at once confinement and concealment, punishment and expiation, and, most damaging for the psyche, an imposed search for an impossible atonement.

One form of prison from which Blouin cannot extricate herself is the pattern of her relationships with men, beginning with Pierre Gerbillat, her own father. Her complex, conflicting, ambiguous feelings toward him include much resentment, especially as he represents the despicable colonial authority. He discarded her, sending her to the orphanage, and so the orphanage comes to represent rejection by the father as well as the power he wields in the colonial arrangement of reality. His power to create and use institutions is instrumental in his rejection of her, thus turning it into sophisticated, institutionalized rejection that is even more painful and more difficult to endure. In addition, through the orphanage Gerbillat robs Blouin of a childhood she could have spent happily with her loving mother. He denies her financial support at a time she needs it most; he rejects her a second time for having a child out of wedlock, and it is only after she is a grown woman and a mother that he "legitimizes" her by allowing her to carry his name. Despite all of this, Andrée Blouin loves her father and desperately wants to believe that this love is reciprocated. That belief is never verified, but only once do her hidden feelings surface. Almost inadvertently, and with an apology immediately thereafter, Blouin explains: "I never thought of throwing those things in his face. I hadn't dreamed that I would make such a scene. It had simply escaped me" (170–71). This is the only time she records speaking up to her father, and even here she quickly provides a disclaimer. Her silence is self-imposed on this point, and as a result the father-daughter relationship is marked by considerable covering; Blouin hides her real feelings toward her father behind a wall of restraint.

That pattern continues in Blouin's love relationships. Her first involvement is with Roger Serruys, a Belgian director of a mining company. They meet on a boat, fall in love, and decide to live together; however, even before they reach their destination, Blouin begins to understand what life holds for "the mistress of mixed blood" (94). The facts of life are different from the rules for love. She cannot ride in the same car with her love but hides in a separate car that he arranges. Nor is she welcomed by the white officials at his new post. Of this life of entrapment she says: "In spite of myself, I was repeating my mother's humiliating history. . . . I was now to learn, through love, the degrading existence of the African concubine" (96).[16] She adds: "I felt as though I were plunging into a trap. It was a trap of my own choice. . . . already, I was relegated to a second class position . . . the bad had already been done. There was nothing I could do but continue recklessly, in pain of despair" (97). The confession conjures up the image of the chain that cannot be broken, for Andrée Blouin is well aware that she is reenacting her mother's life, but she cannot find ways to escape from the cycle. And the paradox is carried into the confines of her home, which is yet another prison: "It was ironic that after years of longing for freedom at the orphanage I found myself *a prisoner* again in this fine house with elegant rooms and servants. . . . This *sequestered life*, cut off from the society of both white and blacks, was not to my taste at all. Still, it was my option entirely" (100; emphasis added).

The relationship with Roger is short lived, even though they have a daughter named Rita. Later, Blouin meets a second man, Charles Greutz. He is of a lower social status than Roger, but she admires him for his hard work, even while admitting that he is "brutally racist" (125). Blouin confesses that she married Charles because he was a good father to her children, representing the loving father that she never had. Additionally, the nuns conditioned her to accept almost as fate that the métisse woman is to be at the total service of the white man. She acknowledges her own responsibility for accepting this situation, because she realizes that the system of indoctrination and degradation can only work if women adhere to it and remain silent about it: "I did not tell Charles how I felt. He had no idea of the constant duel going on within me between my outrage and my attempt to resign myself to the fate given me as a *métisse*. I was constantly sad, because I knew I was cowardly, that I was putting up with things that I should not. I knew that as a witness of his racism, I was an accomplice to it" (126).

Social silencing and her self-imposed silence do not remove Blouin's outrage when, except for the servants, Charles will not stand the presence of blacks in his household. He pushes this tyranny so far as to prohibit Josephine, Blouin's mother, from visiting. Blouin and Charles have a son, René, and when the boy is very sick, Josephine is prevented from seeing her grandson and caring for him. Even when the little boy dies, Charles does not allow Josephine to attend the wake and funeral. Regarding these prohibitions, Blouin says: "We *métisses* had to make a terrible choice in our relations with our men; if we insisted on bringing our black mother into our homes, it was likely to destroy our relationship with the men; the alternative was to sacrifice our mothers and live by the mens' terms" (126). This exclusion of her mother reflects the double standards of colonization, and Blouin's silent consent makes her complicit. Yet these experiences are the turning point of her understanding of the colonial racism personified by Charles, whom she eventually divorces. Blouin then marries yet another white man, André Blouin, a prominent, highly educated engineer who graduated from the Ecole Polytechnique in Paris.[17]

Inevitably a question arises as to Blouin's choice of three white husbands, given her dedication to African political freedom and her unhappy experiences in her first two marriages. Her mother was chosen by a white man and accepted being chosen, even coming to adore and feel quite proud of her husband. Blouin, however, feels she is *herself* responsible for her marriages, and tries to explain her racial choices: "I was never courted or asked in marriage by a black man, I should explain. If I had fallen in love with such a man, of course I would have married him. But my ways were not those that would attract an ordinary black who was accustomed to expect a docile, long-suffering wife. One who, having borne much from the whites, would accept in her home further injustice from her black husband. My fierce independence undoubtedly set me apart. I was not cast in the usual mode. This is not something I regret" (157).

Of course, perhaps Blouin did not place herself in a situation where she could be courted by a black man. Certainly, her thirst for freedom was hardly being fulfilled in her first two marriages, where she was little more than a prisoner. And two other rather problematic assumptions appear in her statement, that all African women are "docile and long-suffering wives," and even that it is "better" to suffer injustice from a white man than it is from a black man.

The group Blouin seems to identify with most closely is the métisses; she even usually speaks of herself using the plural pronoun "we," marking herself as a spokesperson for them.[18] But she is almost silent on the existence of métisse men. Luc Pacoteaux, the young man picked out by the nuns for her to marry, is mentioned briefly. She rejects him because she feels most arranged marriages between métisses are unhappy ones. Finally, her explanations of her choices in love are not entirely convincing. Her marriage to Charles, the extreme racist, is contradictory for both sides; can she imagine that a man who rejects her mother for her race and who detests everything remotely connected with blacks can genuinely love her? About André, the man she finally marries for good, she remarks somewhat ingenuously: "I did not fall in love with a white man. I fell in love with André Blouin, who was a white man" (156).

One explanation Blouin gives for her attraction to white men is her conditioning by nuns at the orphanage; she was taught that métisse women were to be at the service of whites. A less sympathetic view would fit other descriptions of métisse women in African fiction, the best known being Nini in Abdoulaye Sadji's *Nini, mûlatresse du Sénégal* (1954). In general these women are depicted as trying to escape their Africanness, scorning everything African and identifying with the white race in every way. And although métisses are rarely given full acceptance by whites, as Blouin's autobiography so bitterly documents, in a racist environment their "in-between" status confuses their relationships to both blacks and whites.[19] (It will be recalled that South Africa, in its racial obsession, created a special legal category for people of mixed blood, the Coloureds, giving a kind of constitutional status to their liminal condition.) Blouin experiences some of this confusion, particularly in her early years, but she does not fit Sadji's model, or Frantz Fanon's in *Peau noire, masques blancs* (1952).

Blouin's connection to Africa, its values, its culture, is stated unambiguously in the epilogue of the book when Jean Mackellar asks her what her message for Africa's youngsters of the year 2000 would be. She answers: "Never give up your African personality. Keep your attachment to the land, to Africa. Wherever you may be, you have one great connection, and that is Africa, with all that this means. In spite of the pressures of modern life, always return to your source. Always be African. Nothing can replace our land. Nothing Ever" (294). This strong feeling of being African has been imparted to Blouin by her mother Josephine, with whom she has a relationship of love and unconditional acceptance that balances her father's rejection. The mother's crucial role recalls Diallo's grandmother and Bugul's mother as powerful influences for better or worse, but Blouin's portrait is the most detailed and the most effectively drawn. Blouin recalls her mother as extremely beautiful, always elegantly dressed and smelling good. More endearing to Blouin, however, is her mother's personality: she is loving, warm, attentive, lively with a tremendous joie de vivre, spontaneous, "irrepressibly sociable" (76), and, for her, happiness is a natural state of being. Blouin is only four years old when she is separated from her mother, and five years elapse before Pierre Gerbillat finally allows Josephine to see her daughter and gives her the financial means to do so. From Oubangui-Chari, Josephine travels to the Congo to visit Blouin in the orphanage for a week, a blissful period for the young girl. The moment of reunion is one of intense feelings: "With a cry of joy she swept me into her embrace. She hugged me close, close. For many moments we just held one another, she laughing, I sobbing with happiness. My face buried in her breast, I no longer felt like an orphan. I had my mother to touch and love" (28).

During that short time and even later, silence often characterizes Blouin's relationship with her mother, but unlike Ken Bugul's experience, this is a silence that is communion rather than separation. At a later time, Blouin again lives with her mother for a while. She discovers then how important material things are for her mother, and this, along with her mother's view of how to choose men in relation to their financial status, creates the only friction between the two.

In spite of the restrictions in her life, Blouin belongs to another generation. She is a survivor, proud of being able to do things for herself, proud, despite her meager means, that she works for herself. Her mother, on the other hand, is used to being cared for by men and sees them only in terms of their financial power. This difference of point of view, however, does not affect the close relationship that exists between mother and daughter. Blouin devotes a whole chapter to her mother affectionately entitled: "Little Josephine, My Own *Maman*." In contrast to Ken Bugul's experience, the mother in *My Country, Africa* is indeed a repère for Blouin, to whom she gives a strong sense of belonging and a lasting connectedness with her African culture.

Josephine's reaction to the news that Blouin is expecting her first child illustrates the nature of the relationship between mother and daughter: "Immediately my mother told me to take off my clothes. Everything. She wanted to see my whole body, to have it entirely free, in the air. Tenderly, she stroked it, pressing my stomach where the child was now alive. To fulfill an important ritual, she hastened to the river for a handful of fine white sand. This she let fall like a gentle rain over my belly, which protruded just a little. Passively I stood there, accepting my mother's loving ministrations, feeling connected through them with my ancestors" (109)

This ritual is highly symbolic: the nakedness is a reaffirmation of Blouin as child, as well as her affirmation as a new mother. With the sand, symbol of the earth on which the child is coming to live, the child is connected to the land and to the ancestors, and the gesture also reconnects the mother-to-be to the same land and ancestors. Finally, because the ritual is performed by Josephine, there is a connection between grandmother, mother, and child, showing continuity and sealing the sense of belonging to the same land and to a common ancestry. The ties between Blouin and her mother remain very strong throughout life, and Blouin explains that even dead, her mother is still very alive: "Each morning when I awaken, my first thought is for my mother. Speaking to her in the language of our country, I greet her, I tell her she will share my day. I tell her my problems, I remember things we have shared, I tell her that I love her" (134).

Her attachment to the African soil and the love for the continent transmitted to her by her mother prepare Andrée Blouin for the political role she is to play as an adult. Historically and politically ignorant at the orphanage, Blouin finally begins to discover the social structures of racism and colonialism, though as a young woman she still does not understand colonization in political terms, or even in terms of justice. When she learns the dynamics of the system, she becomes sensitive to the pain inflicted on Africans and understands the experiences of her childhood in a new light. Her newly acquired awareness in turn leads her to political action.

The distressing images of colonization were first imprinted on her mind when she was eight years old by an experience so traumatic that she narrates it in the first chapter of the autobiography as an important

point of reference. She had heard screams that "only an inhuman suffering could have wrenched . . . from a human throat" (17). These
screams came from a line of African prisoners being beaten to death,
their skins streaking with blood as they shouted over and over, "We
want to be French citizens" (17), which meant, as Blouin was to understand later, that they wanted to have equal rights with the French. Their
revolt was cruelly suppressed and the nuns accused them of committing
"a terrible sin of pride" (18). This disturbing image of grown men being mercilessly beaten, with their agonizing screams and the nuns' in-
ept explanation, haunted Blouin for a long, long time.

Later, traveling throughout the Belgian Congo with Roger, Blouin
came to see the exploitative maneuvers of those whose duty it was to
implement the colonial system. The colonizers took the best lands and
pillaged the mineral and forest resources, always buying raw materials
at minimal prices. In the name of the *mission civilisatrice,* they created
new tastes and new needs in their laborers in order to sell to them, at
high profit, goods imported from Europe. They introduced taxes and institutionalized forced labor, which was only a new variation of slavery.

Andrée Blouin describes these and other brutal aspects of colonialism, most of which are well known and documented by historians and
social scientists. What she brings to her text, however, is the testimony
of experience, the circumstances and details of what she actually saw,
witnessed, suffered. The power of her narrative arises from its autobiographical nature, an act of uncovering. For example, Blouin interprets as
an adult an image of colonization similar to the one that caused her so
much pain as a little girl. She discusses this incident with Roger, who,
with an unthinking double standard, addresses *her* with terms of en-
dearment while trivializing her people's suffering:

> "These files of workers we sometimes see by the roadside—they seem to
> be all the same people."
>
> "You are right . . . It's the Moupende people . . . In 1933, the Moupende
> staged an uprising against the Belgians. We put them down, made prison-
> ers of them."
>
> "But my dear, this is 1940!" I said.

"They were sentenced to forced labor for 20 to 30 years, *angel.* That's the punishment for rebellion."

"Forced labor for so long!"

"Their work is useful *my love.* They build our roads and railways." (103; emphasis added)

Although these experiences accumulate, Blouin is most devastatingly struck by the iniquities of colonialism following on her son's illness. The little boy had developed malaria, but was denied a life-saving dose of quinine because the medication was exclusively reserved for European children. He died, and that moment constituted the turning point that politicized Blouin and propelled her into action:

> I understood at last that it was no longer a matter of my own maligned fate but a system of evil whose tentacles reached into every phase of African life. I experienced this evil in the grief particular to a female—in an orphanage for girls, as a repudiated mistress, and most of all, as the mother of a dying child. . . . The difference between my new attitude and the old one was a matter of clarity of vision. . . . When I lost my bronzed little boy I saw finally the pattern connecting my own pain with that of my countrymen and knew that I must act. (153)

Her political involvement begins in Siguiri, Guinea, where she had followed André Blouin, her new husband. In contrast to Charles, André "had escaped the colonial mentality" (157) and encouraged her commitment to help in the process of decolonization. In Guinea, she hears about the RDA, or Rassemblement Démocratique Africain, "a political group formed to arouse and prepare the people of all the French colonies for independence" (168). She becomes acquainted with their leaders and is particularly inspired by the charisma of Sékou Touré, the president of the RDA in Guinea who was to become the first president of that country. Blouin starts by sending money to the RDA and staging little shows whose proceeds go to a charity for abandoned children. Then, in 1957, she completely throws herself into the campaign for the referendum on independence, the same moment of history grippingly fictionalized by Sembène Ousmane in *L'Harmattan* (1964).

Once Andrée Blouin commits to this calling, she is indefatigable. She works in Guinea in support of the RDA, is exiled to Madagascar by the

French colonial administration and only returns after Guinea obtains independence in 1958. Then she is drawn into the Belgian congo's struggles and the early organizing efforts of the MPLA (Popular Movement for
the Liberation of Angola) freedom fighters. When the Belgians abandon
the Congo in 1968 and Mobutu replaces Patrice Lumumba, she helps
create a commission to aid Congolese children. Even the French press is
moved to give her the name Black Pasionaria, a measure of her ceaseless
efforts for African liberation.[20]

If the second part of Andrée Blouin's life is summarized in my analysis, it is because my concern is with the influences in her early life that
led to her actions as an adult woman. All the potential for resistance was
present in her life, but it is her grief as a mother losing her son for the
erroneous notion of racial superiority that pushes her to the political action that consumes a significant part of her adult life. It is in that death
that she sees clearly how her métisse situation is connected to colonialism and racism, and how the condition of being a woman is an important factor in all these intersections. As it is with Nafissatou Diallo's
and Ken Bugul's autobiographies, the inscription of gender is prominent
in *My Country, Africa.*

This continues to be true in Andrée Blouin's life of political involvement. When she first meets Fulbert Youlou and speaks to him in earnest
about critical political concerns, all he does is to compliment her on her
beauty, making it impossible to carry on any form of dialogue. Blouin is
accused of being a witch because she speaks several African languages,
and also of being a spy. She is said to be a "kept woman," who spends considerable amounts of money being dressed by the best Parisian designers.
Finally, she is charged with being the mistress of the political leaders she
is working with, as if a woman cannot be driven by political convictions
only. To compliment her on work well done she is called "a man," as if
that were the very embodiment of all virtue. Andrée Blouin reflects on
her situation as she closes the autobiography: "I consider myself very
handicapped, being born of the female gender. . . . If I had been born a boy
I would never have accepted the way I was treated at the orphanage. . . .
I would not have to bear in silence, whatever they [the nuns] chose to inflict on me. . . . When one wants to express admiration for a great leader,
one says 'There is a *man!*' The compliment is that he does not act like a

woman. But the fact is that women can be very strong . . . women, too, are capable of great sacrifices and bravery" (277). Thus, Blouin has destroyed one kind of silence, and the bravery, here, is to have written an autobiography that denies the limitations imposed on women for no other reason than that they are women.

Yet this autobiography is not without its own contradictions. Some are particularly related to Blouin's relationships with white men, as have been discussed earlier. Others also emerge from her depiction of the African women around her as "docile, long suffering" wives (157), a portrayal further developed in chapter 15, entitled "An Invitation to Help the Congo's Women." She rightly uncovers how polygamy is designed for men's convenience and aggrandizement and to keep women in servitude, yet she attacks the institution as well as the dowry system, without placing these traditions in their sociohistorical context. Also, although she speaks of prostitution in the Congo, she fails to place this phenomenon in the urban framework in which it occurs. Finally, using her own mother as an example, she moves from the African woman to African people in general: "She [my mother] was so unequipped for life, so unconscious of many of its realities. They escaped her, as they do many Africans" (179).

If these images of African women are presented in a problematic and even misleading way, it is rather easy to contradict them by finding within the text itself pronouncements to the contrary. Indeed, how unequipped for life can her mother be when "whatever was painful she lived only for the moment. Then she forgot it, thrust it aside in some riotous new joy. . . . She made life live" (179)? In the same way, there are many instances where Blouin shows that African women are never totally silenced, precisely because these women are not as submissive as she describes them. Perhaps the ambiguities here come from Blouin's position as an insider / outsider, or from what sometimes seems to be an imposition onto the African situation of paradigms that are unsuitable to African contexts. This might be due to the circumstances in which she wrote her autobiography, in the English language and with a collaborator, a mediation that emphasizes the insider / outsider position. Moreover, it is not clear that all this happens at the conscious level. Blouin has a profound attachment for the continent, a real love for its people, and a deep concern for its future: "The truth is, speaking of my life has been my way of speaking of Africa. I want to share my Africa with people who do not yet know what Africa may mean to them. I want Africa to be loved. I speak of my country, Africa, because I want her to be known. We cannot love what we do not know. Knowing comes first, then love follows" (286). As we have seen, Andrée Blouin has gone far beyond her stated goal in *My Country, Africa.*

It should be apparent from the analysis of Diallo, Bugul, and Blouin that for African women autobiography is not entirely, as Lejeune would have it, a focus on individual life or merely the story of the writer's personality. With these three it is not possible to make such a generalization, for the focus shifts from one writer to the next. With Ken Bugul in *The Abandoned Baobab*, the self is prominent; in *A Dakar Childhood*, Nafissatou Diallo emphasizes the social order and how it affects women's lives; and the political dimension is central to Andrée Blouin's *My Country, Africa*, which can be seen, among other things, as a political history of the Belgian Congo (Zaire).[21] In addition, Blouin's book especially exhibits the complexity of the intersections of race, class, and gender. Thus, concepts of selfhood, of society, and of politics are intimately related in this writing. There can be no separation of the self from the group because the individual works within the framework of group identification. This is established through the dialectical motion of women who merge to emerge. They merge into society to analyze it from within in order to emerge from that very society, infinitely richer in awareness.

There has been abundant discussion of the subject of *écriture féminine*, not in the particular sense of the fluid dislocated writing described in French feminist theory, but simply meaning a female way of writing. Some critics believe that écriture féminine exists as a distinctive trait of women's writing, and some argue it is only an illusion; still others stay clear of the controversy to avoid the pitfalls of essentialism.[22] I believe that while it may be difficult to "prove" that women write differently, there is at least a female sensitivity, a different way of beholding the world, which is reflected in women's writing. Without wanting to reopen the debate, it is obvious that in each autobiography studied here there exists an all-pervasive female consciousness. Each of the authors produces, in various ways, what Domna C. Stanton refers to as "auto-gynographies."[23] Even though these women, with the exception perhaps of Ken Bugul, have not taken an overt feminist stance in their lives, the issue of gender is at the very center of their writings. Leah D. Hewitt makes a valid point when she affirms that "a female name attached to an autobiography particularizes the text in ways that a male name does not. Whatever position a contemporary woman autobiographer takes . . . , she is aware that gender affects the reading of her position, whether she likes it or not" (2).

If autobiography is a way of knowing, a mode of cognition of the self, it is also a mode of recognition of the social and political constructs and ideologies in which not only the self but the *gendered* self evolves. It is precisely this cognition / recognition that makes possible the dé/couverte, the process of discovering as covering / un-covering / recovering. In that sense, my initial belief that autobiography provides for women a "safe" entry into writing becomes untenable. It is, on the contrary, a daring undertaking that cannot even cover itself under the guise of the novelistic form, which is rightly or wrongly seen as the "real" fictional mode, and which will be the subject of the following chapters.

CHAPTER TWO

SPEAKING UP,

DISCLOSING FAMILY LIFE

Although in their autobiographies women maintain that they "simply" record their lives—and we have seen that the level of sophistication and of narrative strategies in their work belies this claim—they clearly use the genre to disclose how their lives are affected by patriarchy and colonialism and how they respond to this situation. As we move from autobiography to the novel, we find women continue to use textual constructions to map the conditions of their life and decode the organizing principles underlying the cultural and ideological structures that nurture or smother them. The novel becomes a public forum for discussing private life, and disclosure remains the primary end of representation, even as the genre is putatively different. Ken Bugul, for instance, claims that there is in fact no difference between the two genres and says that she is more preoccupied with expression than with the literary genres that allow that expression.[1] But although genres may allow expression indiscriminately, as I have suggested, societies and governments are less inclined to do so. Certainly within a patriarchal and politically authoritarian atmosphere the advantages of fictional representation over autobiography are significant. The novel offers a different mode of *dé/couvrir*, covering while yet uncovering, while still allowing the transformation of experience into art.

The three novels discussed in this chapter make that transformation. Calixthe Beyala's *Tu t'appelleras Tanga* [Your name will be Tanga] uses the dynamics of *telling* multiple life stories for disclosure and self-representation. The striking interplay of telling and naming is a means of securing sanity and achieving mere survival in a fictional world where the whole concept of womanhood needs to be revised and the mother-daughter relationship confronted anew. Angèle Rawiri's *Fureurs et cris de femmes* [Cries and fury of women] exposes one of the basic tenets of patriarchy, which considers a woman only as a womb, essentializing her and confining her to a reproductive function. Encompassing gender, race, class, and culture, Mariama Bâ's *Un Chant écarlate* [Scarlet song] contemplates woman from a more global perspective, and by showing the devastating effects of its lack, emphasizes the need among women for a solidarity that would transcend divisive social and racial considerations.

Calixthe Beyala: Becoming a Woman / Resisting "Womanhood"?

Calixthe Beyala's first novel, *C'est le Soleil qui m'a brûlée* [It is the sun that burnt me],[2] was a controversial book written against the grain, disclosing the plight of contemporary African women in an extremely trenchant manner, and *Tu t'appelleras Tanga* continues the same themes. This last novel is set in imaginary Iningué, a monstrous new African city where life is harsh for the underprivileged classes that Tanga, the main character of the novel, is part of.[3] The story begins in a prison cell where Tanga is dying. Before her death, however, she pours both her life and her psyche into a French-Jewish cell mate, Anna-Claude, by sharing her life story with her. Tanga eventually dies, but the telling of her story provokes a metamorphosis whereby Anna-Claude becomes Tanga; she resurrects Tanga, in effect, by assuming her identity. Tanga's death is the novel's origin, initiating a circular pattern unfolding through a long, detailed analepsis.

Even this brief synopsis points out the two narrative features of the text that move its story—naming and telling. Naming begins in the very title of the novel, though the narrator avoids disclosing her identity and never flatly says, "*My* name is Tanga." In African cultures, a name is usually given at birth, with additional names added when significant events occur in one's life.[4] Here, the crucial naming takes place late in the novel, where the story focuses on naming as a means of survival, that which figuratively gives a new life. Thus, Tanga pronounces her own name for the very first time when she tells Anna-Claude, "Your name will be Tanga"; before that moment all references to identity are ambiguous. When Anna-Claude first meets her and wants to know her name, Tanga replies, "Ma mémoire s'est fermée sur lui" [My memory has closed itself over my name] (10). Later, when Cul-de-jatte, one of her lovers, asks her name, she retorts: "J'ai perdu mon nom" [I have lost my name] (163). Instead of using "Tanga," the narrator constantly refers to herself as *femme-fillette*, which means "woman-child" or more precisely, "woman–female child."

By identifying herself as someone without a name, Tanga strips herself of a human essential: without a name she is disembodied, neutralized, silenced. Having "lost" her given name, she deliberately assumes a generic identity—that of the woman-child, a compound term that knots the two strands of her being into one, for the name reflects the socialization or coercion of child into woman. At the end of her story (placed at the very beginning of the novel) we close the circle (though without yet realizing this) through a reappropriation of her name, "Tanga." Even though the name is given to another woman, it is Tanga who carries out the renaming, a triumphant reaffirmation of self. The tension between being a woman and resisting "womanhood" is contained in this process of rejecting one's name (Tanga), adopting a new name that is generic (woman-child), and then repossessing one's name in a different person (as Anna-Claude becomes a new Tanga).

The second important narrative feature of the novel is the *act* of telling itself. Not only Tanga, but also Anna-Claude and a character who appears later, Camilla, tell important events of their lives to each other. But this telling must be induced, just as Anna-Claude encourages Tanga: "Qu'as-tu de plus à rester scellée à l'intérieur de toi? . . . Donne-moi ton histoire. Je suis ta délivrance. Il faut assassiner le silence que tu traînes comme une peau morte" [What advantage do you derive from being enclosed within yourself? . . . Give me your story. I am your deliverance. You must murder the silence you let cling to you like a dead skin] (17). The act of telling produces extraordinary results in the novel. It brings forth life, liberates, restores sanity, and ensures immortality. Its potency is such that it even turns a white woman into a black one by means of a veritable transfer of identity.

The telling of the story is sustained by physical contact. Indeed, each time Tanga stops her narration, Anna-Claude takes her hand, or squeezes it, as if to rekindle language in Tanga's dying body. The touching has a vital restorative effect, propelling Tanga deeper into a story that must be told to the end. The act of telling transcends the telling itself. Coupled with the touching it is not only catharsis, and exorcism, but a means of sustaining life. As Arlette Chemain suggests: "Les liens entre les femmes permettent de 'tenir' dans un univers social destructeur" [Only the links that bind these women allow them to "hang on" in a destructive social environment] (163). And like the transfer between osmotic membranes, Tanga discharges her life into Anna-Claude, who will continue it. The act of telling becomes a simultaneous narrative movement, the story that is poured into Anna-Claude and the story that we, as readers, are reading.

The twofold movement reflects another duality, as the novel is marked by the double quest, the same for the two main protagonists. Tanga seeks a life fulfilled by the love that nobody ever gave her; Anna-Claude, who, in many ways is Tanga's double, aspires to the same fulfillment. In another place, and for other reasons, Anna-Claude followed some of the same paths as did Tanga. A victim of discrimination because of her Jewish origins, Anna-Claude is so deprived of love that she lives intensely in an imaginary utopian world where everything is possible and all desires are certain to be realized. Tanga's story, then, is also a means for the disclosure of multiple women's stories. In addition to Anna-Claude's life, Tanga painfully discloses her own mother's life, as well as Camilla's. Finally, the telling of Tanga's story, which goes back to infancy, is a means of giving the children of Iningué a voice.

The process of becoming a woman, which is a central concern in Beyala's novel, involves a development from childhood into adulthood, and so inevitably brings "the voice" of children into the narrative. Tanga's story recounts how children are exploited and victimized in Iningué, silenced by an absolute parental authority: "Je suis une enfant. Je n'existe pas. Mon âge m'annule" [I am a child. I do not exist. My age annuls me] (47). As a child she has no rights whatsoever; she can only be the embodiment of obedience. And if being a child is an "inferior" state, being a female child represents yet a greater liability. Tanga's body can be used, abused, and even commodified as a source of revenue to her mother and family. As she repeatedly says, this process makes her "l'enfant-parent de ses parents" [the child-parent of her parents] (34).

Tanga vividly recalls the ways in which she is forced to "become" a woman. One of the first images of adulthood engraved in her mind, and even more so on her body, is the excision performed on her by "l'arracheuse de clitoris" [the clitoris snatcher]. Tanga remembers the excision as a happy moment for her mother, who expresses her joy with the jubilant words: "Elle est devenue femme, elle est devenue femme" [She has turned into a woman, she has turned into a woman] (24). But Tanga is consumed by the pain inflicted on her, and as "reward" for her *rite de passage* she has only blood and a hole between her thighs. The difference between the two women's reaction to excision is very sharp. Seeking to perpetuate a tradition imposed by patriarchal dictates and having forgotten the pain of the operation, the mother is elated, whereas Tanga, in pain and wonderment, can only attempt to adjust to "cette partie de moi qui s'était absentée" [this part of myself that had become absent] (24). The use of the metaphor signifies that neither the performer of the excision nor the institution that allows it is given any blame; it conveys the helplessness of the woman-child, who must submit to the law without understanding its implications.

As painful as the operation is, it is only the first of a series of terrible incidents that accompany her passage into womanhood. At the age of eight, Tanga is pushed into prostitution by her mother in order to help support her family; it is this act that explains the name—la femme-fillette—she gives herself. Still a child, yet forced to use her body like a woman, she is reduced to a source of ready cash, a process in which her feelings are unimportant: "Personne ne me demande mon avis. D'ailleurs je n'en ai pas. Pauvre mortelle et femme de surcroît" [Nobody asks for my opinion. In any case I have none. I am only a poor mortal and, to make matters worse, a woman] (10). At age twelve, her father rapes her and then poisons the infant he has conceived with his child-daughter. Still a young girl, Tanga suffers multiple rapes by various other people, so that by adolescence she has become numb, incapable of feeling or thought. The woman-child's life is enacted in a dream she records, a nightmare in which she passes in an instant from infancy to adulthood, an image reminiscent of the "old man-child" in Ayi Kwei Armah's *Beautyful Ones Are Not Yet Born.*[5]

The brutalities of Tanga's situation mean that she never experiences childhood, or at least the simplicity and innocence that are ordinarily assumed to fill a child's world. Tanga's indictment of the exploitation of children becomes another central theme for this novel, and it marks a new concern in African fiction: until recently, little attention was given to children as central characters. It is interesting to note in this regard that children become more evident because women as writers give them a larger place.[6] Here, Beyala chooses the harshest words to characterize the exploitation of children, whom she describes as being "slaughtered," "disembowelled," "mutilated." Considered primarily a form of security for old age, children are their parents' slaves, and, in another image of stolen time, they have become "des enfants veufs de leur enfance" [children widowed of their childhood] (76).

As a woman-child, Tanga is not so much defined by her sexuality as she is by other people's demands on it. Coerced into prostitution at an early age, she can say: "A seize ans, j'ai habité tant de lits, jour après jour, avec des hommes de tous les pays, de toutes les couleurs, tous ces hommes qui ondoyaient sur moi, recherchant la silhouette de leurs rêves . . . " [At sixteen, I have lived in so many beds, day after day, with men from all countries, of all colors, all undulating on me, in search of the shadows of their lost dreams . . .] (160). Tanga's childhood is sacrificed to both her parents and the men who use her body to fulfill their fantasies. She is coerced into a "false womanhood," which is only economic and sexual, with no emotional, intellectual, or spiritual dimensions. Tanga detects that same false womanhood in the many other femmes-fillettes who roam the back streets of Iningué, and wishes she could at least save her own sister from this degradation: "Pute-enfant je le suis depuis le début. Mais je voulais pour ma soeur une vie à la dimension des rêves dont ma tête s'emplissait" [I have been a child-whore from the beginning. But for my sister, I wanted a life with the dimension of the dreams that filled my head] (106). That wish in a sense defines a turning point for Tanga, because by speaking to herself she initiates the act of telling, and in that telling is her escape from the imposed silence of childhood. The wish for a different life for her sister also reflects what I call the "community of women," that is, a sense of solidarity that many Francophone women have their female characters share. Indeed, Tanga commiserates with all other femmes-fillettes and does not want them to follow the same painful path she has.

Tanga becomes a woman, in the sense of becoming aware of the community of women, when she witnesses other women's existence—just as Bugul did. She begins with her own mother's life, then Anna-Claude's and Camilla's. To tell her mother's story, Tanga goes back to her grandmother Kadjaba Dongo, who after being raped, brings Tanga's mother into life only reluctantly. Wanting nothing to do with that "illegitimate child," she gives it to her own mother to raise, while making the decision to "tuer sa fertilité" [kill her own fertility] (43). It is not surprising that Tanga's mother develops a confused relationship to her "illegitimate" body—which she regards as an "objet maléfique"—the word *maléfique* combining both ill luck and evil. But meeting Tanga's father she decides she can drive the curse away and with him escape her misfortune. Things do not go as planned: Tanga is born and the husband proves unfaithful, progressing from a few hours absence to whole nights away, and later even bringing other women into the family home.

Turned into the shadow of herself, Tanga's mother accepts all this without rebellion, finds excuses to explain away the situation, and fits herself in the mold of the betrayed woman. Eventually, however, the mother's rebellion comes to the surface in a powerful way, a demented laughter that she passes on to the father: "Eve avait conduit l'homme au péché. Ma mère l'avait entraîné dans la folie" [Eve had dragged man into sin. My mother had dragged him into madness] (49). After her husband dies, the mother has a loveless relationship with a man who has sex with her but has no love for her: "Il la possède très vite, tel un insecte" [He takes her very swiftly, like an insect] (79). He too betrays her, though this time she at least expresses her pain by shouting and kicking him. From that point on she concentrates on her business of working her daughters as prostitutes.

Camilla is another woman whose life is defined by the misfortunes of her gender. Tanga meets her in a bar where they strike up a conversation, and gradually Camilla tells Tanga her story. As a youngster in France, Camilla married Pierre, who was from Iningué, and followed him to his country. An outsider, Camilla's life in Iningué was boring to her, and seeking escape she began to drink and quickly became an alcoholic. Without warning, Pierre abandoned Camilla, and after his departure their two children died tragically; disillusioned, distraught, and alone, Camilla turned to prostitution. All of these later events grow out of a history Camilla doesn't tell, of a childhood scarred by alcoholic parents and a series of foster homes. Although she tells her story in order to understand better how she has become who she is, she cannot shake free from the demons of her past and is unable to tell her whole story.

The way Tanga describes Camilla and reproduces their dialogue reflects the idea of that community of women that is at the center of this novel. But if that community can only come into existence through storytelling, which produces the necessary empathy and self-knowledge, neither Camilla nor Tanga are entirely ready for this. Camilla withholds part of her life, and twice Tanga lies about herself. She tells Camilla that she (Tanga) is not a prostitute, and she tells her boyfriend, Hassan, who comes into the bar, that she does not know Camilla. Here the tension within Tanga comes across vividly. She suffers for / with Camilla, and yet she wants to distance herself from her, because "Camilla est la femme, la morte d'hier qui m'aurait, à moi femme-fillette, légué son histoire. Elle est mon futur refusé" [Camilla is the woman, the dead woman of yesterday who would have passed her story to me, the femme-fillette. She is the future that I refuse to have] (119). The communal meeting of the two women is broken by shame and by a fear of "contamination."

In contrast, when Anna-Claude tells Tanga the story of her past to "tuer le vide du silence" (17), she is able to create an empathy that in turn allows Tanga to speak with complete openness. As Anna-Claude's story unfolds, one understands that she is able to hear Tanga out, to absorb the suffering disclosed by the process of telling, because she too suffered a great deal growing up as a Jew in France. The first time her schoolmates throw her Jewishness at her like an insult, with the phrase "sale juive" [dirty Jew] (148), she goes home and naïvely asks her mother to wash her clean of that Jewishness. The following day she returns to school renewed, thinking that repeated baths have cleaned her of that "dirt." Of course, she is wrong, and so, "dès ce jour, elle apprit à ne plus être juive, à ne plus être, à s'habiller de rêve pour tuer l'angoisse" [from that day on, she learned to stop being a Jew, to stop being altogether, and to clothe herself with dreams that killed anxiety] (149).

Because that state of suspended identity is unbearable, Anna-Claude looks for places where she might find acceptance, and ironically lands in Iningué as a teacher of philosophy. The students find her ideas strange, for she believes that chance does not exist, that the meeting place of humanity is the imaginary world. Nor do her students believe her claims that she lived a previous life in Africa, where she buried her husband alive because he had been unfaithful to her, or that she had twelve children and lost two. In the streets she tells men that she is married and pregnant. But Anna-Claude invents these stories to escape reality and to simulate fulfillment, even as she has constructed her ideal man, Ousmane, whom she travels all the way to Iningué to seek. And Anna-Claude's imaginary power is not only escapist, for despite her seeming ineffectualness, her imagination is a measure of women's suppressed empowerment.

The students listen to her and laugh in disbelief. Nonetheless, because of these students, she is imprisoned. In the politically oppressed Iningué, she dares inquire about students who suddenly are reported missing. As no one will listen to her, she writes on a picket sign "OU SONT NOS ENFANTS? EGORGES PAR UN BOUCHER!" [WHERE ARE OUR CHILDREN? SLAUGHTERED BY A BUTCHER!] (16) and walks across town with it for a whole day. She is arrested and put into jail as an "élément subversif et uncontrollable" [subversive and uncontrollable element] (16). In prison she meets Tanga, accused of helping children to forge money: both women are in prison because they wanted to help dispossessed and voiceless children, deeds of generosity considered "subversive." They will commit together a greater act of subversion, however, by telling their story and by the preservation of that story through the written word.

Although Tanga's childhood is a terrible negation of maturing, of the passage into adulthood, in the act of telling her story she uncovers possibilities of resistance that point toward a different end. She repeatedly says that she wants to be at least a woman, as she has been robbed of her childhood; she is overwhelmed, in fact, by the desire to claim her own identity. Yet she must find a definition of womanhood free of the destructive elements that marked her own upbringing.

Tanga's confusion over what it is to be a woman shows most painfully in her divided sexuality, for although the commercialization of her body is the aspect of womanhood she resists most intensely, it is through sexual degradation that she finds fulfillment: "J'existe là aux yeux de l'homme, juchée sur son désir" [Perched on his desire, I exist in a man's eyes] (27). Tanga is trapped between her moral rejection of prostitution and her physical acceptance of it when she enjoys the pleasurable reactions of her body in contact with her numerous lovers. She is torn between disgust and a reluctant *jouissance.* Her disgust isn't merely a superficial morality; it is rooted in her absolute reduction to an object of sexual pleasure only, to the obliteration of all her human qualities but that one.

Because her womanhood is lived only through the body, she wants to desexualize herself by "removing" those parts of the body most directly associated with sex appeal. Alluding to excision, she tells Hassan that her sex was buried under the banana tree years ago, a removal ordained by patriarchal order; because she was a helpless child then, she could do nothing about her mutilation, but as a grown woman she resolves to complete the job of desexualizing herself. In a cemetery (a setting which, of course, magnifies the symbolic value of her action) Tanga chants: "Je m'accroupis. Je ramasse une motte d'argile incrustée de graviers. Je l'enfouis dans mon sexe. . . . J'enfouis une vipère dans mon sexe. Il distillera le poison. Il envenimera quiconque s'y perdra" [I squat. I pick up a lump of clay inlaid with gravel. I bury it in my sex. . . . I insert a viper in my sex that will distill venom and poison anyone who is lost in it] (152). Not only does Tanga seek her own desexualization, but also punishment for the men who violate her body.

Tanga is filled with "le désir de couper mes seins, d'embrigader mes fesses, de trancher des noeuds gordiens" [the desire to cut off my breasts, to box in my buttocks, to cut the Gordian knots] (91). This desire arises from the repulsive images of women whom she abhors and wants to separate herself from, women like hens who are only "pondeuses" [good layers] or, like heifers, "bâillonnées" [muzzled]. In the novel, images connected with sex often include unyielding inorganic materials such as marble and stone. Of Anna-Claude, who was unable to find love, she says: "Elle avait fini par sculpter son sexe en marbre" [She had ended up carving her sex in marble] (14). To express how she resists the invasion of her body by men, Tanga says that she reached a point where she felt nothing because "mon corps s'était peu à peu transformé en chair de pierre" [my body's flesh had gradually turned to stone] (20). When Tanga rebels and refuses to comply with her mother's demands on her body, her mother curses her with what she thinks is a terrible insult: "Ton sexe est devenu un mur de pierre" [Your sex has turned into a wall of stone] (193). These analogies between a woman's sex and stone create a literal image for the emotional complexities that surround every woman in Beyala's novel. Sexual love, which should express human attachment, softness, and warmth, is transformed into a calculated, indifferent act ("Il la possède très vite, tel un insecte"); and the stone vagina is an objective correlative not only of the alienated woman but also of a social milieu that denies every essential human contact.

The reader does not know that Tanga actually inserts gravel into her vagina. Such an act may have been imagined by her delirious mind, for Tanga is balancing between madness and sanity, but its reality to *her* is part of the story she tells, and that story has a metaphorical truth as well as a literal one. She constantly lives on the edge, wanting to both embrace and resist a madness she feels her mother has passed on to her—at age thirteen, for instance, her mother filled her own vagina with palm nuts. Though Tanga reenacts events from her mother's life, she also recognizes the necessity of freeing herself from these destructive patterns, which involves her in attempting to understand her mother's life, mingled as it is with her own.

Thus, resisting a destructive womanhood also means escaping from the mother who is the custodian of womanhood. Nowhere else in Francophone West African fiction has the mother-daughter relationship been explored so deeply, in such a tormented, sorrowful manner as in *Tu t'appelleras Tanga*.[7] Tanga's mother is never mentioned by name; the only time that her name, Ngâ Taba, appears is at the end of a letter sent to the governor responsible for distributing medals to the "good layers," and the letter, mailed without stamp or address, goes nowhere. Having no destination, the letter will arrive nowhere, erasing the mother's name a second time. The point of the letter's commendation, that the mother brought twelve children into the world, matters little, for ten died in infancy and Tanga and her sister are killed figuratively.

Tanga prostitutes herself for her mother, who supervises the way she dresses when she is to meet with important, rich men. This becomes a parody of the parent's function in socializing their child: here the mother teaches her daughter what to do to attract men and urges her to take advantage of her young body to do so: "Quand le temps va te manger, hé hé . . . Personne ne va plus t'attendre, même pas un chien" [When time eats you up, huh, huh . . . Nobody will wait for you, not even a dog] (109). The goal of this attraction, however, is only a whore's assignation and money for the mother's support. Tanga believes her mother's behavior also reflects her desire to be young again, and consoles her mother, promising never to abandon her and always to provide for her. When disgust about her way of life overwhelms Tanga and she decrees that she needs to take care of herself, her mother feigns sickness and refuses to take medication, as if longing for death. Then Tanga always resumes her degrading job, and when she brings home money and material things, the mother is miraculously restored. During these times of calculated sickness, Tanga looks after her mother dutifully, bathing her, clothing her with newly bought pagnes, performing all of the domestic chores. Afraid that her mother will die, Tanga is subjected to continuous emotional blackmail, and so she becomes, indeed, the child-parent of her own parent.

Tanga understands the dynamics that make her mother act as she does, realizing that her violence against Tanga soothes the pain inflicted on her by her husband. Tanga initially believed that her mother pushed her into prostitution because of an inordinate love for money, but she comes to realize that her mother is simply caught up in a larger, more complex situation in which sexual and economic exploitation are interconnected. As a consequence, her mother is driven by "le désir forcené d'arrêter les bourrasques du malheur . . . de contourner le destin" [the frenzied desire to control the turmoil of adversity . . . to circumvent destiny] (41). Tanga loves her mother despite being so cruelly treated. At one point, when her mother laments that "life is hard," the daughter collects stones and smashes them with a hammer, literalizing her desire to soothe her mother's feelings. Her action expresses the pathos of a child's love, as well as the powerlessness of their situation.

Despite her love, Tanga sees her mother as a coward who allows her husband to betray and hurt her, and because she is determined to escape her own situation, Tanga also comes to perceive her mother as a danger. She represents especially the danger of a silence that manifests itself as denial and madness, a powerful silence that extends its influence to the children. Tanga realizes that to insure her own survival she must escape her mother: "Ce soir, c'est la vieille la mère que je veux interdire de séjour dans ma mémoire. . . . J'ai décidé de vivre, je n'ai plus rien à voir avec la vieille la mère" [This evening, it is the old woman my mother that I want to expel from my memory. . . . I have decided to live; I no longer have any connection with the mother of my past] (58). So Tanga refuses a command to accommodate Mr. John, the rich lover her mother had forced on her; the mother reacts with accusations of ungratefulness and threats of death,[8] but Tanga's resolve to live finally takes precedence: "Je ne veux pas l'entendre, je ne dois pas l'entendre. Il faut chasser l'image de la vieille ma mère secouant sa natte sur les ruines de ma vie" [I do not want to hear her. I must not hear her. I must erase the image of the old woman my mother shaking her mat over the ruins of my life] (82). And she goes so far as to say: "Je déstructure ma mère! C'est un acte de naissance. . . . Je lui échappe, je l'évacue" [I destructure my mother! It is an act of birth. . . . I escape her. I evacuate her] (64–65). And this she must do to avoid being prey to a mother whom she compares to a leech that sucks her blood.

It is extremely important to note that Tanga does not resist all versions of womanhood. It is only a perverted view of womanhood, an aberration of womanhood, that she resists with her extraordinary willpower. Tanga wants to be a "normal woman," not forced to go with a multitude of men. She dreams of loving one man, "la même voix d'homme qui me réveillerait chaque matin" [the same man's voice that would wake me every morning] (30). She dreams of a man who would work all day and come home in the evening, to a house where she will be waiting for him with delicious food set on a beautiful table. One could argue here that Tanga frees herself from her mother's materialism only to resort to a middle-class, Westernized ideal; yet one has to remember that this *is* a dream, that within Tanga's circumstances this is what might constitute happiness.

When Cul-de-jatte, one of her lovers, asks her to give him a child, however, Tanga replies: "Je ne veux pas me multiplier. . . . Je ne veux pas prêter mon ventre à l'éclosion d'une vie" [I do not want to multiply myself. . . . I do not want to lend my womb for the birth of another life] (176). Here she is not against giving birth, but she laments the condition of children born to parents who have nothing to offer them. "A Iningué, la femme a oublié l'enfant, le geste qui donne l'amour, pour devenir une pondeuse" [In Iningué, women have forgotten the children, they have forgotten the gestures of love, they have become layers] (89–90). The implication that one should not have children if one cannot love them is also found expressed in *Elle sera de jaspe et de corail* [It will be of jasper and coral], in which one of Werewere Liking's protagonists contends that those who do not have the force of character necessary to raise a child should refrain from doing so. These are not necessarily commonplace observations in African literature.

Tanga wishes to give motherhood a more loving, more human face. This is why she adopts Mala, an abandoned child: "J'adopterai Mala le fils de personne, je lui donnerai l'enfance oubliée et tout le monde se souviendra car il faudra se souvenir de l'enfant-roi celui qu'il faut porter sur son dos, vers la clarté, vers plus de lumière" [I will adopt Mala the son of no-one. I will give him the childhood that has been forgotten and all the world will remember that a child is a king to be carried on one's back, toward radiance, toward more light] (76). Mala becomes a symbolic child for Tanga, who, by adopting him, is attempting to give to him what was stolen from her. Symbolically she is also giving a mother back to every child in need. It is not by chance that Mala is an abandoned child, nor that his second name is Pieds Gâtés, "Bad Feet." His deformity accentuates the fact that, like Tanga, Pieds Gâtés is a cripple, an outcast. Neither one of them has been able to function as a "normal" human being in a social environment that has nearly destroyed them.[9] Adopting Mala, then, is also adopting herself. She does it for the child no doubt, but also to be able to at last be connected with love, tenderness, and uncalculated joy. Her joy is complete when Mala gives her a present, a drawing representing her recurrent dream: a house, with a magpie in the meadow. Tanga is elated and says: "J'existe. Un cadeau certifie ma naissance. Il me situe. Il viole le malheur. Il me place dans l'enfance gâtée" [I exist. A gift authenticates my birth. It situates me. It rapes misery. It places me among the children who are indulged] (178). Tanga's generosity is thus rewarded, and her relationship with Mala becomes the single happy relationship between child and adult in the novel.

Tanga's effort to redefine womanhood is largely expressed in negatives. Besides her adoption of Mala, she can hardly conceive how to work toward a better state for herself, except her mental sketch of imagined middle-class life. But her resistance may also function moment to moment, as a kind of fantasy mechanism; another way to deny the distortion of womanhood is to escape into an imaginary world. Some words that appear again and again in the text—*absenter, ailleurs, fuir / fuite, dormir, oubli / oublier, mémoire, partir, rêve / réver* (to absent, elsewhere, to escape, to sleep, to forget, memory, to leave, to dream)—indicate that imagination plays a very important role in Tanga's survival, as it does in Anna-Claude's. For both of them imaginary power is a response to the powerlessness of women. Through imagination Tanga can resist her mother, and even escape her, simply by refusing to be present mentally: "Elle peut gueler, j'ai déjà plié bagage" [She can bawl, I have already packed up and gone] (63). Taking a multitude of forms, imagination allows Tanga to leave her place of abode and sorrow and take refuge "dans l'ailleurs" [in a place elsewhere]. She escapes to Paris periodically, for Iningué is a place of intolerable socioeconomic conditions, and Tanga there belongs to the "wretched of the earth."[10] Paris, which of course she has never seen, is a world where she pictures herself as a rich woman; there she knows the meaning of love, has the ability to stop time, and there she has a future.

Not seeing something can mean it does not exist; becoming something else means you cannot feel pain. Vision is Tanga's sophisticated form of escape. She either looks intently at something or closes her eyes to find an inner distraction. She either looks inside of herself for strength or outside of herself to move to different places. She uses sight to avoid the humiliation of prostitution: "Je regarde le mur, rien que le mur, afin d'en prendre sa dureté" [I stare at the wall, only at the wall, so I can take on its stoniness] (33). She moves outside of her immediate reality to become so hard that she can remain motionless, rigid, if not frigid. More radically, imagination even allows Tanga to abstract her body entirely from the reality of prostitution: "J'arrêtais les images . . . Je ne sentais rien, je n'éprouvais rien" [I stopped images . . . I was feeling nothing, nothing] (19). The escape is total, and Tanga can ignore the invasion of her body by men, repossessing herself and regaining control of her sexuality.

Tanga has other means of escape in her ordinary life: she tells herself folk stories, writes, sleeps, anything to block memories, to embrace forgetfulness. Above all she dreams, in broad daylight or at night. A specific dream—which involves a house, a bird at the edge of the meadow, a dog, children, and a man—functions as a leitmotif, repeated twelve times in the story, with slight modifications for each version. The poignancy of this repeated dream is that it asks for little and yet is so far beyond the reach of Tanga's grasp. But Tanga is not alone in her efforts to forget, for each of the women in the novel chooses her own particular form of escape. Anna-Claude escapes into the imaginary world of her own utopian fantasy. Camilla escapes through alcohol and prostitution. Tanga's grandmother declares herself deaf and blind following rape and unwanted pregnancy. Tanga's mother goes mad.

All forms of escape illustrate the long history of resistance by women. This is women's way of rebelling, of challenging patriarchal oppression. What Tanga seems able to do is to distinguish between escape and escapism. Tanga at least avoids the fate of Camilla or of her mother. In her death she leaves her life to Anna-Claude, as a name and as a story, and although it is not certain Anna-Claude will be able to overcome her own madness, her best hope seems to be the example of Tanga's endurance. Perhaps the two women, black and white, are meant to represent one whole new woman, with the vision of Anna-Claude and the will, intelligence, and compassion of Tanga. The story's conclusion imagines this unity, though it leaves its fulfillment provisional.

As the power of the imagination, escape is not only the weak resistance of the oppressed, it is the same impulse that leads to storytelling or to reconceiving the terms of one's life. When Tanga speaks to Anna-Claude she tells a story that reconceives her own life, and the elements of the unlikely or the fantastic that enter her narrative become, as I have said, poetically true, true as metaphors of Tanga's experience. What has happened to Tanga is similar to the experience of Anna-Claude or Camilla or her mother, but Tanga's story refashions events to give them a different meaning. Her mother's life of unredeemable "facts," of events unremarked beyond expediency, has a deathly silence around it. Part of the evidence of Tanga's new meaning is in the fact that her story is being spoken, a story that will remain alive.

Beyala destroys any romanticized or distorted visions of womanhood. For Tanga, becoming a woman has nothing to do with the rite of excision or of being recognized as a sex object. Faced with the extreme situations of her life, Tanga finds her own definition; for her, becoming a woman is to be able to have genuine family relationships in a family that includes a man and children, a family in which love, caring, and tenderness are present. Becoming a woman is to discover the community of women, to recognize the universality of women's oppression and seek ways of resisting that oppression. If these seem very ordinary aspirations, that should only make them more worthwhile, more powerful in their appeal, more necessary in their articulation. Even if Tanga is obliterated, what will endure is the example of her voice, traversing the walls of the prison cells, defining and redefining womanhood: destroying the emptiness of silence.

Angèle Rawiri: "I Have Children, Therefore I Am"

A Cameroonian proverb says that "children are the reward of life," and any survey of women's fiction clearly indicates that for an African woman, children are not only the reward of life, but life itself. To have children is seen as a woman's primary function, her raison d'être, and as a result a woman who has no children does not really exist.[11] She is scorned, discarded, made to feel totally inadequate and so will go to any length to try to "produce" children, not only for herself but also for her husband and to gain acceptance and recognition within society.

Because African women have to deal with the unwritten coercion of "compulsory" childbearing, it is a recurrent theme in their writing.[12] Many women have fictionalized the yearning for children that is embedded in cultural ideology, either making it the focus of their novels or emphasizing its importance,[13] but the special case of barrenness and what it means in a woman's life is particularly emphasized by a novelist from

Gabon, Angèle Rawiri, in *Fureurs et cris de femmes* [Cries and fury of women].[14] The novel's central character is Emilienne, a middle-class, intellectual woman who for more than ten years has been haunted by the wish to give her husband Joseph the son he desires. The fact that they have a daughter does not quench that desire, of course, because a female child is only slightly better than no child. The daughter, Rékia, is largely unappreciated, but when she dies at age twelve, the relationship between husband and wife worsens. Joseph's mother encourages him to divorce his wife and marry his mistress to solve the problem of childlessness. The novel's plot, then, is moved by the absence of children in Joseph and Emilienne's marriage, and by the interference of Emilienne's mother-in-law and the threatening shadow of Emilienne's "rival."

These themes are established immediately; the first chapter, "The Disintegration," deals with one of Emilienne's many miscarriages, and the title alludes to a double disintegration that is taking place, the decomposition of the fetus and Emilienne's near mental breakdown. The narrator muses: "Tout en elle serait-il en train de se désintégrer et de la renier? Son sang, ses larmes, le contenu de son estomac, jusqu'à sa propre image?" [Was it possible that everything in her was disintegrating and renouncing her? Her blood, her tears, the contents of her womb, even her own image?] (26). In this opening the mood of the novel is set, and it is developed as a record of Emilienne's suffering when her desire to have children is frustrated.[15]

Emilienne's goal is not only to give her husband a son. In one of her frequent interior monologues she tells herself, "Il faut que je lui donne un garçon qui lui ressemble" [I must give him a son who will look like him] (25). It is not only a child at stake, for Emilienne and Joseph have the little girl, Rékia (and at first they are happy to have any child). Of course, it is not important whether Rékia resembles Emilienne. As it becomes clear she is going to be an only child, both parents increasingly regret that she is not a boy. Rékia is neutralized because of her gender, made less important; her existence becomes insignificant. What Emilienne wants to "give" her husband is a *male* child, because it is the reproduction of male children that is valorized by patriarchy and by women themselves. Even at that, it is not sufficient to have a male child: Emilienne prefers a son that resembles his father. In this final requirement, she must create for the man a young self-reflection, as if to deny his mortality and prove her own obeisance.

To understand the full meaning of Emilienne's statement, "I must give him a son who will look like him," requires a cultural and psychological perspective. Lauretta Ngcobo rightly points out that motherhood is so important to African societies that it is often institutionalized through fertility rites, taboos, and beliefs. She goes on to explain in cultural terms why childlessness is associated only with women and why they are faulted for not having children:

> Central to many African beliefs is that there are three states of human existence—the land of the unborn, the land of the living, and the land of the ancestors and the dead. Belief has it that the children of any given family are there waiting for the mothers to come and rescue them from oblivion and bring them to life in the land of the living. Failure therefore, to "rescue" the children is a sorrowful capitulation and betrayal. In cases of childlessness, people . . . hear the echoing cries of the unborn child that she (the mother) will not "rescue" and bring to life. (142)

Seen in these quasi-religious terms, it is not surprising that the insistence on childbearing is not only part of cultural ideology but also something that has been absorbed into the individual women's psychology. Women have internalized the primary biological tenet of patriarchy, which posits reproduction as *the* essential act of women's lives. By adhering to this patriarchal command, women place a tremendous psychological burden on themselves, a situation emphasized by the very title of Rawiri's novel, *Fureurs et cris de femmes*. The *cris*, here translated as "cries," are the ones Emilienne cannot even utter because the pain is overwhelming. The word *fureur* has three meanings, each indicating an intense emotional state. *Fureur* can be a madness that leads to violent acts; it can be extreme passion, creating a state close to madness; or it can be extreme rage. The passion and anger that pervade the novel might lead to madness, if they cannot be controlled.

Psychological conditioning for motherhood affects women across class divisions. *Fureurs et cris de femmes* does not involve the "underclass" described in *Tu t'appelleras Tanga*. It depicts a family belonging to the new African bourgeoisie and living in luxury, with an impressive array of servants and a gardening staff. Emilienne belongs to a new generation of African women. She is educated, well-to-do, and professionally successful. She holds a position of high visibility and commands a larger salary than that of her husband, Joseph, whom she chose to marry in spite of family disapproval on both sides. In accordance with this background, and as a member of this new class of African women, Emilienne regards marriage and marital relationships very differently from the traditional cultural belief. Her ideal of domestic arrangement is no longer based on the polygamous model, in which men and women often live parallel lives, but on the notion of *the couple*, involving the sharing of ideas, feelings, and way of life within the parameters of monogamy.[16]

The crisis for Emilienne, however, has to do with the gap between her "new" ideals and the old cultural demands she still accepts. When the family is gathered, waiting to hear from Rékia, who is missing, Emilienne recalls only one event in Rékia's life, which she shares with her own mother, as if to ward off the possibility of the girl's death: "Sais-tu maman . . . qu'elle a eu ses premières règles la semaine dernière? Oui, elle est précoce. Elle est en âge de donner la vie à son tour. Bientôt tu seras grand-mère car elle ne sera pas stérile" [Do you know, Mother . . . that she had her first period last week? Yes, she is precocious. She too is old enough to give birth. Soon, you will be a grandmother because she will not be barren] (42). A girl's life takes on significance only in so far as she can give birth, and Emilienne is so caught up in the patriarchal belief system that she cannot think of a greater loss, should her daughter pass away; all the potential that a human life holds is thus reduced to the possibility of procreation. Because nothing else is so central for her, Emilienne unthinkingly contributes to the circumscription of her daughter's life. Through the novel's narrative, the neutralization of the girl is fully realized in Rékia's actual death.

The centrality of childbearing as a theme in *Fureurs et cris de femmes* is particularly developed with references to the female body. At one point, Emilienne, depressed by her repeated miscarriages, says, "A quoi me sert d'entrenir un corps incapable d'assumer son rôle vital?" [What use is it to look after a body which is unable to fulfil its vital role?] (27). By referring to her body as vessel for children and to procreation as the primary function for her body, Emilienne reveals how completely she subscribes to the dictates of patriarchy, even to the extent that she is willing to neglect her health because she is barren. If this is not exactly self-hatred, it is at least a guilt-induced self-punishment; she alienates her body from herself and then maltreats it for its imagined betrayal.

The novel is constructed around the leitmotif of the womb. Its first sentence refers to Emilienne's "aching womb," and the word *womb* then acts as the perfect synecdoche: a woman *is* a womb. Emilienne is said to be "frappée de stérilité" [struck by barrenness], to have a "chair inféconde" [a barren flesh], a "problème de ventre" [a womb problem] that requires her to finds ways of "débloquer son ventre" [unblocking her womb]. The womb is likened to the earth. When Rékia dies, Emilienne says: "En la choisissant comme leur victime, ils ont percé mon ventre à coups de couteau. En l'assassinant, ils ont tué puis enterré mon ventre déjà mort. Dorénavant, mon ventre lui servira, comme à tous ses frères et soeurs qui n'ont pas réussi à sortir de moi, de cercueil et de tombeau. Ils seront enfin tous réunis dans les confins de mon corps" [In choosing her (Rékia) as their victim, they (the murderers) have pierced my womb with a knife. In murdering her, they have killed and buried my already dead womb. From now on, my womb will be a coffin and a tomb for her as it is for all her brothers and sisters I could not bring to life. Finally, they will all be reunited in the confines of my body] (45). Her statement recalls the remarks of Lauretta Ngcobo; because Emilienne has not been able to "rescue" children from the realm of the unborn, she feels as if she had actually "killed" them. Emilienne later extends the analogy between womb and earth even to reflections on the political upheavals that plague the African continent when she notes: "Le ventre de l'Afrique deviendra bientôt aussi stérile que le mien" [Africa's womb will soon be as barren as mine] (124).

Both of these analogies to the earth have a mythic and a symbolic significance. One is predicated on the well-known "Mother Africa" myth, in which Africa is compared to a nurturing mother and the African mother is given the proportion of the whole continent. This notion magnifies her, but only as an idea, a concept, for it is far removed from the reality of women's daily existence. The other analogy is representative of woman seen as "nature." These analogies, of course, are not complete, for unlike the earth, which can represent the antithetical conditions of life and death, the woman is allowed nurturing qualities only. Following this logic, Emilienne believes that her many miscarriages were caused by past failures on her part and that because of her maternal failings, she deserves to suffer.

The social pressures that reinforce Emilienne's obsessive yearning for children are evident in the way she is treated by the people around her. Her secretary Dominique states bluntly: "Si j'avais été stérile . . . j'aurais pactisé avec le diable pour avoir au moins un gosse" [Had I been barren . . . I would have made a pact with the devil himself to have at least one kid] (100). Dominique then compares a childless woman to a one-armed individual, a cripple to be pitied or ridiculed. Emilienne's mother-in-law, Eyang, believes that Emilienne is a "useless" woman because she cannot have more children. Consequently, Eyang feels justified in looking for a second wife for her son, and plots with this mistress to end Emilienne's marriage. When the plot fails, she can still tell her daughter-in-law: "Au lieu de faire des enfants comme toutes les femmes, tu élèves des chiens et des chats. . . . Tu ferais mieux d'utiliser tout cet argent pour soigner ton ventre malade. Il existe des médecins pour les femmes anormales comme toi" [Instead of making babies like every other woman, you raise dogs and cats. . . . You would do better to use all that money to cure your sick womb. There are doctors for abnormal women like you] (59).

Eyang makes these statements although Emilienne had given birth to a child and is only suffering from a secondary barrenness. According to the social view Eyang presents, Emilienne's dead child does not count, an idea even her sister Eva, who is otherwise very supportive, uses in a harsh attempt to shock Emilienne into seeking medical help: "Tu dois savoir que tu ne seras jamais une femme à part entière tant que tu n'auras pas des enfants que tu élèveras et que ton entourage verra grandir. . . . Ton enfant qui est mort ne compte plus, et dans quelques années on aura oublié que tu as été mère comme toutes les femmes normales" [You must know that you will never be a complete woman as long as you do not have children that you can raise and that people around you can see grow up. . . . Your child who died does not count any longer, and in a few years, people will have forgotten that you have been a mother like all normal women] (89). With these words Eva also completes the erasure that Rékia has been a victim of, erased by her gender, physically obliterated by murder and finally expunged from society's memory. Because many African societies believe the dead remain alive only as long as there exist on earth people who *remember* them, these words would finally dissolve Rékia's social existence. In Rawiri's novel the daughter's death seems to be ordained by the absent, longed-for son; the death is perhaps a melodramatic plot device, yet in terms of a gender ideology that devalues women it has bitter logic. As the desire for a son becomes paramount, Rékia gradually disappears.

Childbearing for a woman is equated with normalcy. Having been told so often that she is not a *femme normale*, Emilienne begins to believe it, particularly as she senses her increasing social isolation. She sees much less of her husband, who spends more and more time with his mistress. Joseph was very sensitive to his wife early in the marriage, and was even present when she delivered their baby—though sharing birth was a rare occurrence among men of his generation. Now, his relationship with his wife has deteriorated to such an extent that "il lui fait l'amour comme un ivrogne se jetant sur une prostituée ramassée sur un trottoir obscur" [he makes love to her like a drunk throwing himself on a prostitute he picked up in a dark alley] (29). This mechanical lovemaking, as in Beyala's novel, is a measure and a reflection of the severance of emotional ties, of the soullessness that has crept into the relationship. It is obvious that Joseph's actions and reactions have a tremendous impact on Emilienne's state of mind.

However, the break between them reflects other tensions about gender roles, some of them peculiar to their class. To be certain, his mother's negative influence plays an important part in Joseph's behavior. But Emilienne's personal achievements also seem to make his own inadequacies more obvious. Joseph resents the fact that Emilienne earns twice as much money as he does, and when he discovers that she has revealed that fact to his mother, he becomes furious and feels he must assert his maleness: "Apprends que je ne me laisserai jamais dominer par une femme" [Be advised that I will never let a woman dominate me] (70). Joseph, who has a very traditional attitude toward marriage, after all, feels that although Emilienne may not need the financial support of any man, it is precisely her financial independence that will bring her downfall. Keeping a mistress flatters Joseph's male ego, and he says that he now understands why well-educated men marry unlettered village women who see the world through their husbands' eyes, are obedient, tolerant, and ever so grateful.

The most alienating incident in the marriage occurs when, after learning that *she* is not barren, Emilienne suggests that they both pay a visit to Dr. Paul. Challenged to prove that he is not sterile either, Joseph discloses that he has two children by his mistress—the older one now being nine years old. Emilienne is devastated by what she sees as a double betrayal. Not only has Joseph led a secret life, but he did so during the period she considered they were most happy together. The realization causes Emilienne to reassess her relationship with her husband, who, living in a man's world, feels justified because his mistress *had succeeded* in giving him a son. He can even feel sorry for himself for having married Emilienne, who turned out to be a "mauvais numéro" [bad number] (95).

Emilienne's isolation extends beyond her husband. Her mother-in-law, of course, thinks nothing of her, but in addition, in a roundabout way, Emilienne feels isolated from her own family, because of her parents' and sister's insistence that she do something about her "womb problem." Sensing that even her parents are ashamed of her, Emilienne cuts herself off from them, curtailing her fields of activity and reducing her living space. At the worst of her depression she does not quit her bedroom, circumscribes her range of movement within the room, and finally confines herself to the bed for days. She falls into a state of physical and mental lethargy, one of the many forms of confinement that appear in the novel. At one point she says that her life with Joseph is nothing but a trap, and she speaks of being a prisoner, as if in a cell (a restrictive psychological space recurrently described by women—Bugul, Blouin, Beyala) where she is sentenced for life.[17] In a rebellious moment, she reminds Joseph that her wedding contract does not include the stipulation that she has to produce children or else be subject to capital punishment.

At this point in the story Rawiri introduces something almost unheard of in African women's fiction, a lesbian relationship that develops between Emilienne and her secretary. Miserable and depressed, Emilienne accepts Dominique's advances to put an end to her hopeless isolation, then finds, as the two women become closer, the physical contact creates a new kind of stir in her. Yet Emilienne, while thinking of how she trembled in Dominique's arms, still denies her feelings; she refuses to analyze "les nouveaux besoins de sa chair" [the new needs of her flesh] (113). In time Emilienne realizes that her relationship to Dominique has become much more fulfilling than her connection to her husband. In the rare moments when he does approach her, she recoils, seeing her sexual relationship with him in a quite new perspective: "Elle se considère le dépotoir des déchets de son époux" [she sees herself as the garbage dump of her husband's refuse] (117). Gradually she comes to feel that she does not have to put up with her husband's duplicitous life, and she begins to delight in her newly found joy and vitality, in her desire to be attractive not to her husband but to a woman like herself.

In the midst of their new intensity of love, Dominique asks Emilienne to obtain a divorce so they can live together. In spite of her feelings for her secretary, Emilienne immediately finds this proposition preposterous. She realizes they do not live on a deserted island, and their society does not tolerate this kind of relationship. Nevertheless, Emilienne is torn. She knows that something has changed within her from the contact with Dominique's body: "Il s'agit . . . d'un réveil physico-sentimental. . . . Et le corps de Dominique, semblable au sien, lui permet non seulement de se redécouvrir, mais également lui procure un certain équilibre" [It is . . . a physical and emotional awakening. . . . And Dominique's body, which is like her own, not only makes her rediscover herself, but also provides her with a certain balance] (146). Emilienne realizes that this "liaison interdite" [forbidden relationship] has become a drug she can no longer do without.

Romantic relationships between women are rare in African women's fiction. They may exist in an ambiguous, metaphorical manner in Beyala's *C'est le soleil qui m'a brûlée* and *Tu t'appelleras Tanga;* however, with Rawiri the relationship is more explicit, and one is tempted to cite Sara Mills's analysis of *The Color Purple* by Alice Walker: "It is also one of the few texts where lesbianism is portrayed not as something which is necessarily biologically determined, but as a choice women can make as an alternative to oppressive sexual relations with men" (64). If this choosing is true of Emilienne, though, it seems to provide a short-lived and inadequate fulfillment, for she realizes that "ce n'est pas l'échange de caresses avec une autre femme qui comblera l'absence du contact charnel de Joseph" [it is not the exchange of caresses with another women that will fulfill my need for physical contact with Joseph] (158–59). And still later, after making the decision to put an end to the relationship with Dominique, she will ask herself, "Comment ai-je donc pu descendre si bas?" [How could I have possibly fallen so low?] (161). As we shall see, this apparently simultaneous acceptance and rejection of socially prohibited behavior is something Rawiri does at various places in her novel. Her inconsistency itself perhaps illustrates the confusion of values in the new urban milieu she writes about, though it can also make the story seem cheaply sensational.

Dominique, it turns out, has used the relationship as a ruse to get Emilienne to seek a divorce. Rawiri so crafts the narrative in *Fureurs et cris de femmes* that the suspense is maintained until the last chapter—even though there are numerous clues to alert the informed reader. We learn finally that Dominique is Joseph's mistress, and when Emilienne refuses to comply with her demands, Dominique grows desperate and tapes a compromising dispute with her lover. She then confronts Joseph with the tape and serves an ultimatum: obtain a divorce or the world will learn that his wife is a lesbian. Dominique's opportunism and complete lack of feeling for Emilienne emerge in this scene; she has simply used Emilienne's plight in a base and cunning manner to advance her own prospects, and so in the end the relationship between the two women is made trivial.

The novel's denouement is instructive in its depiction of the fates of the three main protagonists. When Dominique confronts Joseph with her tape, he is outraged and tells her she is the embodiment of the devil himself. He slaps and kicks her and drives her out of his office, thus putting an end to their relationship. This treatment relies on a "traditional" cultural pattern, which exonerates the man and portrays the "bad woman" as a villain. The explicit violence against Dominique seems to betray the narrator's ideological stance, an allegiance to the patriarchal order and to conservative cultural norms in general. This stance appears elsewhere in the narrative; it poses for a reader the problem of trying to differentiate between the class and cultural bias of the story and a defensive attitude related more to gender politics.

As for Emilienne, in spite of everything she has accomplished as an individual, she has remained emotionally dependent on Joseph. Her happiness is based on him, for she gages herself through his eyes, admitting at one point that "sans lui, ma vie n'a plus de sens" [without him, my life is meaningless] (99). Because she wants his child, she has accepted constant humiliation from him, unable to find the strength to ask for a divorce. Even though her capacity to embrace suffering is astounding, she must drown her pain in alcohol and suffers from bulimia; in her sober moments she does everything she can, as do the other women in the story, to "keep" her husband, regardless of the cost. The cultural reasoning behind her attitude has been concisely summarized: "On the whole a wife will do everything to endure even a stressful marriage, for in a divorce she comes out the loser: even when her husband is the offending party, society sees her as having failed to hold him in place—therefore his failure is her failure as well" (Ngcobo, 149).

Yet at the end of the story, Emilienne completely, and suddenly, reverses her position of emotional dependence. She suddenly achieves an awareness that gives her the strength to end the hurtful life she has been living with Joseph. Realizing how foolish she was to think that having a child would bring back her husband, Emilienne determines she will not put up with Eyang's insults or with Joseph's duplicitous behavior. With a rediscovered confidence, she throws her husband and all his family out of her house. Joseph is thus pushed into the background as the novel ends with the intimation that he has lost both his wife and his mistress.

A proverb from the Ivory Coast claims that "a woman's rebellion is like a glass of hot water—you only have to let it cool off," but it certainly does not apply to Emilienne's deliberate and final decision.[18] Her transformation is not entirely unprepared for in the novel, for she has shown streaks of rebellion intermittently throughout the story. She was proud of her personal achievements as a professional and of the material rewards and the security her economic independence allowed her. She could even be occasionally critical of the idea constantly imposed by everyone, that having a child was her essential purpose and would resolve all of the problems in her life. In one instance she recognizes that "la maternité et les enfants ne représentent pas le bonheur absolu" [motherhood and children do not represent absolute happiness] (92). Yet there remains a crucial, perhaps unresolvable, ambiguity in the story of Emilienne when, three lines from the end, it is obliquely disclosed that she is again expecting a child. Her resistance to the oppressive stereotyping of motherhood is abruptly undercut, and the author seems to be having her ideological cake and eating it too.

In fact, the modus vivendi of Rawiri's novel is based on establishing strong cases for social criticism or weaving shocking events into the narrative, and then effectively undermining them. Rawiri portrays a lesbian relationship—a daring undertaking in African fiction—only to make a mockery of it the novel's finale. Dominique begins as a figure to free Emilienne and then is reduced to an almost stock "other woman," a creation of melodrama. Emilienne seems to break out of her prison of cultural expectations, to become the liberated modern woman of the new class, only to be at the last moment redefined yet again by her pregnancy. I do not believe that the contradictions, which run through the entire novel, can be completely resolved. Rawiri's novel, intentionally or not, reflects somewhat realistically an actual confusion that exists in many African cultures attempting to find a new harmony between the old and the new.

Thus the narrative reveals a series of "blind spots," almost in spite of itself;[19] it can also be seen as an effort to manage that balancing act of African women I have mentioned, an act that allows for progress in a gradual manner, rather than creating rifts between men, in their strongholds of patriarchy, and women who must attempt to demolish those strongholds. A rift is not desirable between either the old and the new or the "traditional" and the "modern." Perhaps the way to resolve these two seemingly contradictory elements is to do just what Rawiri has Emilienne do. She *will* have another child, therefore she *will* exist, but this time it will be on her own terms.

Mariama Bâ: Intersections of Gender, Race, Class, and Culture

After she gained widespread attention with her first novel *Une si longue lettre* [So long a letter], for which she won the 1980 Noma Award for

Publishing in Africa, Mariama Bâ wrote *Un Chant écarlate* [Scarlet song], which was published posthumously in 1991. Divided into three parts, *Scarlet Song* is set in Dakar, Senegal, and Paris. Part 1 revolves around two young students of philosophy who are in love and want to be married. The male protagonist is Ousmane Guèye, whose father, Djibril Guéye, is an important figure in the Muslim community of Dakar, and whose mother, Yaye Khady, is a woman rooted in her African traditions. Mireille de la Vallée, Ousmane's girlfriend, is the female protagonist, a young French woman from a bourgeois family, whose father is a diplomat working at the French embassy in Dakar. His beautiful, official speeches about breaking racial barriers are tested when he discovers that his daughter is in love with a black man. His reaction is instantaneous: he sends his daughter back to France the same day. The separation only serves to strengthen Ousmane and Mireille's relationship, and part 2 describes how at the end of their studies they are secretly married in Paris. Following the traditional Muslim ceremony, they return to Dakar and settle into a domestic life, which is soon disrupted by serious cultural clashes; their relationship begins to deteriorate, a breakdown that is closely and painfully described in part 3 and leads to the novel's tragic denouement.

In *Scarlet Song*, a complex web of relations is uncovered by showing how gender intersects with race, class, and culture in a meeting of Africa and Europe. I have elected to use Mireille, one of the novel's pivotal characters, to explore these intersections, all of which profoundly touch Mireille's life and define her relationships with the other characters (see diagram 3, p. 100). Thus, even Mireille's relationship with her parents, Jean and Mathilde de la Vallée, is marked by gender, race, and class configurations. One of the strengths of Bâ's writing is how she moves easily in and out of both African and European contexts, allowing her to show similarities where differences usually have been depicted. If this novel is about a clash of cultural values, it nevertheless is able to demonstrate how that clash is fought with the same weapons on both sides.

Mathilde de la Vallée, often called Madame de la Vallée, enters the narrative in a revealing breakfast scene: "Madame de la Vallée kept her appetite well under control with a strict diet. In this way she fought against a tendency to put on weight, as her husband's position de-

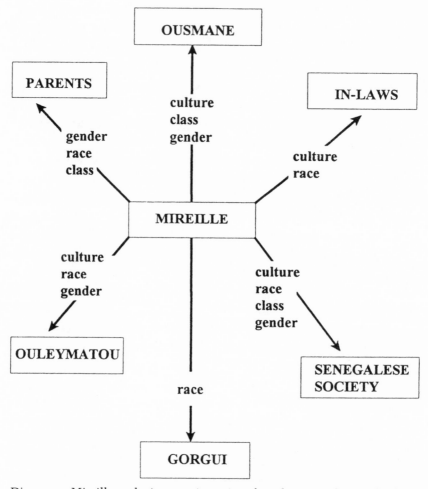

Diagram 3. Mireille as the intersecting point of gender, race, class, and culture in relation to the main characters of the novel *Scarlet Song*.

manded that she retain her beauty and poise."[20] This initial description of Mathilde offers a basic insight into her behavior. She is on a diet not for herself, but to fulfill the demands of her husband's position. As the novel unfolds, other incidents expose Mathilde's position as a woman, as a wife, and as a mother in a similar light. After finding Ousmane's picture in his daughter's belongings, Mathilde's husband calls a family meeting to interrogate Mireille. On entering the room, Mireille "glimpsed her mother sitting stiffly, hardly recognisable" (25), putting a hard shell around herself not to let her feelings show. During the inter-rogation, Monsieur de la Vallée is the only one who talks. His wife does not utter a single word. The decision to send Mireille back to France is made by the father alone, so Mathilde is denied any kind of influence even in the matter of her own daughter's future. Jean de la Vallée can make all family decisions because acceptance from his wife is assured; and not only does she accept his decisions, she also accepts all of his opinions. When her mother comments on the students' re-bellion that shook France in May 1968, Mireille observes this "commonality" of views: "As for Mother, she accepts everything that her husband says. She repeats to visitors whatever she can remember of his diatribes against 'these lunatics' (father's expression), without giving them a chance to air their opinions about what father calls 'this tidal wave' " (43). Madame de la Vallée is thus reduced to be a hu-man parrot, a reso-nance chamber, not capable of thinking or making judgements for her-self. Her husband's words become gospel, the truth, her truth. And her part becomes self-effacement, self-repression, and withdrawal.

Madame de la Vallée's behavior stems from her sociopolitical back-ground. She was raised as a young woman of bourgeois French origins. No explicit time frame is provided for Bâ's novel, but an important clue to the setting is that both Mireille and Ousmane participated in the May 1968 rebellions, in Paris and in Dakar, respectively. It is reasonable to assume that Mireille and Ousmane must have been born in the early 1950s or the late 1940s, and that their parents were born in the twenties or the thirties, important assumption for gender-role analysis, as Mariama Bâ skillfully shows how Mathilde's behavior represents the era in which she has been raised. After Mireille had become the renegade daughter who dared to challenge her father's authority with an act as "vile" as marriage to a black man, and her father has decided to cut all ties with her, Mathilde's background affects her thinking: "She had been brought up in a convent for girls of good family and had learnt, among other things, the principle of obedience. . . . When she heard talk of the problems of women's liberation, she remained indifferent. In her life, only her husband counted. She pampered him, obeyed him and antici-pated his slightest whim" (77–78).

Through careful grooming then, Mathilde was prepared to become an obedient, subservient wife, and the relation she has with her husband underscores the inegalitarian gender politics prevailing in her time. Mathilde lacks any freedom; she cannot do what she wants and, even more damaging, she cannot think independently. She cannot hope to express her own feelings openly. Rendered mute by sexual politics, Madame de la Vallée fits exactly the image of the middle-class French woman described by Simone de Beauvoir in *The Second Sex*.

When Madame de la Vallée reads the letter Mireille had sent to her and her husband informing them of her secret wedding, her heart goes out to her daughter. Filled with memories of her own life, she feels a close bond with Mireille; the mother is ready and willing to forgive her daughter:

> But Jean de la Vallée was planted in front of her, inflexible in the face of this attack on his honour, this assault on his dignity. He exclaimed loud and furiously, "Snake-in-the-grass! Slut!" by which his wife understood that there could be no reconciliation. And then, out of habit—thirty years during which she had not had a thought of her own, no initiative, no rebellion, thirty years during which she had simply moved in the direction in which she was pushed, thirty years during which it had been her lot to agree and applaud—then, out of habit rather than conviction, she sobbed, "Snake-in-the-grass! Slut!" and fell into a faint. (78)

Trapped in a male-defined concept of womanhood, Mathilde speaks with borrowed words; with no voice, she is a mere echo, only reduced to "spinning around the axis of maleness," to borrow Molara Ogundipe-Leslie's phrase.[21] Because the pain of submission is too difficult to bear emotionally, her body gives way and she repeatedly faints as a means of escaping her reality. What makes her situation tragic is that reality always returns: "On opening her eyes, her only feeling was one of total isolation. Her daughter had disappeared into the night. She was sure she would never see her again. She felt plunged into mourning. The only person she had left was her husband, this cold man whom she must wait on, satisfy, applaud, till her heart broke" (78).

Mathilde feels isolated, yet she has no one to turn to except her husband—the very one who isolates and represses her. The use of the word *mourning* (a term that Yaye Khady, Ousmane's mother, will also use later into the novel) has a twofold significance. It constitutes one of the narrative's many clues, which Gérard Genette calls *amorces*.[22] The word *mourning* is such an amorce, which prefigures the novel's denouement and also suggests that Jean's rejection of their daughter is tantamount to "killing" her.

Indeed, Mireille's existence is erased by her father, who cannot stand what he perceives to be her ultimate betrayal. Following his direction, Mathilde erases her daughter as well, in spite of the raw pain that this brings to her. This is neither her decision nor her will, but she knows she is not equipped to rescue Mireille, and she cannot even show her support by maintaining a minimum contact. The mourning, therefore, is a deeper expression of loss, which goes beyond losing her daughter to include the loss of the children that Mireille might have, another amorce that prepares for the conclusion of the novel. Madame de la Vallée has no agency, no way of representing herself as an identity outside of her husband's. Her life, governed by oppression, repression, and deprivation, is a paradigmatic example of the workings of sexism.

As we will see in the analysis of this novel, one of the notable characteristics of *Scarlet Song* is the expert way Mariama Bâ handles characterization through a third-person narrative. Given this fact, it seems appropriate to draw on narratology for an analysis of the relationship between narration and focalization in the novel. Whereas narration reveals who the speaking agent is, focalization determines who is "seeing" characters and events; it determines whose point of view informs the narration at any point of the novel. *Scarlet Song* is replete with narrators and focalizers who allow Mariama Bâ multiple viewpoints, making the novel even more structurally and ideologically complex and challenging.[23] For example, Mathilde is never allowed a direct speech; her ideas and attitudes are focalized by either other characters, Mireille in particular, or the narrator. This reinforces her lack of agency in the novel, for the only time she is the focalizer is within an interior monologue, a voiceless mode, with no interlocutor.

Jean de la Vallée's relationship with his daughter consists only in strictly applying the law of the Father. Jean is the paterfamilias, sole ruler of the household, the exclusive decision maker, the unquestioned Authority. He is the one who knows, understands, orders, and is obeyed. A member of the bourgeoisie, of the dominant class, he is a firm believer in hierarchy and adheres to the status quo that privileges his class. His attitude toward the 1968 students' rebellion in France is characteristic, set against what he feels is a senseless display of anarchy, believing that youngsters have moved away from the "right" path because their parents (read: their fathers) are no longer strict or vigilant. But beyond this usual bourgeois response, he adds: "If I was the Minister, they'd be picking up the dead bodies of their offspring! Then there'd be no more demonstrators, no more barricades! No more protests!" (43). Here, his discourse is framed so as to make it seem ridiculous, because while he is making indignant speeches about parents' lax behavior, his own daughter has elaborated a clandestine device to escape and participate in the riots. Even worse, she is preparing a greater escape: her return to Senegal as the wife of a black man.

Monsieur de la Vallée is three times privileged; he is male, he is bourgeois, and he is white. These advantages are magnified in the Senegalese context, where he holds an important diplomatic position, and where the vestiges of colonialism, well internalized by Jean de la Vallée, still exist and are, in fact, at the root of his racism. On discovering Ousmane's picture, he asks his daughter with utmost disdain: "Do you recognize this object?" (25), referring, of course, not to the picture, but to Ousmane himself.[24] At that moment Mireille, in complete outrage and disbelief, cannot recognize her father as the same man who makes speeches preaching fraternization with the indigenous people. She sees instead, in the most naked and brutal way, her father's hidden racism.

Audre Lorde defines racism as simply "the belief in the inherent superiority of one race over all others and thereby the right to dominance" (45). Jean de la Vallée realizes that open dominance is no longer possible in a postindependent Africa, but set in his neocolonial mentality, he still believes in the European right to control basic economic and political arrangements.[25] Eloquently and from her heart, Mireille reproves the absurdity of his racism, condemning the anachronistic nature of colonialism and the hypocrisy of the neocolonial system. In a few words, she brilliantly demonstrates how groundless her father's theory of white supremacy is; yet, Monsieur de la Vallée is far too entrenched in his prejudice to be touched by his daughter's argument.

Purposely, Mireille chooses to address the letter announcing her marriage to Ousmane to her father's office, a place where decorum must be maintained. This is her attempt both to cut Monsieur de la Vallée down to size and to force him to reflect on his own hypocrisy; he can hardly give vent to his racist feelings within this official context. But she underestimates the depth and the intensity of his prejudice. As far as he is concerned, his daughter's wedding to a black man is, racially and socially, a marriage beneath *his* station. It is a betrayal, a debasement, a miscegenation. It is an act that only a "slut" would commit. Utterly overwhelmed, Monsieur de la Vallée no longer attempts to control his racism. Reading Mireille's letter—"In your book, one can fraternize with a black man, but you don't marry one"—he repeats to himself, "Of course one can fraternize with a black man, but you don't marry one!" (76). With these few lines Bâ brilliantly depicts an insurmountable gap between the generations.

It is only within a racist, colonial mind-set that Monsieur de la Vallée can recall the Africans he has come into contact with. He considers his domestic servants: "Hideous half-wits, guffawing with laughter, the white of their eyes staring out of their vacant faces!" (76). His educated black "colleagues" are no better: "Even more ridiculous with their affected manners and their panting to catch up with generations of civilization! They're primitive people! They behave like primitives!" (76). These comments, so obtrusive that they hardly need remarking on, do have interesting implications about the colonial use of Eurocentric history. In Jean de la Vallée's view, Africans have no civilization, or if they do, it is not one to compare with the "proven" achievements of Western civilization. Implicit in his remarks is the mission civilisatrice, which justified a colonial enterprise in which humanitarian rhetoric concealed the mission's exploitative and hegemonic nature.

In his righteousness, the father feels that his daughter is doomed; she has become part of the African wasteland, and he will have nothing, *nothing* to do with her. His attitude toward Ousmane is significantly different: he refuses to read Ousmane's letter, throwing it immediately in the trash. He rejects the letter outright, just as he had rejected Ousmane; whereas Monsieur de la Vallée strikes his own daughter out of his life, he will not even admit Ousmane's existence. That "object," that black man, is a non-person, one that does not, cannot, exist in his world. There is a seamless, implacable resolution in his racism; nothing is allowed to divert it, and it extends continuously from civilization to nation to individual.

Mireille is very different from her parents. Despite her bourgeois background, she is far removed from their ideological convictions. She has an egalitarian outlook regarding both gender and race. She sees nothing wrong in loving a black man, but, equally, the practice of totally accepting her husband's desires and whims is inconceivable. Mireille is the new woman, the emancipated woman who "wants to be active, a taker, and refuses the passivity man means to impose on her" (Beauvoir, 798). She is also a modern woman who "prides herself on thinking, taking action, working, creating, on the same terms as men; instead of seeking to disparage them, she declares herself their equal" (Beauvoir, 798).

Mireille's clashes with her parents revolve around matters of gender, race, and class. Because her mother's inaction minimizes her relationship with her daughter, those clashes are mainly played out with her father, who has a strong sense of class, a belief in the indisputable superiority of his race and a sexist conception of how his "women folk" must be treated. In Senegal, Mireille's battles are on a different terrain, involve a strong new element of cultural difference, and bring more clashes with women than with men. By going to Dakar as Ousmane's spouse, Mireille was "undergoing two difficult apprenticeships: that of married life and that of a black man's wife in Africa" (99).

During the courting period, both Mireille de la Vallée and Ousmane Guèye were color-blind and largely indifferent to racial or cultural issues. They genuinely believed that love knows no frontiers, that it could transcend class, race, and even culture. They both felt enriched by their differences, which became assets as they were eager to learn more about each other. But even in this picture-perfect time, the narrator provides amorces that subtly foretell the development of the plot. Prior to their marriage there is a scene where, struggling to reach a decision, Ousmane articulates one of these amorces: "I will never split myself apart for you. I will never lose my identity for you!" (39). Mireille, too, is firmly attached to her culture: "I am determined" she says, "to retain my own identity as far as essentials are concerned—the values that I believe in, the truths that light my path" (41). Each character has a strong sense of identity. Although each is willing to meet the other halfway, they are both determined to preserve the essence of who they are culturally.

In fact, there are already conscious cultural deceptions taking place even before the wedding. While Ousmane is in love with Mireille and will marry her, he hides his involvement with her from his parents. He tells his mother, Yaye Khady, that Mireille's photograph is that of a movie star; then he returns to France for the marriage, telling his parents nothing of his intentions. According to African codes of behavior, to marry without the consent of one's parents is unthinkable, and to do so without their knowledge is unpardonable. Yet Ousmane cannot bring himself to disclose his secret love, because he knows the idea will not be acceptable to either parent.

Thus, from the beginning, all the characters surrounding Ousmane and Mireille in Dakar consider their marriage as a betrayal: Ousmane's parents feel betrayed, as do most of his friends and acquaintances. Before marrying Mireille, Ousmane realized he was running the risk of being called a *guena het,* a traitor to his people, and so his choice was heavy with foreboding consequences: "To choose a wife outside the community was an act of treason and he had been taught, 'God punishes traitors' " (37). Most people surrounding Ousmane feel that to marry outside one's race, outside one's community, is to "come down from [one's] own hill" (74). The reference is to a proverb that captures the central thematic focus of the novel, and provides the thrust of its story. The proverb, which can be linked to the concept of the *guena het,* is first alluded to by Yaye Khady and then repeated several times in the course of the narrative. It is fully expressed only on the very last page of the novel: "Kou wathie sa toundeu, tound'eu boo fèke mou tasse. When one abandons one's own hill, the next hill which one climbs will crumble" (168).[26]

In an excellent article, "The Female Condition in Africa: A Literary Exploration by Mariama Bâ," Mbye Baboucar Cham shows very effectively how Mariama Bâ intertwined elements of Wolof culture to weave her narrative: "The cultural concept embodied in the Wolof proverb, 'Ko wathie sa toundeu, toundeu boo fèke mou tasse' (Quand on abandonne son tertre, tout tertre où l'on se hisse croule), influences much of the form and substance of *Un Chant écarlate*" (32). Further, Aminata Maïga

Ka argues: "L'oeuvre de Mariama Bâ est une mise en garde contre les risques de la désobéïssance et du rejet des traditons. 'Ko wathie sa toundeu, tound'eu boo yeck mou tasse'—'Quand on abandonne son tertre, tout tertre où l'on se hisse, croule.' Ramatoulaye, Aïssatou, Jacqueline, Mireille sont toutes victimes de leur entêtement d'être decendues de leur tertre au profit d'un homme" [Mariama Bâ's works are a warning against the risks that disobedience and rejection of tradition entail. "Ko wathie sa toundeu, tound'eu boo yeck mou tasse"—"When you abandon your hill, any hill you climb will crumble." Ramatoulaye, Aïssatou, Jacqueline, and Mireille are all victims of their stubbornness in abandoning their own hill to please a man] (134).

This proverb takes on a deeper significance when one knows that Mariama Bâ initially wanted to title her book *Le Tertre abandonné* [The abandoned hill]. However, it is also pertinent to note that an analysis of *Scarlet Song* clearly shows that Mariama Bâ's opinion is not as absolute as these critics would have it, for in giving several points of view, Bâ indicates the complexity of the problems she fictionalizes. She is aware not only of the dangers defined by the proverb but also of the new attractions that might draw people off of their hill or the circumstances that might force them to leave.

Chapter 2, part 2, of the novel begins to show in detail the cultural distance that divides the young couple. The entire chapter is focalized by Ousmane, and it is one of the few sections in the story where he appears as a sympathetic figure. He has become increasingly aware of the gap between his wife and himself, and he explains this difference by contrasting the significance that drums have for each of them. For Mireille the sound of drums is synonymous with maddening "noise." For Ousmane, drums are not "noise" or even merely musical instruments; they are the very embodiment of his childhood, the bearers of centuries of tradition, the living symbol of his culture. In his mind drums are linked with a rich heritage of orature—songs, folk stories, legends, myths—that his wife does not share. Hence, his nostalgic lament: "Oh, to find an echo to my own voice! To find a kindred soul, tormented by the same thirst! To find the partner, prepared to make the same fantastic journey through life, receptive even to the howl and the hyena . . . " (93). This longing for African culture becomes so strong that Ousmane desperately clings to what he calls his "Negritude," and he delights when his father and his friends praise him for having remained African in spite of his French wife.

Ousmane's behavior is contrasted to that of his cousin Lamine, whose marriage with a French woman is successful. From Mireille's perspective, this success is possible because Lamine is not encumbered by his negritude. Lamine has abandoned some African traditions and largely adopted a Western life-style. Lamine's family believes he is a lost soul, and Ousmane accuses his cousin of turning into a *Toubab* (a white person), but Lamine retorts: "You can't combine two different conceptions of life. . . . If you're to be honest, you've got to make a choice" (98). In turn he questions Ousmane's behavior: "*You* want happiness without making any sacrifice. *You* won't make any concessions, while demanding concessions from others" (98–99).

Ousmane has chosen to marry a white woman without understanding the implications of his choice. A weak character, Ousmane does not realize that it takes special individuals, with strong personalities, to manage a mixed marriage. In addition to the African cultural elements that he has become inordinately attached to, his male ego comes strongly into play, adding to the picture gender configurations: "For Ousmane, any compromise was synonymous with surrender. He countered Mireille's 'stubbornness' with 'the hardening of his own position.' Even when he was in the wrong, he would not give in. Any compromise, any backing down, seemed to him the abdication of his own personality" (99).

Given these circumstances, Ousmane seeks to satisfy both his emotional and his "cultural needs" outside the home. The woman he selects for this purpose is Ouleymatou, a childhood girlfriend who becomes the symbol of the African culture that he craves to embrace anew. She, in turn, sets a trap to win him back for herself. At first he is somewhat remorseful about his unfaithfulness and tries to improve his relationship with Mireille, a half-hearted attempt that is short lived. But soon he embraces his new love and finds excuses to justify his behavior: fate, atavism, cultural heritage, and blood ties explain away his new obsession with "black flesh." He claims that his ultimate goal is to regain his freedom: "He no longer wanted to resist. He wanted to live, to live at last" (112).

When Ousmane learns of Ouleymatou's pregnancy, he resolves to do the honorable thing and marry her, provided she agrees not to have a "turn,"[27] an arrangement he demands to avoid Mireille's suspicion.

Thus, he uses the same strategies to deceive her as he did earlier to hide her. Indeed, Ousmane deliberately keeps his second marriage from his first wife, confident that she'll never come to know about it because she is not prone to lending an ear to gossip.

Ousmane clearly prefers Ouleymatou, who rather than claiming to be an equal partner like Mireille, will wait on her husband hand and foot. In principle Ousmane appreciates equality, but in practice "a man doesn't refuse the prerogatives he is granted . . . " (148). He is too much of a coward to let Mireille know about his actions and his feelings, so his strategy is to isolate her, to become so indifferent that she will be driven to quit the marriage and probably the country as well: "Cut her off . . . let her eat her heart out from neglect and boredom. . . . Don't react to her everlasting fault-finding. Make it easy for her to leave, and then there'll be no ambiguity about the role I shall be able to play; I'll be guaranteed a free hand . . . !" (150). Escaping responsibility, he tries to exclude Mireille from his life.

Just as Mireille wrote her parents to break the wedding news to them, so did Ousmane, who wrote reaffirming his love for his mother and stressing Mireille's conversion to Islam. Ousmane was full of anxiety because he knew that his parents would react to his marriage with horror and disgust: "Djibril Guèye has had experience of white folk. But he had never forgotten that he was different from them, and he was proud of that difference" (38). As for Yaye Khady, he was convinced she "will fight tenaciously . . . fight . . . to her last breath . . . " (38). His predictions are right. Knowing nothing of Ousmane's feelings or plans, the letter announcing Ousmane's marriage to Mireille comes upon Djibril Guèye like a bombshell that leaves him totally devastated. Yet he takes the news stoically, seeing the hand of God in the fateful wedding. Because he is a good Muslim and a leader in that faith, he submits to God's will. When he goes to meet Mireille at the airport, he greets and hugs her warmly, signifying his acceptance.

Yaye Khady's reaction is very different. Having always had a loving, happy relationship with her son, she cannot comprehend how this "calamity" has descended on her. She is furious at herself for not detecting the ominous signs that now seem so evident. Yet she did have a premonition. When Ousmane announced he was going to France, she said, "I've heard that white women are on the look out for black men. Be on your guard. Don't bring us back one of them" (59). It is no wonder then, that when she hears the news Khady is astounded and inconsolable, and from the day she sets her eyes on Mireille, her look is extremely cold. She is against her instantaneously, showing her hostility by alluding to Marième—one of Ousmane's former girlfriends. But Ousmane's retort is direct, to the point, unmistakable: "My wife knows Coumba and Marième by name. . . . And Ouleymatou, and plenty of others as well . . . but she's the woman I love and that I chose to marry" (80). Silenced, Yaye realizes that she will have to act on her own "to get rid of the usurper" (80).

Yaye Khady reacts to Mireille as a mother who has lost her son and who is confused because the mores she is accustomed to are repudiated. Indeed, according to custom, Yaye Khady should have a say in the choice of a daughter-in-law. Similarly, the daughter-in-law is supposed to know the rules and regulations governing the mother-in-law / daughter-in-law relationship:

> What a world of difference between a black daughter-in-law and a white one! A black woman knows and accepts the mother-in-law's rights. She enters the home with the intention of relieving the older woman. The daughter-in-law cocoons her husband's mother in a nest of respect and repose. Acting according to unspoken and undisputed principles, the mother-in-law gives her orders, supervises, makes her demands. She appropriates the greater part of her son's earnings. She is concerned with the running of his household and has her way in the upbringing of her grandchildren. (72)

Yaye Khady is well aware that such rules will have to change with Mireille,[28] and that she will be painfully frustrated in her expectations: "And I who dreamt of a daughter-in-law who'd live here and relieve me of the domestic work by taking over the management of the house, and now I'm faced with a woman who's going to take my son away from me. I shall die on my feet in the kitchen" (66). Yaye feels robbed of her prerogatives and resents Ousmane, and more so Mireille, for having made the unhappy choice.

Yaye Khady truly believes that by marrying a white woman, "Ousmane was introducing an anomaly" (72) into their world. Even before

Yaye had met Mireille, she was calling her a "she-devil," a term that recurs frequently as she describes her daughter-in-law. Not once does Yaye Khady call Mireille by her given name (a form of denial and a way of excluding her from the realm of reality). She also refers to her daughter-in-law as a Jinnee—a spirit that does not belong to the human world—a reference that, ironically, Ousmane contributed to by presenting Mireille as a movie star. For Yaye Khady, however, Mireille is not only the she-devil, the jinnee, she also is the Toubab, the stranger, the usurper, the intruder. She is "this white woman who 'came down from her own hill' to intrude into the black people's world" (74). Yaye Khady finds the intrusion unforgivable.

The complex cross-cultural comparisons Bâ has woven into her narrative produce frequent ironies and contradictions, with shifting points of view. Thus Yaye Khady has lived a good life as a wife and as a mother. Her relationship with her husband seems far happier, and freer, than that of Mme de la Vallée. Contrary to what custom usually allows, Yaye Khady married the man she loved and maintained a loving relationship based on harmony, sharing, and laughter. Being a holy man, filled with a profound sense of duty and responsibility, Djibril Guèye never took a second wife. As Yaye proudly says: "I may have to stay in the kitchen, but I remain queen in my own home" (66). Yet she cannot understand that her son, too, married out of love. She feels betrayed, but cannot put herself in the place of Mireille's mother, whose feelings she dismisses because white people don't have the same attachment to family as "we" (blacks / Africans) do. She falls easily into racist assumptions: "Yaye Khady cared little for the torment of that mother. White people for her were 'abnormal,' not subject to the same laws and the same servitudes as black people" (74).

The most candid accusation of racism against Yaye Khady comes from Soukeyna, her own daughter. Soukeyna is the only member of the family who has made friends with Mireille, and, as the young Frenchwoman is increasingly isolated, she suffers to see her in so much agony. Soukeyna confronts her mother with the truth: "By your selfishness you're driving Ousmane to eventual disaster; and simultaneously, you're killing another woman's daughter, as Mireille also has a mother" (152). This remark is important because killing another woman's daughter is yet another amorce, and because it reveals the character-narrator-focalizer's insistence on the importance of a sisterhood of women in which solidarity should be paramount, binding women together in spite of racial or cultural differences. With her selfishness, Yaye Khady does not admit that the bond exists; by her actions she is "killing" another woman's daughter, just as M. and Mme de la Vallée "killed" their own daughter.

In the same way that Mireille confronted her father, Soukeyna makes her mother acknowledge her racism by telling her: "You reject her because she's white. . . . Her colour is the only reason you've got for hating her. I can't see anything else you can have against her" (152–53). Driven to the wall, Yaye Khady's answer is similar to M. de la Vallée's: "And what if I can't stand Mireille with her white skin among all our blackness? You want my opinion: well, I'm ashamed of my grandson with his skin that's neither black nor white. Go and tell her so. You can despise Ouleymatou and take a foreigner's part" (153). Indeed, both grandparents are rather indifferent when Gorgui, Ousmane and Mireille's son, is born. Djibril Guèye simply says: "This is one of God's creatures; he is born of parents chosen by God and will become what God wishes" (124). Yaye Khady is mesmerized by the resemblance between Gorgui and Ousmane, but the lightness of the baby's skin is a sad reminder that prevents her from receiving the child with joy. Prejudices intact, she is elated when she hears about Ouleymatou's pregnancy. Her reaction is immediate: "Any African woman rather than this white woman. Any African woman would show respect and consideration for me. God is sending me a child to bring Ousmane Guèye back to the right path" (126).

In addition to Yaye Khady's hostility, Mireille must deal with the Senegalese society represented by Ousmane's friends, who use the young couple's household as a meeting place to visit without invitation. They sense Mireille's disapproval but ignore her because, as they put it, "Ousmane is the master of the house! Ousmane is the voice that counts" (86). They praise Ousmane's courage for rejecting neither family nor friends, and argue that marriage in itself is difficult enough without adding the burden of racial differences. They commiserate that he would never know the "titillating little *djité laye*," unless he deceives his wife (86).[29]

Providing yet another amorce, which prefigures his later marriage to Ouleymatou, Ousmane retorts that he need not deceive his wife because both Mireille and he are Muslims, and he could therefore have more than one wife and marry a black woman if he were so inclined.

The question of interracial marriages comes up repeatedly during the conversations of Ousmane's friends. Before falling in love with Mireille, Ousmane himself was not comfortable with the idea of mixed marriages. His friends, who saw that his relationship with Mireille was getting increasingly involved, did not approve: "The bearded member of the group had warned him: "No, no and no again! The reign of mixed marriages is over. . . . A man should look for a wife among his own people. These whites are racists. Their former humanitarianism was nothing but a snare, a shameful weapon of exploitation to lull our consciences" (38). Concerns of class join those of race or nationality as with Boly, the guitarist, who is also against mixed marriages. Boly belongs to the griot caste, and because of long-standing prejudices against his group, his marriage choices were so limited that he chose a Christian woman. He simply cannot understand that Ousmane, who comes from nobility, would go out of his race to find a wife, and he considers Ousmane's choice a betrayal.

Even men who themselves had married white women condemn Ousmane's choice: "We chose this way during the colonial period, out of self-interest, laziness, weakness or opportunism. But you! With the rebirth of our country and the evolution of the black woman! You were the black woman's hope" (122). Ousmane argues that, beyond historical factors, people will always be attracted to other people regardless of race. There is, at this point, a reflection on mixed marriages mostly focalized by Ousmane. He sees two kinds of marriages. The first offers the image of the husband assimilated by the West, with his children as outsiders to the Senegalese family and society. As far as Ousmane is concerned, "this cross-breeding impoverishes and exploits Africa" (122). In the second case, the woman is assimilated by Africa with her children who consider themselves black: "This type of cross-breeding enriches Africa" (122). Neither of Ousmane's arrangements fit the ideas of Mireille, who envisions a third scenario in which difference is accepted and children can choose which of the cultures they want to embrace. The question of mixed marriages is also raised by Guillaume, a French neighbor and colleague to the couple. His racism is so visceral that he cannot stand the idea of seeing Mireille with Ousmane. He makes an effort to honor their invitation to dinner but tells his wife, Genevieve, that he will not return the favor: "I can stand them in their own home. But here, in my place it is unthinkable!" (90). The nickname he has for the couple—"Beauty and the Beast"—is revealing.

Lamine and Ali (Ousmane's cousin and friend, respectively) are the only two Senegalese men who try to make Ousmane come to terms with his choices. Disgusted by the turn of events, Ali tries to get his friend to understand his responsibility toward Mireille, but Ousmane can only think of his responsibility toward Ouleymatou. Ali believes that Ouley-matou might have used supernatural devices to "tie" or bewitch Ous-mane, and he takes his friend to see a diviner, but Ousmane does not respond to the treatment: even before reaching home, Ousmane longs to see Ouleymatou again, because "he no longer saw Mireille as the goal of his desires" (147).

Perhaps Mireille's hill would not have crumbled if it were not for Ouleymatou, whose presence dominates the third part of the novel. A childhood friend of Ousmane's, she adheres to traditional African gen-der roles, and as a young girl rejected Ousmane because he performed women's chores, doing the dishes and sweeping the floor for his mother. But when Ousmane returns to his former neighborhood a successful and overly generous young man, Ouleymatou, divorced after a forced mar-riage, is free and open to the possibility of a renewed relationship with him. She knows of his marital problems, and motivated by love, and per-haps more by ambition, she elaborates a sophisticated plan to win him back. The fact that he is married is no deterrent, as "sharing a man was the common lot of women in her circle and the idea of finding a man for herself alone had never crossed her mind" (106).

Ouleymatou first schemes to win Yaye Khady over to her camp, vis-iting the older woman and asking with feigned surprise why Yaye should be ironing clothes when she has a young daughter-in-law. Yaye Khady sulks: "My daughter-in-law! Hasn't your mother told you? She's white! And for a white woman, the only person who counts is her husband. So, I do the ironing" (106). Promptly, Ouleymatou offers her services, as though substituting in the work for the missing daughter-in-law. She is encouraged in her designs by her own mother and soon by Yaye Khady. Almost immediately, the three woman are in league against the "stranger," who is defenseless in a foreign environment, a physical and emotional exile.

Seductive and manipulative, Ouleymatou organizes her plan around the cultural attributes and habits that Mireille does not possess or cannot understand. She wears beautiful Senegalese *boubous*, uses Senegalese make-up complete with *gongo*, a powerful aphrodisiac perfume, cooks hearty Senegalese dishes for Ousmane, calls him by his pet name "Oussou," makes the beads around her hips jingle, and, to top it all, hires a griot who comes prepared with a well-chosen praise song:

> "Oussou, prince of culture!
> But before you were a prince of culture
> You were and are a Lebu prince
> A white woman forsook her country to follow you
> But better than the white woman
> The Black girl is worthy of you
> Look, look at Ouleymatou, your sister by her blood and by her skin.
> She is the one for you." (118)

Ouleymatou is everything that Mireille is not. To her, entertaining Ousmane's friends is an honor, and in conformity with African hospitality she makes them comfortable and welcomed. Her financial resources are obviously limited, but this too makes Ousmane feel important: she is not on an equal footing with her husband and she has no desire to be. Above all, whereas Mireille seems to pull him away from his culture, he experiences a cultural symbiosis with Ouleymatou, though she can hardly read. In time even her illiteracy is turned into an "asset," because Ousmane decrees that she needs to be "raised" to a higher level and he is delighted to take on the role of teacher and prophet: "In his mind he confused Ouleymatou with Africa, 'an Africa who has to be restored to its prerogative, to be helped to evolve!' " (149–50).[30]

With the efforts of Ouleymatou, Yaye Khady, and others, the estrangement between Ousmane and Mireille is almost complete by the third part of the novel. Several times, Mireille tries to manage a reconciliation with Ousmane, at one point her determination strengthened by the fact that she is expecting a child. Euphoric, she believes that the child will save her marriage and decides to work toward a transformation of her marital life. Wanting to turn a new leaf, Mireille asks her friend Rosalie to teach her Senegalese etiquette—especially as it relates to the mother-in-law / daughter-in-law relationship. But Mireille's efforts remain unappreciated and ridiculed; all her plans fail, a failure reflected in the novel's narrative structure, which hardly touch on Mireille's pregnancy and the birth of her child. It is only through a flashback that we learn about Gorgui's birth, and thus the structure itself trivializes the child, as he has been trivialized by everybody in the story. Not even Ousmane is shown to have felt any thrill, any enthusiasm about Gorgui's birth, and we have already examined the grandparents' lukewarm reaction to the little boy.

At first, Mireille transgresses Senegalese social codes out of ignorance, but now, discouraged and frustrated, she takes a firm stand against her husband's culture and retreats even further into her own. She notices more glaringly Ousmane's bad habits and idiosyncracies, and she cannot stand Yaye Khady. She loses patience with Ousmane's friends, determined to resist the pressures of her environment: "She felt as though they wanted to bury her alive and resurrect her as another woman who would have nothing in common with her except her physical appearance. But she resisted. She made it quite clear that she saw things differently from the people around her. She was shaken in her most firm and innermost convictions and every day eroded a little more of the courage with which she had armed herself when she left her own country and turned herself into a rebel" (99).

Mireille senses that Ousmane has a mistress and confronts him with the idea, but he flatly denies it. Mireille's state is described with powerful metaphors difficult to convey in translation: "Mireille vivait son calvaire," translated as "Mireille put all her courage into surviving her ordeal" (153), loses the connotation of Christ's suffering on the cross and the whole idea of martyrdom contained in the word "calvaire." Another powerful image is that of Mireille caught in a labyrinthian spider web, hugging her son closely, "feeling him her only link with the world" (155). It is not surprising that when the child can no longer fulfill the role of linking Mireille to life, he is not allowed to live.

Mireille's friend and sister-in-law, Soukeyna, is the only person who tries to alleviate her pain, the only one Mireille can really talk to. Soukeyna sympathizes with her sister-in-law and she is tempted to tell her about Ousmane's double life, but cannot quite bring herself to do so. Out of guilt, but also out of compassion, she resorts to writing Mireille an anonymous letter that simply reads: *"You have got a Senegalese co-wife. If you want to know more about her, follow your husband"* (155). Soukeyna sincerely believes that this disclosure will put an end to Ousmane and Ouleymatou's relationship, which she believes would be for the best, but fate will not have it that way. Ironically, Ousmane's plan for isolating Mireille, and keeping her ignorant of his second wife, is thwarted by his own sister.

Before following her husband herself, Mireille has him followed by a taxi driver. She then goes with the driver through a torturous journey, and after waiting for long hours, she finally sees the second wife. She notes that the woman has a baby and is expecting a second one; she realizes that Yaye Khady, who is playing with the little one, approves of this "betrayal," and most significantly she discovers that her husband can still smile and look happy with another woman. At a later visit she witnesses a gesture that will leave an indelible mark on her mind: "One evening, Ousmane's hand had openly fondled the tart's backside, in the street. Instead of repulsing him, the black woman had giggled and stuck out her behind" (158). The image haunts Mireille so much that "she could not open her eyes without seeing Ousmane's fondling those deliberately provocative buttocks" (160).

The sexual element plays an important role in Mireille's wounded psyche: "In her imagination she pictured the amorous frolics from which she was excluded. She was mortified by the glimpses she had of erotic pleasures, which took place to her detriment. Made worse by the fact that nobody made any bones about commenting in her presence on the hot blood of black women. The woman she had spied upon reeked of experience in the arts of love" (159). Mireille is convinced of that "experience" because, earlier, she had seen Ouleymatou's *djité laye* "[fluttering] on the washing-lines, evidence of the care that the 'tart' lavished on her sex-life" (158). Here the sexual elements are linked with cultural attributes that she knows she does not possess. Mireille has no *djité laye,* she detests the smell of incense, she has no way of calling in the *diali* or griot to sing Ousmane's praises. She feels that it is on that terrain that she is losing her husband, because "a powerful magnetism was at work, dragging him back to his own world" (158).

Faced with her husband's dual life, Mireille is deeply hurt and extremely angry. In disgust she exclaims, "Dirty nigger! Liar! Cheat! Adulterer! It's better with your nigger woman, isn't it? Answer me! You love your little-Blackie better than your Gnouloule Khessoule!" (164). Her outburst is significant because Mireille's rage is expressed in terms of race and reveals the deep-seated racial conditioning that individuals are not aware of when life takes a "normal course." The only other time Mireille expresses an opinion in racial terms is when Ousmane and his friends ignore her presence in the living room. If Mireille does not verbalize her feeling, the narrator clearly focalizes her perceptions: "She felt that she was treated with less consideration than a black woman" (86).

Yet, in spite of her devastation, in spite of the mixed feelings she experiences, Mireille is still in love with Ousmane and tries to find strategies to save her marriage. She will seduce her husband all over again to regain his love; she will remain in Senegal:

> She would live, she would fight, upheld by an ideal that did not sink to its knees. Her love and her pride together collected the crumbs of her dead happiness, to build with them some elements of hope. While her reason still argued the pros and cons, while her conscience told her that she must leave, her love and her pride refused to yield an inch of the territory they had won. Pathetically, Mireille chose to stay. She attributed no greatness to her attitude. Her choice was not an evasion nor cowardice, but the only possible choice for a woman in love . . . for a woman with a black child on her hands . . . for a woman who has burnt her bridges behind her. (162)

Mireille is very realistic about her plight and she realizes, perhaps a little too late, that it is not wise for a woman to be so consumed by a man that she burns all bridges behind her, leaning on him solely.[31] This is indeed another example of the danger inherent in leaving one's hill.

The last chapter is the denouement and describes Mireille's decline into madness. Bâ analyzes the mystery of insanity, searching for answers as to how it happens, where the cracks open in people's minds and then widen to deprive them of rationality. This chapter is a masterful presentation of the characters' psychological depth, and of a suspense skillfully maintained until the end of the story; it draws together the amorces in that conclusion and dexterously brings the novel to a dramatic close. It begins with Mireille rereading Ousmane's love letters. There is such a hiatus between the words of yesteryears and the reality she is living at the moment that his words seem unreal, devoid of meaning. These letters—which represent the culmination of the important part letters play in the narrative structure—act as so many blows that unhinge her reason.

Mireille suddenly feels the desire to glue his letters all over the wall, as a rather pathetic testimony to the fact that she once was loved. She does this in a mechanical manner, repeating again and again the sentence "Quick, the glue! The glue, quick!"—a refrain that gives the scene a dramatic rhythm; it is like an incantation celebrating a strange ritual of madness, of exorcism, and it culminates in a demented ritual of death. Raving that her son Gorgui will never fit in either black or white society, Mireille gives the child an overdose of medicine. As she kills the baby, she chants yet another song, this one taken from a lullaby Yaye Khady used to sing to the little boy: "Gnouloule, Khessoule! Gnouloule, Khessoule!" [You're not black, you're not white!]. The infanticide is directly linked with Gorgui's *métissage,* and in killing him Mireille in a sense kills her ideal of a pluralistic society. The fact that the death song is Yaye Khady's lullaby of course emphasizes the mother-in-law's large responsibility in this drama. Following Gorgui's death, Mireille attempts to kill her husband. The French embassy takes charge of her and sends her back to France, where she ends up in a lunatic asylum; the reader is left to imagine what will happen to Ousmane.

Presumably Ousmane's children will live, and he will remain with Ouleymatou, reclaiming his male power and privileges of the past, pampered by a woman who lives up to his ideal of the perfect wife, and free of the conflicts imposed by a woman struggling for independence and equality within the marriage. It is interesting that Ousmane is attracted to Ouleymatou because of her adherence to traditional roles prescribed for women by men. He does not seek an African counterpart of Mireille, and it is clear that his disillusion with Mireille is rooted in more than differences of race and culture—he cannot accept her independence, her desire for equality. Ouleymatou's relationship with Ousmane and Ousmane's mother is one of submission, whereas Mireille had refused to be dominated.[32] Mariama Bâ dramatizes in *Scarlet Song* beliefs she expressed in an interview: "The man must abandon a part of his power, his privileges from the past. The woman who lives with him must not be a slave as he has learned to expect in his childhood" ("Mariama Bâ," 210). This is precisely the kind of marriage / partnership to which Mireille aspired and which Ousmane denied (the parallel with Emilienne and Joseph's situation in *Fureurs et cris de femmes* is striking). In the interview, Mariama Bâ goes on to say that it requires a great effort for the man to abandon these advantages and want his wife to be happy.[33] She declares that all men, regardless of race, are inhabited by a polygamous desire ("Mariama Bâ," 211), and Ousmane illustrates that.

Where do Ousmane's attitudes and actions leave Mireille? In trying to stay true to herself, Mireille loses herself. She "retreats" into madness (another type of exile) as her mother retreated into fainting and illness. Her incoherent speech and withdrawal from the world around her are another example of self-silencing, and finally the fact that she kills her son obliterates all social trace of herself. Mireille's alienation is also gender oriented: where is the female role model of independent thought and action for her to follow? Certainly it is not to be found in her mother or mother-in-law, and not in Ouleymatou, her rival. There seems to be a strong idea of contamination in this novel: Mireille and Ousmane's son is contaminated by his métisse status and by the fact that he belongs to neither culture; the marriage of Mireille and Ousmane is contaminated by the mother-in-law's ill will, as well as by more apparently innocent factors—Mireille's ideals of love transcending race, class, and culture (love sees no color) and of a marriage based on equality and partnership between man and woman.

What Mariama Bâ has brilliantly shown in *Scarlet Song* is the intersection of gender, race, class, and culture in ways that subvert our received notions of them. She does so particularly well when she shows that classes are culture-specific and are constructions that can easily be dismantled. In France, Mireille belongs to an upper-class family, but that distinction means absolutely nothing in Senegal. Ousmane is said to belong to nobility—a category not based on material comfort, only on birth. This is a nobility that Monsieur de la Vallée denies and one that Mireille cannot see. Mariama Bâ also shows Africans, who have been subjected to a long history of racism imposed on them by the West, that racism is not the prerogative of a specific race. It is found among Europeans (Jean de la Vallée; Guillaume) as well as among Africans (Yaye Khady, in particular, but others too). Mariama Bâ also emphasizes finally how insidious racism is when she describes Mireille as not realizing that she could be a racist until her furious outburst at Ousmane. The implicit commentary is that it is erroneous to think that love does not see color. One must see color, but it should not matter.

However, perhaps the strongest meaning of *Scarlet Song* is found in an insistence on the redeeming potential contained in the idea of a community of women. Mariama Bâ, who is deeply committed to the cause of women everywhere, has remarked that "there is a fundamental unity in all of our sufferings and in our desire for liberation and in our desire to cut off the chains which date from antiquity" ("Mariama Bâ," 213). For an effective transformation of the female condition, women need to recognize the potential of that true community of women, based not only on a shared existence of suffering but also on solidarity, understanding, and support for one another. If *Scarlet Song* seems primarily concerned with the obstacles to that solidarity, that does not make the idea less powerful. Perhaps in Bâ's sight all women are gathered on a single hill.

CHAPTER THREE

W/RITING CHANGE:

WOMEN AS

SOCIAL CRITICS

As we have seen in earlier chapters, women writers deal with a wide array of topics centered on the female condition, a condition always played out in society within a sociopolitical context. Accepting a correlation between women's actual and textual lives, these writers have been aware that for women's position to change, society has to change, and therefore they have become social critics trying to create insight into, and a vision of, what the future could hold. Their perceived mission is to offer ways and means of bringing about the advent of a new social order, linking their immediate concerns about the status of women to a critical focus that includes the whole of society.

In Africa, as in other "traditional" societies, art was never separated from general life, but always integrated and purposive. Francophone women writers have received and continued this tradition: "Considéré comme essentiellement fonctionnel dans la tradition africaine, l'art a servi facilement de moyen de contestation entre les mains des femmes. Le chant, la danse, le théâtre, dépourvus de finalités exclusivement ludiques, traduisent, outre leurs désirs et leurs frustations, outre leurs joies et leurs aspirations, leur opposition à l'adversité, leur rejet de l'impérialisme" [Being essentially functional in traditional Africa, art was considered a means of protest in women's hands. Songs, dances, plays do not simply entertain. They serve to express women's desires and frustrations, their joys and aspirations but also their opposition to adversity, their rejection of imperialism] (Ekoto, 142).

Francophone female writers find their inspiration in all elements of tradition, but particularly in ritual, which remains at the center of daily life in "traditional" Africa. Ritual punctuates the important moments of the life cycle—birth, puberty, marriage, and death. Marking personal events in life, ritual acts as a means of including individuals in the community. It calls for group participation in purification or commemoration rites and so reinforces the cohesion of the group, strengthening the ties between individuals and giving them a renewed sense of belonging. Obviously, the social benefits of ritual are manifold.

As a preventive and curative device in society, however, ritual cannot be dissociated from belief systems that seem to be disappearing in contemporary urban Africa. Ritual reasserts the spiritual sense of the community, and it is this form of spirituality that Werewere Liking in particular wants to restore. In this restoration the link between past and present is clearly made: "Le rituel d'hier permettait au groupe décidé à ne pas déchoir, de redécouvrir des rapports profonds et d'assurer sa propre thérapeutique: il revivait ses angoisses et ses maladies devant ses Dieux et ses Esprits depuis la cause première jusqu'au retour de l'harmonie. Aussi s'est-on demandé pourquoi de nos jours où le monde est particulièrement bouleversé, et le monde africain en particulier, le rituel a disparu alors qu'il devenait plus que jamais nécessaire" [Yesterday, ritual made it possible for a determined and confident group to rediscover deep relationships and to perform its own therapeutics. Before its Gods and Spirits, the group reenacted its anxieties and its ailments, moving from the primordial cause to a restored harmony. We then wonder, since in our day the world (especially the African world) is in turmoil, why ritual has disappeared just when it is more necessary than ever] (Ma Njock, 75–76).

The three writers I have chosen to look at in this chapter are important social critics. Of course, as it is difficult to divide autobiography from fiction, it is equally problematic to isolate Liking, Fall, or Tadjo as social critics. Their work is complex and multilayered. I start with Werewere Liking of Cameroon, who is a pioneer in the incorporation of ritual elements within her writing. This technique provides the basic structural order for *Orphée-Dafric* (1982), in which Liking takes the classic myth of Orpheus as a metaphorical and archetypal foundation, and revises and transforms it to weave an African "tale" in which the motif of the quest is central. Part 2 deals with Aminata Sow Fall, a novelist from Senegal whose work exposes the political maneuvers of post- or neocolonial ideologies. In an attempt to comprehend how autocracies come into being and are maintained, her book *L'Ex-père de la nation* [The ex-father of the nation] (1987) probes the conditions for political responsibility, not only for tyrannic leaders but also for the people who let themselves be tyrannized. Part 3 of this chapter examines Véronique Tadjo, a poet and novelist from Côte d'Ivoire whose criticism of African life focuses on the loss of social ideals. In *A Vol d'oiseau* [As the crow flies] (1986), a book composed as a series of discrete vignettes, Tadjo isolates the problems of contemporary Africa from ecology to political dictatorship; as does Liking, she emphasizes the need to rediscover cultural foundations.

Werewere Liking: Initiation as a Tool for Social Change

Werewere Liking is a Cameroonian artiste in the fullest sense of the word; poet, playwright, theater and movie actress, novelist, essayist, painter, jeweler, and researcher. She stands out among African writers, male and female alike, for the diversity of her oeuvre, as well as for the innovative nature of her writing.[1] Liking is also a woman with vision. She has been very critical of contemporary African society, where she can see no plan for the future, either in individual lives or within a larger community that lacks political leadership. Therefore, she has devised a personal plan of cultural revival in which art and ritual play a pivotal role. Living in Côte d'Ivoire, she created a community of nearly fifty artists—sculptors, dancers, actors, and painters—who live and work in her Villa Ki-Yi, (*Ki-yi* meaning "the ultimate knowledge" in Bassa, Liking's native tongue).[2] In this setting the artists, coming from diverse parts of Africa, support themselves through their art and nourish one another through a shared artistry.

The initial assumption of the writing of Werewere Liking is the belief that social change in contemporary Africa can be mediated by a modern adaptation of traditional African ritual. She has put this belief into action working in close collaboration with Marie-José Hourantier, a French writer and sociologist also known as Manuna Ma Njock. Liking, who is herself from the Bassa ethnic group, teamed up with Hourantier to do extensive research on the rituals of the Bassa in southern Cameroon. Among the works produced by this collaboration was *Du Rituel à la scène chez les Bassa du Cameroun* [From ritual to the stage among the Bassa of Cameroon] (1979), in which Liking and Hourantier developed the concept of the ritual-theater, an art form described by Njock:³ "En Afrique toute idée qui s'ébauche, toute philosophie voulant s'imposer avait besoin de ces rituels qui redonnaient à la pensée toute sa puissance, aux mots toute leur force, aux gestes toute leur efficacité. Nous avons réinterrogé les techniques rituelles et en avons fait la base d'une esthétique théâtrale adaptée à l'expression dramatique négro-africaine, le théâtre rituel" [In Africa any budding idea, any philosophy seeking to take root, needed to go through rituals that made thought forceful, words potent and gestures powerful. We have called upon these ritual techniques and used them as a basis for a theatrical esthetics adapted to the black African dramatic expression—the ritual theater] (75). This theatrical form dramatized traditional Bassa rituals for the stage, part of an effort to empower contemporary Africans by creating what Liking called an "operational" theater, one which would restore African values for the individual as well as for the larger community.

The concept of an operational theater, which Liking hopes to make as functional as was traditional ritual, can be traced in all her works. Well known for blurring categories and mixing literary genres, her writing is essentially polyphonic, characterized by a multiplicity of voices and a plurality of texts on which she works to invent a unique fictional universe in which the reinscription of ritual is as significant as the presentation of themes. Her concept of art is a strategic didactic approach that her novel *Orphée-Dafric* illustrates very well. The novel's title explicitly reveals her use of the ancient Greek myth of Orpheus and its adaptation to African culture.⁴

Liking's novel centers on Orphée and his wife Nyango, mythic lovers who are trying to make their hostile families accept their marriage and to coax the Gods into blessing their union. To this end they agreed to undertake the trial of the canoe, a test in which their safe passage across the White River would signify the Gods' acceptance of their marriage. But they undertook the trial during the flood season and their canoe capsized; Orphée was able to swim to the shore, but Nyango never emerged from the river. Tradition had it that the river would always return its victims on the third day after a drowning, but even after the ninth day there was no trace of Nyango, and she was presumed dead. Still, Orphée would not accept her death and, as in the Greek story, embarked on a journey to search for his beloved. With this quest as the central action, Liking transforms the Orpheus myth into a veritable initiation journey in which Orphée follows a carefully outlined pattern of ritual, each stage requiring completion before the next can be confronted. As in any quest or ritual, this progression is meant to culminate in a discovery or resolution. Repeatedly, Orphée is said to be a "chercheur," a word with the double meaning of an academic researcher and of an individual who is in search of something. As the story develops, one discovers that Orphée's search for Nyango is also a search for his own identity.

Orphée's ordeal begins with a difficult choice. At the fork in a road there are two different paths that Nyango could have taken. After six hours of deliberation, Orphée finally chooses the path on the left, but no sooner has he stepped onto it than he is dragged away by the cart of Ngué (God). Ngué leaves him at the foot of what appears to be twin hills, but what are actually the thorax and abdomen of a giant ant having the shape of a figure "8" lying on its side. At the junction of the two loops a dagger is poised in midair, and the giant ant speaks to Orphée, saying he must go through a test that involves weighing himself. Only if Orphée's soul is heavier than his body will he be lifted, presumably with Ngué's help, high enough to see the ant's granaries and so pass the test. If he is not lifted high enough, the balance will be broken and the dagger will kill him. Orphée passes this first test, rising above the hills, because his love for Nyango has given weight to his soul ("fardeau intérieur"); however, this success is only the beginning of his trials.

Orphée's quest is a magical one, taking place in a timeless and dimensionless space. To find Nyango he will have to climb up seven steps of a stairway suspended in midair. When he is told this, he sees at his feet a stick with seven knots and a small, dim lamp. When he picks them both up, the door to the stairway opens and his quest has truly begun. The stick or cane will serve as a measure of Orphée's progress; each time he is distracted or moved by unworthy desires, the knots on the stick swell and he is unable to continue ahead; but when he is moved by love and worthy ideals, the knots loosen and he can advance to the next step of the stairway. In this way Orphée may finally reach the seventh and final step, where he will be able to see Nyango. He will hear a final voice, "la voix du tout" [the voice of the whole], and meet with the ancestors who will impart their knowledge to him. They will also explain to him the purpose and meaning of his journey before allowing him to be reunited with Nyango.

Orphée must do what most Africans, torn between their own traditions and the temptation of the West, have to do: select a path, a direction, that is, a political system, a philosophy, a code of conduct, a way of life. The choice of a path is all the more crucial as it involves adequately measuring advantages and disadvantages in every situation, as if on a scale. That is why Liking's novel is based on the notion of *équilibre,* a recurrent word meaning "equilibrium" or "balance." Indeed, Orphée's journey is a quest for the indispensable balance that will enable him to live a fuller life, for himself, for the people he has relationships with, and for the community at large. If Ngué's cart plunges Orphée into a breathtaking descent, he must make an ascent on his own, climb up the seven steps of a stairway hanging in midair.

The idea of balance and the peril involved in losing it are important even before the actual journey begins. Nyango disappears because turbulent waters upset the canoe in the initial ordeal—balance is lost, causing the canoe to overturn. In the description of the twin hills and the double-edged sword is the image of a scale, and before he starts the journey, Orphée must weigh himself to prove there is a balance between his body weight and his "fardeau intérieur," defined in part as "toutes les énergies mise en movement par des grands sentiments, des passions diverses, des combats . . . " [all energy activated by noble emotions, various passions, struggles . . .] (37). For Orphée, the love he so strongly feels for Nyango has become his inner weight, and he is confident that even should the sword wound him he will not be killed; his love will secure the life-saving balance and symmetry.

Finding a balance between body weight and inner weight reflects the necessity of balancing body and soul, the material and the spiritual. Liking emphasizes this connection by use of a political metaphor, when her narrator predicts the arrival of a strong wind, the typhoon that will blow away all injustice, notably in South Africa, Chad, Western Sahara, Namibia, in all the "coins piégés" [booby-trapped places]. However, in order to create something out of the chaos that will be left in all these places, people will have to be prepared to assume power. And that preparation will demand, among other values, a reestablishment of balance between body and soul because "la matière a trop longtemps régné, l'emportant de plus en plus sur la vie intérieure" [the material has reigned for too long, increasingly supplanting the inner life] (57).

If the concept of balance structures Orphée's entire journey, it is most importantly present in steps one, three, and six. This presence creates balance within the text itself, at a starting point, in the middle, and again at the end. In the trial of the first step, a balance must be found between sexual drive and real love. When Orphée's entire body is driven by sexual desire only, that desire drags him down dangerously: "Toute la vie de mon être semble être descendue dans mon bas-ventre, trop petit pour la contenir. Et plus mon sexe enfle, plus le premier noeud de la canne s'alourdit, me déséquilibre" [My entire life seems to have fallen into my loins, which are too small to contain it. And the more my sex swells up, the heavier the first knot on the stick becomes, pulling me off-balance] (40). Any unbalance will cause Orphée to fall and thus jeopardize his chances of ever seeing Nyango again. Therefore, ardently holding her in mind, he diverts his thoughts from sexual desire, transforming them into love for Nyango: "Subitement, le premier noeud se défait et mon corps s'allège. Je me hisse à la deuxième marche" [Suddenly, the first knot comes loose, my body becomes lighter, and I heave myself onto the second step] (40): the deep love he feels for Nyango provides the propelling force that moves him ahead on his quest.

In the third trial, when Orphée doubts Nyango, thinking that she may have deceived him with other men, he once again loses his balance, but then remembers his father once telling him, "La meilleure façon d'enrayer une forme-pensée était d'en créer une autre, plus forte qui puisse absorber la première" [The best way of erasing a thought was to create another one, strong enough to absorb the first one] (45). During this trial, Orphée feels a tension surrounding him: he soon realizes that it emanates from a hostility within himself, and will only disappear if he can succeed in overcoming the jealous and mistrustful part of his character. The idea of changing himself frightens him, but the remembrance of his father's advice as well as the strength of his love for Nyango will save him: "Dès que mon amour me quitte, je ne suis plus moi-même, je perds l'équilibre . . . Me revient-il? Et je me libère de toute épaisseur, de toute pesanteur, et je m'envole allègrement" [As soon as love leaves me, I am no longer myself, I am off-balance . . . As soon as it comes back, I feel free of all barriers, of all gravity and I can fly away, lightheartedly] (45). The third knot then loosens and Orphée passes on to the fourth step.

The greatest crisis for Orphée is the sixth and final trial, because at that point he finds for the first time that his love is not sufficient; it cannot lift him to the last step. His reaction to this is at first surprise and shock, finding love no longer works: "Il n'a pas su ramener l'équilibre" [It did not succeed in restoring balance]. But the realization that love is not enough sets him free; he moves onto the seventh step as he moves beyond his personal love into a vision of a whole human society, one in which he is praiser, critic, observer, participant, leader, follower. Once he reaches this level of consciousness, his senses are far more acute: he exists, he sees, hears, feels, and now knows that the six knots have disappeared, that gravity has no hold on him. He has a revelation of how he can remake his life and achieve a new beginning. Only then does he have a vision of his reunion with Nyango.

Joseph Campbell has argued that "it has always been the prime function of mythology and rite to supply symbols that carry the human spirit forward, in counteraction to those other constant human fantasies that tend to tie it back" (11). In African societies, initiation rites were a privileged mode of cognition; individuals learned to abhor vile, shameful acts, to shun greed, and to attempt to uphold honesty and build a life based on communal moral values. This is the path taken by Orphée in his initiatory ordeal, a *rite de passage*. He finally finds the balance he has been seeking, not only because of his strong desire to do so but also because he had been preparing himself to fulfill this task. In his village, he was perceived as being a "case": "Le seul jeune homme qui s'achar-nait à suivre les voies de la tradition, tout en vivant avec son temps" [The only young man who was desperately trying to live according to tradition, while also living in his time] (43). The task was arduous and gave rise to much suspicion within his community: "Du coup, je passais pour marginal des deux côtés, on m'avait à l'oeil: ma vie était connue de tous" [Consequently, I was branded as marginal by both sides; I was spied on, my life was an open book for everybody to scrutinize] (43). Yet this resistance did not deter Orphée's continued quest for knowledge.

But Orphée could not have overcome the initiatory trials and acquired knowledge in the process only by his own volition. He was assisted throughout the quest by more experienced members of his community. Taken in a large African cosmologic sense, the community includes not only human beings but also the "living-dead" or ancestors and even the surrounding forces of nature. That is why, in addition to Ngué's voice, Orphée hears the twin hills, the dead leaves, the blue and red moons, and above all the voice of "the whole." Orphée's father can be seen as the rit-ual leader, though all his interventions occurred *before* the protagonist's journey actually started. First of all he had given Nyango and Orphée two highly symbolic gifts. One was the Book of Thoth, the Egyptian God of learning, letters, and wisdom and the inventor of speech and writing. This gift is meant to underscore the significance of learning, which is seen as a strong instrument of regeneration, as the highest "weapon" against all forms of violation. The prominence of ritualistic speech is bal-anced with that of writing, and it is not by chance that when Orphée and Nyango are reunited they write down the lessons derived from the initi-ation and their plans for the future. They must commit the learning to memory, but they also must have a document to consult in case they be-come forgetful.

The second present was a stone that they were to keep in their wed-ding room. After the nuptial night they were to examine the stone to see if it underwent any transformation; if it did, Nyango and her hus-band would know that they had received the blessing of the whole community. The stone was not an ordinary one, of course. It had nine layers of increasing value, from the surface—a light clay, to the core—a diamond. When they woke, they found that seven layers of the stone (reminiscent of the seven steps of the stairway) had disintegrated, making it possible to see the diamond through a surrounding block of crystal. They knew then that they had obtained "la bénédiction cosmique, seule capable de permettre la véritable créativité" [the cosmic blessing that alone is capable of bringing forth creativity] (67). Symbolically the stone teaches them to go beyond obvious appearances, to discover the more profound nature and significance of things. In other words, it teaches them to see things rather than just look at them, another way of coming to a more profound knowledge.

Orphée's father also plays the role of the archetypal Wise Old Man whose words assist the hero throughout the trials and terrors of his quest. During the journey the words of wisdom once pronounced by the father become a source of action for the son. Orphée's father taught him how to think, to question assumptions, and to sharpen his critical mind. He compelled Orphée, for instance, to reassess his concept of "African humanism" by asking him pointed questions and demanding concrete definitions of what that phrase is supposed to stand for. Even though Léopold Sédar Senghor's name is not explicitly mentioned, this is clearly an intertextual reference to some of the ideas contained in his negritude philosophy.[5] Orphée realizes that he has been an uncritical disciple of Senghor when he finds himself unable to provide his father with a coherent explanation. He is forced to admit, "C'était vrai que je ne savais pas en quoi il consistait ce fameux humanisme que le nègre était censé avoir apporté au monde" [It was true that I did not know what the much-vaunted humanism that blacks were supposed to have contributed to the world was all about] (42). This realization further encourages Orphée to critique his received knowledge, questioning it and testing it, before integrating it into his life.

Orphée's father had given his son therapeutic knowledge by showing him the virtues of plants and teaching him how to use them to heal the body. He did not, however, neglect the healing of the soul. He instructed his son on the necessity of being oneself, of living with integrity, of adding a spiritual dimension to one's existence. He taught him values by contrasting what they had meant in the past with how they are adulterated in the present:

Autrefois, disait mon père, le verbe "être" prédominait: il fallait être digne de son clan, de sa tribu, être fier de soi ou être honteux de ses actes. L'ambition la plus haute? Etre un ancêtre, c'est-à-dire maîtriser suffisamment de connaissance à transmettre à la tribu, pouvoir la protéger et lui permetre plus de créativité.

Aujourd'hui, nous n'attendons de la vie que ce qui entre dans le cadre de l'avoir: avoir des honneurs même si on en est indigne, avoir des richesses même si on est un égoïste et ingrat, même si on est idiot, avoir l'amour des autres même si on est un salaud, avoir la puissance même si on est un danger public. (35; emphasis added)

[*In the past,* said my father, the verb "to be" was predominant: one had to be worthy of one's clan, of one's tribe, to be proud of self or ashamed of one's actions. The highest ambition? To be an ancestor, that is master enough knowledge to pass it on to the tribe, be able to protect the tribe and allow it to be more creative.

Today, we only expect from life what falls in the realm of the verb "to have." To have honors even if one is unworthy, to have wealth even if one is selfish and thankless, even if one is an idiot, to have other people's love even if one is a bastard, to have power even if one is a public danger.]

His strong message is a lesson in character building, in understanding one's aspirations. It is meant to teach what is essential: to *be* a total person rather than *have* things, especially when they are undeserved or ill-acquired. Therefore the father, who acts as a spiritual leader, teaches his son how to balance speech with silence, conveying "la puissance de la parole" [the power of the word] (22) and the "culte du savoir-dire" [the cult of knowing-how-to-express-oneself] (23), which were once so important in African life and which, Liking emphasizes, need to be rediscovered. He reminds Orphée that speech was indeed the seat of ancestral wisdom and a tool for creativity, a vital impulse in the process of regeneration: "Tout fils de ce peuple était artiste dès qu'il prenait la parole" [Every son of this land became an artist as soon as he started to speak] (23).

Yet words are not to be used lightly. It is vital also to know how to remain silent in order to fathom the significance of speech and to feel God's presence. As the father says: "Chaque homme devrait s'imposer au moins un mois de silence dans sa vie, pour prendre conscience, pour comprendre la vie, et pour savoir pourquoi il y a un Dieu" [Every man should impose upon himself at least one month of silence in his life, to reach consciousness, to understand life and to know why there is a God] (20). And, having done this, Orphée suggests that the reader do the same: "Quand on se tait, on est assailli par le bruit. . . . Faites donc l'expéri-ence: taisez-vous! Bouchez vos oreilles, et écoutez de l'intérieur. Le bruit est en vous. Il aspire à la vie. Vous devez la lui donner. Vous êtes né pour créer, pour donner, pour renouveller la vie" [When one remains silent, one is assailed by noise. . . . Try it: keep silent! Block your ears and lis-ten from within. The noise is within you. It aspires to life. You must give it life. You were born to create, to give, to renew life] (20).

The apparent contradiction contained in the idea of remaining silent in order to bring forth "noise" is in fact a powerful way of describing how the silence of the body may create the necessary space for the "noise" of the mind, which is creative energy. Silence then serves a creative func-tion by opening up the imagination and bringing about innovation.

The quest for an inner silence is also a form of spirituality capable of replacing the so-called African humanism, which has proved ineffectual: "Et ton humanisme? Ne pourrais-tu pas te réjouir de trouver Dieu en toi alors que le monde le cherche au ciel? N'es-tu pas heureux d'éponger la souffrance et de toujours essayer de la remplacer par l'harmonie et la paix?" [What about your humanism? Could you not take pleasure in finding God within yourself when the world is looking for him in the sky? Are you not happy to wipe away suffering, and always try to replace it with harmony and peace?] (42–43). Yet it is important to emphasize that the spirituality advocated here has little to do with a specific God. Fur-thermore, it is not synonymous with waiting passively for help from above: "Il faudra une puissance supérieure pour régler nos problèmes, mais elle n'est pas ailleurs qu'en nous-mêmes. Elle gît-là, au bas de la canne à sept noeuds. Il s'agit de la réveiller, de la mettre en action, et les arbres pousseront à notre appel, et les montagnes se déplaceront au son de notre voix" [We will need a superior force to solve our problems, but it is nowhere else but within ourselves. It lies there, at the bottom of the seven-knotted stick. What we need to do is to wake that force, to put it into action: then the trees will grow at our call and the mountains will move at the sound of our voices] (58).

Finally Orphée is initiated by the ancestors who, forming a link between the living and the dead, have the ultimate knowledge of life and death. At the end of his journey, Orphée experiences the "Grande Rencontre" [Great Encounter], where he meets the ancestors, who tell him that *they* had hidden Nyango from him in order to drive him to his quest, to make him realize the scope of his own possibilities. Thus, at the end of his initiation, Orphée comes to realize that his very survival depends on a transformation of self, on a metamorphosis. To begin that change, he subjects both himself and his society to a harsh critique, an interlude that allows the author to examine the social ills of Africa and to suggest the necessity for change.

African writers often closely link poetics with politics, and Liking is no exception to that general rule. She has said: "Je me préoccupe de l'Afrique, de ses contradictions, de ses aspirations conscientes ou inconscientes, de ses échecs, de ses tares. . . . J'ai mission d'utiliser les outils dont je dispose pour la défense de la collectivité. Je ne sais pas si un artiste de mon genre peut se passer de la politique. C'est la politique qui opère tout et pour réorienter nos destinées, l'artiste doit la suivre" [I am preoccupied by Africa, her contradictions, her conscious or unconscious aspirations, her failures, her shortcomings. . . . I have a duty to use the tools that are at my disposal to defend the community. I don't know whether an artist such as myself can do without politics. Politics regulates everything and to give a new orientation to our destinies, the artist cannot ignore it] (Liking, "Werewere Liking: Créatrice," 195).

Today's political situation can only be explained by history. Orphée's society was disrupted by colonization, referred to as *La Mort Blanche* (White Death), which came with both the "Holy Book" and the "Holy Gun" to establish itself as a sort of semigod, rewarding only its worshipers—who were traitors to their own people—with promises of eternal bliss in heaven. Nonworshipers were crushed mercilessly, so that La Mort Blanche could impose its institutions, from the seven-day week to an ideology in which "la plus grande ambition est . . . d'atteindre ce niveau où l'on a tout pour soi, et tous en dessous de soi" [the greatest ambition is . . . to reach the level where you have everything for yourself and everyone below you] (35). The most brilliant innovation of La Mort Blanche was the school, even though it was inadequate and substandard: "Une école où l'on apprenait à tracer des signes et à dire des choses qu'on ne comprenait pas, Mais qu'importe? C'était les mêmes signes qu'on traçait chez lui [le civilisateur], les mêmes choses qu'on disait là-bas. On demandait à Dieu un pain quotidien qu'on ne connaissait pas; tant pis, nos ancêtres les Gaulois en mangeaient" [A school where one learned to write signs and to say things that one did not understand. But did it matter? They were the same signs that were written in his country (the civilizing man's), the same things that were said over there. One asked God for a daily bread one did not know, but it did not matter. Our ancestors the Gauls ate of that bread] (31).

The satirical tone is unmistakable, and it brands both the colonizers and the colonized. No doubt, colonization was a formidable factor of disequilibrium, but the colonized did little or nothing to restore the balance, particularly after they became independent. On the contrary, they let themselves be seduced by the West. They emulated its practices and adopted its values, even if those were not fully understood and were not suitable for African societies. In an ironic tone, Liking gives multiple examples of this kind of behavior. On the first page of the novel the narrator describes the way children used to be named:

> Traditionnellement, chaque nom voulait dire quelque chose, quelque chose qui était en rapport avec les circonstances de la naissance, le caractère et le destin de son porteur. Et au fur et à mesure de l'évolution, on acquérait de nouveaux noms. . . .
>
> Aujourd'hui, dès la naissance et irrévocablement on nous affuble d'une demi-douzaine de noms en ignorant leur intention première. Ne suffit-il pas de savoir qu'ils furent portés par des Saints? (9)

> [Traditionally, each name meant something, something having a link with the circumstances of birth, the character and the destiny of its bearer. And as one grew, one would acquire new names. . . .
>
> Today, right from the day of birth we are irrevocably clothed with a half-dozen mock names whose original meaning we are ignorant of. Is it not enough to know that they were Saints' names?]

Liking's criticism of society is all-encompassing, touching social mores, social structures that allow shameless exploitation, political leaders with no commitment, and the plethora of nouveau-riches who contribute nothing to their country's economy. Women are not spared in this diatribe, because they too are guilty of the pervading degeneration; too many of them are consumed by materialism.[6] Nyango's mother, for instance, is described as an "intellectual" woman, but her sole preoccupation is helping her husband maintain his privileges, by any means necessary. Hence the narrator's dream of a different role for women: "Et si les femmes ralentissaient la course au pouvoir et aux richesses, elles ne conseilleraient plus à leurs enfants de chercher tel parti nanti, ne feraient plus pression sur leur maris pour qu'ils adhèrent à tel parti en place, et briguent tel poste d'honneur. Parce que l'honneur ici se place à un autre niveau, un niveau qualifié de rétrograde et d'antiprogressiste" [What if women curbed the rush to power and riches? They would no longer advise their children to look for a good match and would cease pressuring their husbands to join the political party in power and to seek honorific positions. Because in this society honor is now viewed differently, as backward and antiprogressive] (12).

Women, therefore, should not accept the contemporary confusion of values. They should, on the contrary, uphold and redress lost values. Their role is all the more important as Liking believes that "l'Afrique n'évoluera vraiment que quand ses femmes auront choisi la voie vers laquelle leurs enfants doivent aller" [Africa will only move forward when her women choose the path on which their children will walk] (Liking, "Une femme mystérieuse," 10).

In the society described by Orphée in his criticism, traditions have been stripped of their significance and value, and replaced by practices that make no sense. This has created a society of dispossessed people who have lost "the code" and with it their balance, their harmony, and their sense of dignity. They now live in a kind of vegetative state, constantly being "assisted" because they are void of substance and filled with "non-desire." Their stagnation threatens to lead to a "collective suicide," but that is where ritual can be instrumental, for its ultimate goal is rebirth: "Only birth can conquer death—the birth, not of the old thing again, but of something new. Within the soul, within the body social, there must be—if we are to experience long survival—a recurrence of birth . . . to nullify the unremitting recurrences of death" (Campbell 16).

Because ritual serves as a means of reinstating the psychic and psychological balance for the group and the individual, it can be used as a redressive principle to avert collective suicide. This explains the strong intimation in *Orphée-Dafric* that it will be necessary to go back to the past in order to recapture the positive values contained in African traditions. The venture must not be construed as a romanticized *retour aux sources* on Liking's part. Going back to the past is no indication that everything in that past was perfect. Yet faced with the inability of current sociopolitical systems to solve crucial problems in Africa, Liking's is an invitation to examine tradition and extract the best it can offer as an alternative. Through her writing, Liking already carries into practice the innovative venture she advocates. In *Orphée-Dafric* the narrative structure is most intriguing in terms of characterization, temporal and spacial strategies, and imaginative use of language. Orphée is no doubt the main protagonist, but his father and his wife Nyango are key characters without whom Orphée's initiation could not come to fruition. Certainly Nyango is lost in order to begin the search. Yet her very absence is fictitious because she is constantly present in Orphée's mind. She plays an important role as the source of inspiration, as the force that makes the journey possible, a journey that will ultimately redeem the community. And at the final reunion Nyango, who had merely been an object of quest, becomes an active agent capable of making sense of the journey with Orphée, of envisioning a new future.

The temporal and spatial strategies in *Orphée-Dafric* work in such a way as to create a story that seems to occur in a dream. The strong suggestive force of this mood allows Liking to condense a nine-year initiation into a few hours, manipulating time as well as space, as Orphée has a number of out-of-body experiences and travels on his long journey without ever leaving the nuptial room. This manipulation is extended so as to blur the border between dream and reality, the tangible and the intangible, the real and the imaginary, allowing no possible separations, but, instead, a single continuous experience. The last thing the reader learns is that the quest happened in a dream.

The blurring of these distinctions brings to mind the fusion of literary genres that Liking is so adept at making; as she states: "Je n'adhère pas à la scission systématique des genres. L'esthétique textuelle négro-africaine est d'ailleurs caractérisée, entre autres, par le mélange des genres. Et ce n'est qu'en mélangeant différents genres qu'il me semble possible d'atteindre différents niveaux de langues, différentes qualités d'émotion et d'approcher différents plans de conscience d'où l'on peut tout exprimer" [I do not subscribe to the systematic separation of genres. The black African textual esthetics is characterized, among other things, by the mixture of genres. It is only by blending different genres that it seems possible to reach different levels of language, different kinds of emotions and to reach different levels of consciousness from which everything can be expressed] ("A la rencontre de," 18). *Orphée-Dafric* is a novel that blends elements of drama and poetry. The novel has two narrators, Orphée himself and a nonrepresented narrator who often provides supplementary commentaries. Yet there exist a multitude of "voices" in the story, reminiscent of the large cast of a play. In addition, poetic passages are incorporated in the text and even typographically laid out as verse. Orphée's declaration of love for Nyango is expressed:

> Je l'aime
> Je l'aime comme on ne peut aimer que soi-même
> Son souffle est comme la brise du soir
> La salive de sa bouche est un miel des forêts vierges
> Savoureux et odoriférant à envivrer
> Sa peau est un velours de soie
> Je l'aime. (29)

> [I love her
> I love her as I love myself
> Her breath is like the evening breeze
> The water in her mouth is like the honey of the rain-forest,
> So delectable and so fragrant it enraptures me
> Her skin is silky velvet
> I love her.]

Finally, the novel's language is innovative and draws attention to itself; spelling is purposely altered as, for example, in the title. Punctuation is often unconventional or omitted altogether. Liking's combinations of words are arrestingly unusual; she combines or dislocates signifiers to produce words such as "femmesvoituresvillas" [womencarsvillas] or "parti-troupeau-unique" [single-sheep-party].[7]

Innovation and creativity are the conditions necessary for social change, and in Liking's view such change might well come by a restoration of love, balance, and spirituality. Indeed, the initiation completed, Orphée has grown in knowledge, acquired a sense of balance, rediscovered the power of love, the importance of spirituality, and the desire for creativity. He is therefore ready and equipped for a new beginning. Having an acute awareness of what leadership requires, he can become a leader. The narrator cannot conceive of leaders who have not gone through an initiation ritual.

Thus, Orphée becomes the prototype individuals need to emulate in order to effect change in society. In this conclusion, I see a fundamental shift from a community-based search for solutions to societal problems to the advocacy of individual quest. Yet this is not to be confused with a plea for individualism. Rather, it is a move to shift responsibility onto the individual, who is all too often lost in the collectivity. For Liking, renovation of society can only take place if personal transformation is achieved.

Aminata Sow Fall: Political Responsibilities

Initiation and leadership are also part of the political background of *L'Ex-père de la nation* [The ex-father of the nation], Aminata Sow Fall's novel of the rise and decline of a contemporary African politician, President Madiama.[8] Liking's initiation depends on a mythical ritual meant to join individuals to their cultural and social world and prepare them for leadership. Fall constructs a circular novel, beginning and ending in a prison cell where Madiama in a long flashback recounts his eight-year rule of an imaginary African country and the coup d'état that led to his imprisonment. Fall's initiation is not ritual but *politique réelle*, an introduction to the political complexity of the modern nation state in Africa.

Madiama is a male nurse whose rise begins when he is jailed for daring to speak out against the malpractice he witnesses in the health center where he works. After his release he collaborates with a group of militant friends to create a trade union, and so launches his political career. He soon becomes a *député,* then the president of the Government Council, and finally the head of state of his country. An ambiguous and complex character, Madiama is full of good intentions, but somehow finds himself leading a repressive political regime, in fact, one far worse than the regime he once criticized and fought against. Through the exploration of Madiama's relationship with leadership and power, Aminata Sow Fall aims at discovering "comment naissent et se maintiennent les tyrannies" [how tyrannies come to be and how they are maintained] (157).

Told as first-person narration, Fall's story is related in eleven chapters by Madiama, who is at once character, narrator, and focalizer. His perceptions shape the presentation of what is said, though there is a second narrator who intervenes in a few instances. The story itself is linear, centered on Madiama's present role as a leader, and describing through flashbacks his crucial background. Some flashbacks are marked in the typography of the text; thus, each time there is direct speech expressed in the past, but reported in the present, it is rendered in italics, as when Madiama recalls the oath he spoke on being sworn in as the new president, soon to be called the Father of the Nation: *"Au nom de Dieu le Miséricordieux, je jure de gouverner pour le peuple avec la volonté du peuple, pour la dignité et la sécurité du peuple que je ne trahirai jamais"* [*In the name of God the Merciful, I promise to govern for the people, in accordance with the will of the people, for the dignity and safety of the people which I will never betray*] (17). The relation between past and present becomes cautionary or ironic or both through this device; the memory of the past is neither random nor decontextualized, but Fall's way of commenting on Madiama's folly and on an obtuse history.

Fall constructs a fictional universe in which, as the title *L'Ex-père de la nation* indicates, the concept of nationhood is coupled with that of fatherhood. This association draws the reader's attention to the fathers in the novel, and there is, in Madiama's family, a succession of male figures who offer various interpretations of what fatherhood should stand for (see diagram 4, p. 143). Questions of family politics go back to

Mangone, the grandfather who was a lumberman. His ambition and pre-occupation with the role of fatherhood led him to seek more profitable employment. Wanting to provide for his children in the present as well as prepare for their future, he became an executioner for the colonial administration, a fact that his sons, Diobaye and Lansana, did not suspect until a playmate confronted them with the painful truth. The family only knew of his secret occupation for certain after Mangone had passed away, leaving a substantial fortune.

Lansana was not overly disturbed by Mangone's secret, but Diobaye, Madiama's father, would have nothing to do with an inheritance soiled by blood. In reaction, Diobaye became obsessed with cleanliness and made it his mission to wash away his father's sins. Even earlier, when Diobaye only suspected his father's second "profession," he had refused to bathe in the river used by his father and instead walked miles to bathe in the sea. After Mangone's death, Diobaye decided to become a fisherman, irresistibly attracted to the sea, which becomes his metaphor for purity: "Nous devons reconquérir la propreté. . . . Regarde la mer, comme elle est belle et pure. Elle en a charrié, des souillures. Mais Dieu lui a offert ce privilège de n'être jamais corrompue. Je voudrais lui ressembler. . . . Je lui offrirai mes mains et mon corps pour un bain de purification chaque jour renouvelé. En elle, je veux retrouver la paix de mon âme" [We must recover cleanliness. . . . Look at the sea. It is beautiful and pure. It drains an immense amount of filth but God endowed it with an enormous privilege: never to be tainted. I would like to resemble the sea. . . . I will offer it my hands and my body for a cleansing bath renewed each day. It is through the sea that I want to regain the peace of my soul] (88–89).

Diobaye's entire life becomes an elaborate cleansing rite that only finds resolution when he passes on a deep sense of moral cleanliness to his own sons, Bara and Madiama. He specifically asks Bara to prolong the pact he made with the sea and become a fisherman, and he sends Madiama to school, telling him that he has done so not only to provide his son with an opportunity to study, but "pour y acquérir assez de savoir pour laver la terre d'un peu de ses souillures" [to acquire enough knowledge to clean the earth of some of its filth] (95). Both Bara and Madiama become the bearers of their father's ideal, Bara continuing the tradition

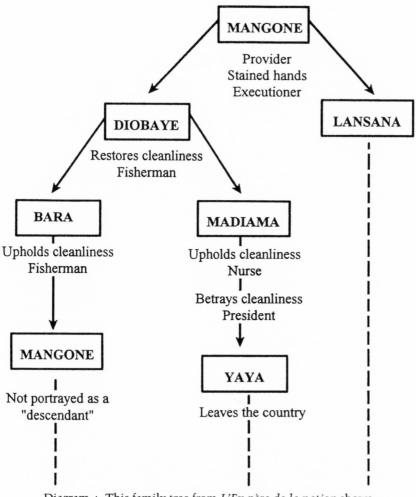

Diagram 4. This family tree from *L'Ex-père de la nation* shows
the males who were, are, or will be fathers.

of fishing, Madiama becoming a nurse; for him, sickness represents the
souillure he will rid people of. The father's ideal was a personal ritual
converted into a code, almost an obsession. Madiama received this high
sense of integrity symbolized by the metaphor of cleanliness and his father reminded him as well that "sans le coeur, le savoir n'est rien"
[knowledge is nothing if it does not involve the heart] (95). Coumba
Dado Sadio, his mother, reinforced this notion, adding, "Le plus grand

champ de bataille se trouve dans le coeur" [The greatest battle field is located in the heart] (60).

Madiama has absorbed these noble values, which would seem to have helped fit him for leadership, but the course of Fall's narrative is to trace how he fails and what that failure says about the collision of personal morality and the entrenched systems of rule in contemporary Africa. Thus the novel's social criticism focuses on both the character of Madiama and on the members of his entourage. Madiama's African collaborators are unscrupulous politicians who steal, lie, and crawl to maintain the status quo. The nation is their very least concern, and they have no qualms about trampling the people in order to preserve their own privileges. But the damage is not only carried out locally; Aminata Sow Fall also creates the character of Andru, to demonstrate how the neocolonial structures work within contemporary Africa. Andru is Madiama's French special advisor, who also holds key positions as director of the Intelligence Service and as the man in charge of the president's bodyguard; The apparatus of the security state is concentrated in him.

Madiama is haunted by the notion of cleanliness, yet he is not able to express this ideal politically when he becomes president. At the beginning of his administration, he sets himself the goal of leading his people into happiness, and genuinely believes he will succeed in doing so. Instead, he slips into nepotism, the father looking out for his family, and then cannot resist the temptation to secure his power by violence and oppression. Once the wheel of repression is set into motion, Madiama cannot stop it and the escalation of violence becomes inevitable. His regime moves rapidly from repression to dictatorship and from dictatorship to tyranny. When an irate crowd descends on his palace, he calls in the army to crush the demonstration. The show of force causes several deaths, including most ironically that of Nafi, Madiama's own daughter.

Nafi's death marks the point at which Madiama consciously turns his back on his people, whom he holds responsible for his loss. An opposition group accuses Madiama of having killed his own daughter, and their underground newspaper daily prints a picture of Nafi, smiling and full of life, with the caption: "Elan brisé par les balles de son père" [Elan broken by her father's bullets] (149). Madiama is devastated, and the newspaper photograph renews his pain every day. He resolves to take his revenge on the people by installing a regime of terror, and has the opposition and its leaders tracked down and thrown into jail, where they are mercilessly tortured before being summarily executed.

Fall's novel poses an essential political question, then: How can such a hopeful beginning end in such a catastrophe? And, by implication, what might be the conditions to produce genuine political change for the better? At the level of power politics, the key relationship is between Madiama and the French advisor, Andru. In addition to his control of the police and intelligence forces, Andru is an expert at manipulating Madiama's opinions and feelings. In one of his most deadly flatteries he likens Madiama to the majestic and powerful sun, so that the merely human leader starts to believe he *is* the sun, able to "mener les hommes, les opprimer, les tordre, les torturer, les acculer comme le soleil" [handle men, oppress them, bend them, torture them—push them to the wall as the sun would] (169). The sun symbolizes the power Madiama has learned to wield: it shines and, according to its whims, it signifies either light and warmth or fatal drought; it is always on the move and people cannot look at it directly without jeopardizing their eyesight. The sun also connotes transcendence, for Madiama is no longer on the human plane, but up in the company of the stars and probably closer to God.

The identification with the sun is in one way only a distortion of Madiama's personal ideal of cleanliness: the sun too may be an agent of purification, of the fire that cleanses. The line between devotion and megalomania is a thin one, and Andru's program for controlling a figurehead president depends importantly on blurring such distinctions. Madiama has to be ousted from the presidency before he can put things back into perspective. In the confinement of his cell, he reflects: "Je pourrais bien comparer mon destin à celui du soleil, mais je ne suis pas le soleil et la plus grande erreur de ma vie aura été d'avoir cédé au mirage et d'avoir cru que je lui ressemblais. Le soleil décline pour prendre le temps de renaître" [I could easily compare my destiny to that of the sun, but I am not the sun and the biggest mistake of my life was to have succumbed to that mirage and believe that I resembled it. The sun sets only to rise again] (8). Madiama realizes rather late that he cannot rise again, and certainly not as the Father of the nation. Vowing never to betray the people, living in fear of being an agent of betrayal and shame, of course, ironically, what he fears is precisely what he becomes in the end.

Madiama always retains somehow a very idealistic conception of his role as a leader; he genuinely wants to rule in an honest, transparent manner, but he also continually discovers to his dismay how dirty politics are. He is both sophisticated and hopelessly naïve. He has high moral standards, but the fabric of his morality is punctured with irregular holes through which leak his good intentions. He knows that his election to the presidency was orchestrated by the "Colonial Authority," but how can he accomplish anything if he gives up his position? He knows that Andru, with whom he has a very ambiguous relationship, is the focus of Western meddling in his country's affairs, but he keeps him as his advisor and always ends by heeding his counsel. He knows that his colleagues ransack the country to line their own pockets, yet cannot bring himself to interfere. He wants to change the country, but he is unable to do so because he sees corruption already so entrenched in the people's ethos. Eventually he joins in the nepotism and corruption.

In spite of all his faults, Madiama sees his own shortcomings very lucidly and is able to analyze the formidable nature of power and its insidious traps. Introspective by nature, he is conscious of his own impotence and even devastated by it. At one point he tries to introduce and implement reforms, but his plans fail miserably. After severe self-criticism, he finally realizes the extent of his failure and decides to resign, but it is too late and he will not be given even that satisfaction. The system he set out to use for change, changes him into a functionary, though all along, his conscience gives him no respite; as a leader, his most common feelings seem to be malaise and helplessness.

As Fall makes clear, however, Madiama has not only failed the people, the people have also failed him, by allowing him to treat them as he did. No doubt Madiama has an enormous responsibility in what happens to the nation he is entrusted to lead. Yet he strongly believes that "c'est le peuple qui fait les tyrans" [it is the people who create tyrants] (165). They do so through passive, fearful acceptance:

> Ça grognait sous cape dans les salons des intellectuels, dans les bureaux, au téléphone, dans les chambres d'accouchées des cliniques, dans les marchés. . . . Ça grognait mais personne ne bougeait. On s'accommodait tant bien que mal de la nouvelle situation et au bout de quelques mois,

on . . . s'était habitué aux chars aux coins des rues, aux policiers armés, partout; aux fouilles méthodiques avant d'accéder à un ministère, aux files interminables au commissariat pour payer l'autorisation de voyager. . . . Tout pouvait faire croire que les restrictions étaient devenues une espèce de routine qu'il n'était plus question de remettre en cause. (150)

[People were grumbling surreptitiously in intellectual circles, in offices, over the phone, in hospitals' labor rooms, at the market. . . . People were grumbling, but no one did a thing. Everybody put up with the new situation and within months . . . people got used to seeing army tanks at street corners, armed policemen everywhere; they had gotten used to the methodical searches they were subjected to before entering a ministry; they had gotten used to the unending lines in front of the Police Building to obtain permission to travel out of the country. . . . One would have thought that the restrictions had become some kind of routine that nobody would question.]

The people are not totally passive; a strong opposition to Madiama's regime is led by Dicko (a name reminiscent of Steve Biko's), but the majority remain acquiescent and allow themselves to be tyrannized, and so they share the collective responsibility of their destiny.

Madiama's fate as a leader demonstrate how both he and the passive majority of the people may be controlled by a power structure that is institutionally rooted as well as sophisticated in its strategies. Perhaps if Madiama had effectively resisted, Andru would simply have dismissed him, but that resistance never develops because Andru so cleverly manipulates him. The important point of Fall's political characterization is not that Madiama fails, but *how* he fails, by his self-delusion and his emotional reliance on the single ideal of his father. His brother Bara constantly reminds him of their father's message: "Souviens-toi en toute occasion de l'héritage de Père. Une voie de paix dans l'effort et la propreté. Je te fais confiance pour l'effort. . . . Pense à la propreté. Tu gouvernes, mon frère. . . . Gouverne dans la propreté" [Never forget Father's legacy: follow the path of peace through effort and cleanliness. I do not doubt you where effort is concerned. . . . Think about cleanliness. You are a leader, my brother. . . . Lead in cleanliness] (79). Evidently that ideal, excellent though it may be, is not enough to rule a country. It has shown itself susceptible of corruption, and at the end of the story Madiama's incarceration represents the demise of fatherhood, a demise suggested in the title of the novel itself, because one is a father or one is not; it is impossible to be an *ex* -father.

Even Madiama's relations with his biological children fail badly: his daughter Nafi is killed and his son Yaya is alienated from him. At the end of the novel, Yaya feels only disgust at the political situation in his country and chooses to emigrate to Asia "pour y retrouver le goût et la raison de vivre" [to rediscover a taste and reason for living] (189). Madiama's brother Bara seems a figure of wisdom and integrity, who might have been a better leader—in fact, Madiama wonders how Bara would have acted had he been president. However, crucially, he is never tested. He remains an outside observer of the situation, and his advice to "lead in cleanliness" is not enough to help. By the end of the story the moral tradition of the fathers is likely to disappear, for there are no viable fathers left.

Because the concept of nationhood is linked with that of fatherhood in Fall's novel, it is obvious that the unfolding of the narrative underscores the failure of that paternity to fashion a society based on usable values. Faced with an impasse that threatens the very existence of the nation, will the women, marginal in political terms and yet with an important impact, moral and otherwise, be able to take over? Presenting a parallel history of the women, Fall goes back only as far as Coumba Dado Sadio, who is Madiama's mother and whose female children are not expected to carry on the family. Sassi, Coumba's daughter, plays a minor role, and the other female characters exist only in relation to the men in their lives and to their children; Coura and Yandé function essentially as Madiama's wives. The tree starts to make sense in terms of descendance only where Coura and her daughters are concerned (see diagram 5).

Coumba plays an important role as mother and educator. Relying on the oral tradition, she tells her children tales and legends that are meant to guide them onto the right path. Madiama fondly remembers the story of the goat that was betrayed by human beings; he also remembers how his mother emphasized the moral of the tale with a tone of great disgust: "C'est vilain! *Tiem!* C'est vilain de trahir et c'est encore plus vilain si ce n'est que pour se remplir le ventre" [Betrayal is ugly! Yuck! Betrayal is ugly and it is even more so when it is done only to fill one's stomach] (38).

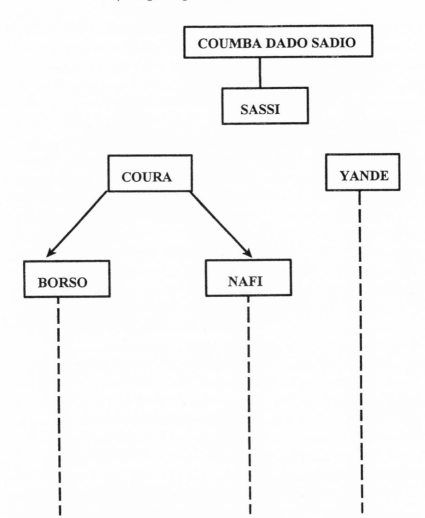

Diagram 5. This family tree from *L' Ex-père de la nation* shows the female characters. The female lineage begins with Coura and her daughters.

Coumba also carries on the rituals that mark important passages in family life. She performs the wedding ritual that unites Madiama with Coura, the niece she raised as a daughter. Coumba wanted the marriage to endure and made the young couple take an oath of loyalty that they were never to betray or abandon each other. Coura reminds Madiama of that oath when he takes Yandé as a second wife, for, faced with a polygamous fait accompli, Coura feels wounded and betrayed. She cannot undo what Madiama has done, but she is aware that she does not have to accept the situation, and using a powerful analogy, she signifies her choice in no uncertain terms: "Je peux pouvoir dire oui ou non. Si de tout l'univers je ne disposais que d'un grain de sable pour asseoir mon corps, je ne laisserais pas l'univers me comprimer sur ce grain de sable. Je chercherais et je trouverais la position la plus confortable sur ce grain de sable, avec l'univers en face de moi" [I have the right to say yes or no. If all I had from the universe was a grain of sand to sit on, I would not let the universe restrict me on that grain. Facing the whole universe, I would seek and I would find the most comfortable position on that grain of sand] (56).

The image suggests that although Coura is aware of the narrowness of the social space in which she can operate, she is determined to use that reduced space to allow herself to make choices. She deals with her husband's betrayal by declaring that she is no longer his wife, and to make that declaration incontrovertible she becomes, in words and in action, the reincarnation of Coumba Dado Sadio, Madiama's mother: "Elle avait fait gicler le lait de son sein et avait dirigé le jet sur ma bouche encore ouverte" [She had squirted milk from her breast and had directed the jet toward my mouth, still opened in disbelief] (59). This symbolic gesture, which is effectively turned into a transformational ritual, carries considerable force and marks a point of no return. Coura keeps to her word and places "a cloth of chastity" between herself and her husband for more than twenty years.

Coura's action is deliberate and shows that she can express her will and find ways to force Madiama to abide by it. Yet she knows that she must remain within the traditional norms of decorum, which she does by keeping secret both her protest and her decision to remain celibate. It is puzzling to see that in punishing Madiama, she punishes herself too; she is the one who is deprived of all sexual intercourse, as Madiama has a second wife. In spite of her claim to the contrary, she silences her body. For Coura, however, this result is less important than preserving her sense of freedom and choice: "Sache que je ne suis pas malheuresuse, au contraire! J'éprouve une joie profonde d'exprimer mon droit à l'existence quand tout apparemment, concourait à m'écraser" [Know that I am not unhappy. On the contrary, I am overcome with great joy at being able to express my right to existence when everything seemed to crush me] (59).

Coura's effective use of her limited power appears in stark contrast to anything her husband can manage in the public sphere. Yandé, Madiama's second wife, is a very different female character. The major events of her life are disclosed in a series of flashbacks, as a teacher, then a housewife married to Boly, then a prostitute, and again, a wife to Madiama. Yandé's first marriage is a traumatic experience that silences and humiliates her. She falls madly in love with Boly, a painter who is handsome, intelligent, talented, articulate, and sophisticated, but is heartless where Yandé is concerned. He dominates her, treats her like a maid, finds fault with everything she does. He causes her to lose her self-confidence and her sense of self-worth, until she indeed begins acting like his maid.

One episode is a particularly vivid depiction of mental cruelty. Boly makes Yandé pose for him every evening, then, each night, he tears his drawing of her to pieces. Unable to complete his work, he says that Yandé is the embodiment of disharmony, because she has a beautiful body but an extremely ugly face. He claims that this unnatural combination destroys his inspiration. Yandé, of course, is hurt by this nightly ritual and comes to desire the completion of the drawings more than anything in the world; she goes so far as to suggest, "Je peux bien m'envelopper le visage dans une écharpe pendant que tu dessines" [I could wrap my face with a scarf while you are drawing] (123). Ready to efface herself, or to symbolically mutilate herself to please her husband, she finds he will not even accept the offer: his artistic ethics will not permit him to cheat and his answer comes phrased as yet another insult: "Tant de désharmonie est contre nature. Tu dois porter en toi une malédiction" [So much disharmony is against nature. A curse must dwell in you] (123). Boly, like Madiama, adheres to an inflexible code that doesn't seem to allow for ordinary human compassion.

Boly refines his cruelty, showing her pictures he has drawn of beautiful women, as if wishing to cultivate her aesthetic appreciation. Yandé accepts these humiliations because she loves her husband deeply, though, receiving nothing in return, she reaches a point where she no longer expects love from him. Instead, she begs for pity as a reward for her total devotion; when she does not get even that, her pain becomes more acute. Blinded by Boly's appearances, neither her parents nor her friends listen to her pain, arguing that she should feel fortunate to have a husband like Boly. Isolated and forced into silence, Yandé rebels when the pain becomes unbearable. One day she makes special efforts to cook a delicate meal and set an attractive table for dinner, but Boly brushes her off, suggesting that she first takes a shower because the kitchen odors on her make him nauseous. This incident, which is minor compared to what she usually endures, is a last straw. She reaches for the kettle and pours boiling water on his face, an act that intends at last to destroy his vanity.

Accused of attempted homicide, she is sentenced to twelve years of forced labor, which she serves among criminals and prostitutes, and in such circumstances, she herself becomes a prostitute. When her family hears of her new profession, her brother Yatma tries to kill her with a machete, shouting: "*Dans notre famille, quand on n'est plus digne de vivre, il faut mourir*" [*In our family, when you're no longer worthy of living, you must die*] (126–27). Covered with blood, she is taken to the hospital, where Madiama cares for her and then falls in love with her, or at least feels compassion for her, and asks her to marry him and give up her life of prostitution.

Yandé is victimized by the patriarchal system represented by her husband's tyranny, by the males of her family who believe that they have the right of life and death over her, and by social institutions such as the judicial system, the prison, and law enforcement, which do little or nothing to help her. Eventually, Yandé recognizes, however, that her fault had been to love Boly to the point of self-negation. As she develops a new consciousness, she recalls a saying that she heard time and time again as she was growing up: "Il ne fallait jamais tout donner, pour garder toujours par devers soi un bout à tenir en cas de naufrage" [One should never give everything. One should always keep one thing to hold on to in case of shipwreck] (122). In her new life she sets out to protect herself first.

After she becomes Madiama's wife, Yandé follows his rise in the government, discovering that her life as a prostitute was clean in comparison with the political life she is now part of. But she enters the political arena with a vengeance, becoming a cynical and unscrupulous political strategist, who develops an unusual expertise at pulling strings behind Madiama's back and at hatching elaborate intrigues. Within Madiama's family, Coura, Sassi, and Nafi treat Yandé as a pariah because of her past, and also because of the way she tries to rule the household. An important part of Coura's decision to stop being Madiama's wife is that she will not share her husband with a former prostitute. For Sassi, Yandé is a "rotten grain"; for Coura she is "a curse," and for Nafi she is "trash." Yandé deserves these names in part, for she has become hateful and vindictive, without compassion or generosity. In this household, there is no community of women; here, each woman acts only for her own advantage and their mutual cruelties are gratuitous and unrelenting.

The impact of the women in *L'Ex-père de la nation* therefore has very mixed results. Coura raises her children to respect right values and forces her husband to respect her values, but although she has integrity and moral strength, her power is limited to what she can do within the home, even though she cleverly negotiates her freedom within patriarchal limitations. Ironically, Yandé, who disregards morals, has the power to intervene in political decision making. Unfortunately, her intervention is not positive: she plays political games and becomes a Machiavellian schemer. Sassi and Borso play insignificant roles, and Nafi, the revolutionary woman who might have brought changes about, dies young. None of the women is able finally to salvage the public morality that the male characters have so dismally failed, and that failure seems even to infect domestic life. Madiama's marriage to Yandé is like his other choices, a perhaps worthy impulse that leads to disaster. In Fall's narrative, this pattern seems to represent idealism disconnected from pragmatic reality.

In *L'Ex-père de la nation*, neither the male nor female lineages have been able to beget the nation, to build it up and nurture it. Fall relentlessly shows how the people betray themselves and in turn are betrayed by corrupt politicians, and the severity of her criticism leaves only a thin margin of political hope, especially as behind the changing figures of presidents endures Andru. Still, it is not by chance that the metaphors of cleanliness, transparency, faith, and beauty are so recurrent in this novel; if the political and social conditions are to improve, these are the values that each child of the nation must cultivate. Thus the "fathering" and the "mothering" of the nation is the responsibility of every individual in society.

Véronique Tadjo: Toward a Loftier Ideal

Véronique Tadjo, a poet and novelist from Côte d'Ivoire, entered the literary world with *Latérite*, a book that can be read either as a collection of poems or as a single long poem.[9] Her first novel, *A Vol d'oiseau* [As the crow flies], is one of the most original pieces of Francophone writing, and one that defies easy classification. It is surely a "text" in the primary meaning of the word, that is, "something woven." Tadjo's cloth is patterned from ninety-two independent yet related pieces, most accurately described as vignettes, that can stand on their own or be put together to form an immense appliqué representing an African social reality.[10] The vignettes are written mainly in prose, but Tadjo's language is never far from poetry, and here it exhibits her ability to use very simple words to create a superb poetic prose. The book comprises twenty-one chapters, each chapter containing a varied number of vignettes (one to eleven), ranging from one line to several pages in length, with each vignette assigned a roman numeral (I to XCII).

Like Werewere Liking, Véronique Tadjo often blurs the genres, and even within a genre she shows great originality in form and structure. In *A Vol d'oiseau*, there is no central figure, but a multiplicity of characters in different situations and belonging to different social classes. There is no single setting, but a variety of loci, no conventional plot, no real successiveness; only the main narrator serves as a unifying agent. This narrative technique, reminiscent of "stream of consciousness" and the *nouveau roman*, makes it possible for the writer to constantly shift directions, to move from one part of the world to another, to speak of the most diverse themes ranging from love and art to social and political issues. In addition, the vignette technique allows Tadjo to disregard the categories of time and space. She does not tell a story but a multitude of stories, some taken from personal life, news items, or reflections, some allegorical, constructed like a legend. Tadjo chooses to disregard chronology, which she views as artificial, distorted linearity and as a rearrangement of reality.[11] The reader is given a glimpse of her poetics

when she says: "Bien sûr, j'aurais, moi aussi, aimé écrire une histoire
sereine avec un début et une fin. Mais tu sais bien qu'il n'en est pas
ainsi" [Of course, I too, would have liked to write a peaceful story with
a beginning and an end. But you know that it does not work that way]
(2). Even though literature is an imaginary construct, it has bearing on a
tumultuous reality, and Tadjo uses it as an avenue for social criticism
aiming at social change.

Two major themes of *A Vol d'oiseau* appear on the opening page,
which functions as a kind of prologue. The first has to do with the importance and power of love, and the second with commitment to self and
society. The prologue commences with a short poem, containing the title of the book, which reads like an epigraph: it urges that love be important enough to warrant total commitment, and that once set on its
path, one must go the whole way, straight ahead, as the crow flies. Perhaps the metaphor can be extended to include not only love, but every
human action:

> Si tu veux aimer
> Fais le
> Jusqu'au bout du monde
> Sans faire de détours
> A vol d'oiseau
>
> [If you want to love
> Do so
> To the end of the world
> With no false detours
> As the crow flies]

The beginning of the prologue is an invocation addressed to the reader
in the second person *tu*, the informal, friendly form of "you." The usage
of *tu* / you serves the phatic function of discourse by which the narrator
maintains a constant contact with the reader, who is addressed directly
and so drawn into the narrative.[12]

The second part of the prologue is written in prose rather than verse.
It starts with the first person (*je* / I), then quickly moves to the second (*tu*
/ you), and back again to *je* / I. The recurrent use of the second person

(*tu* / you) and its alternation with *je* / I complicates the relation between addresser and addressee. Indeed, according to various contexts, the *tu* / you refers to either the narrator / protagonist *or* the reader. The "I" is the producer of discourse, whereas the "you" is the receptor of the same discourse. Yet when the narrator says, "*Tu* dis en te regardant dans le miroir: '*Je* n'aime pas ce que *je* vois'" [In looking at the mirror *you* say, "*I* don't like what *I* see"] (2, emphasis added), there seems to be no difference between the "you" and the "I." Lafont and Gardès-Madray note: "Le passage dialectique du *je* au *tu* fait que *tu* est considéré . . . en *je* éventuel" [The dialectical passage from *I* to *you* results in *you* being considered . . . as a possible *I*] (93).[13] This technique of pronominal interpenetration indicates how there can be in Tadjo's text a double addressee; the addresser and the addressee of her own discourse. The narrator / protagonist is speaking to herself even while speaking to the reader.[14]

The second part of the prologue describes a character looking into a mirror, loathing a self-reflection marked by weaknesses and failures. Tadjo suggests that in order to overcome shortcomings one must be able to imagine one's own decomposition, or to face the idea of being cremated. The word *death* does not appear in the text, but it is generated connotatively with enough force to become the unspoken presence, the oppositional force against which the narrator sets herself. This resistance requires tremendous courage and strength, qualities necessary to survive in the world and to combat the forces that would thwart her life. And she goes on to prophesy: "Ta force surgira de tes faiblesses éparses et, de ton humanité commune, tu combattras les tares érigées en édifices royaux sur les dunes du silence" [Your strength will come from your scattered weaknesses and with your common humanity you will fight the corruption rising like a royal edifice on the dunes of silence] (2). The eye / I that is looking in the mirror does not settle on an uncritical acceptance of self, but aspires to and works for transcendence and seeks to develop a character strong enough to fight for voice and freedom. The phrase "the dunes of silence" suggests that when people are silenced for too long, that silence, which in principle is an abstraction, an absence, becomes concrete, a presence. It accumulates and solidifies like sand dunes on which the corrupt elements of society can erect their monuments of lies and abuse. Speaking up is a way to end this destructive masquerade and dislodge the abusers from their "royal" authority.[15]

The two major impulses of the novel announced in the prologue are woven throughout the text, variations on the two significant sentences, "L'histoire de la misère se raconte" [The story of poverty must be told] (22) and "L'amour est une histoire qu'on n'arrête pas de conter" [Love is a story that one never ceases to tell] (53), that summarize the themes. There exists, however, a third dimension, inseparably intermingled with love and social concerns. It is the pervasive inscription of women's experience that signals a female-authored text and a femino-centric perspective on social reality.

Vignette LXIII, which forms the whole of chapter sixteen, beautifully encapsulates *A Vol d'oiseau*'s tridimensional orientation. Drawing inspiration from the cultural reservoir of orature, Tadjo invents a tale of a man and a woman who love each other so deeply that they decide to have a child. No sooner have they made the decision than the woman becomes pregnant, giving birth to a son before the end of the day. In this legend, the importance of love and the positive impact it can have on individuals is exemplified by the degree of feeling shared by the young man's parents. Their commitment to each other does not undermine their commitment to society, manifested in the way they raise their son, patiently preparing him for a social mission: to travel and to teach. They tell him, "Reconstruis les cités détruites par la violence et l'oppression. Laisse pousser l'herbe folle et n'écrase pas les nuages. Parle-leur de l'eau qui ne tarit pas. Plonge ta main dans la terre et respire son odeur et surtout, surtout, crois en toi-même" [Rebuild cities destroyed by violence. Let wild grass grow and do not crush the clouds. Tell them about the water that does not dry up. Dip your hand deep into the soil and inhale its fragrance. Above all, above all, believe in yourself] (69–70).

This is a message of justice, creativity, hope, and self-reliance, all positive values, but difficult to act on in a world whose social fabric has been badly damaged. The young man finds that the city he travels to is a locus of extreme contradictions. Bright lights inundate the rich neighborhoods, and yet close by, there is nothing but mud and filth. People are dressed like royalty and parade their gold jewelry, but not far from them cripples in rags and abandoned children are a common sight. The teachings given by the young man's parents are difficult to pass on because skepticism and despair have settled in the city: "Le plus grave c'était que les habitants avaient perdu la foi. On parlait de liberté et de changement mais c'était des paroles inutiles. Personne n'y croyait" [What was most serious was that the people had lost faith. People talked of freedom and change but these were useless words. Nobody believed in them] (70). Indeed, the people have been deceived so many times with words emptied of meaning that they have lost all hope, becoming utterly apathetic. More devastating than physical destitution is the destitution of mind and spirit that becomes so contagious that the young man must fight to hold on to his own faith. Furthermore, he finds that the fulfillment of his mission is jeopardized by his own inability to establish contact with others, so that he soon feels estranged, suffering at the thought that he who was supposed to make a difference has become despondent like the rest.

He falls in love, but the relationship is very different from that of his parents because he and the woman he loves are very dissimilar people. The woman has a strong sense of who she is and of what she wants. She refuses to fit into accepted women's roles. Believing that what she can accomplish is limitless, she views love as secondary. She only agrees to a relationship with the young man to share a friendship: "Elle savait que ce qu'il disait faisait partie de la vie mais elle n'était pas prête. Il lui fallait encore du temps. Beaucoup de temps. Des années peut-être" [She knew that what he was saying was part of life, but she was not ready. She needed time. A lot of time. Years, perhaps] (71).

The young man does not have that patience. He is so taken by the woman, his desire so overwhelming, that one night he gives her a soporific drink, makes love to her, and conceives a child. The result of this betrayal is an extraordinary apocalypse: the world is plunged into profound darkness and silence, and people are turned into stone. The woman regaining consciousness immediately says: "Cet enfant n'est pas de moi. Il amènera le malheur" [This child is not mine. It will bring misfortune] (72). The young man, now panicked, places his hand on the woman's navel to see if the child is alive, but this touch unleashes a fury suggestive of nuclear disaster across the earth, laying waste the land and its people, as "un énorme nuage-champignon sculpta l'horizon incendié" [an enormous mushroom cloud was sculpted against the blazing horizon] (72).

This story is compelling in its force and effective brevity, and it illustrates some of the main ideological bearings of the novel. It is no accident that the young man was raised in the best possible conditions to fulfill his mission; similarly to Fall's Madiama, his failure indicates that the best conditions may not be sufficient to produce human virtue: something else is required. The young woman attempts to escape the stereotypical notion of womanhood, even disowning the child she is carrying because it was conceived against her will. Before that conception she had decreed that she had no gender, caring neither for skirts nor for breasts, significant symbols of rejection as they involve the semiotics of clothing and of gender difference. Most importantly, the story implies that to betray a woman, even in the name of love, is to risk total destruction, and Tadjo's surreal visions of the world's end emphasizes how the unhindered presence of women is vital to the survival of the cosmos itself. This deliberately grand vision of women's role and place in the world, though located at the phantasmagoric level of the tale, reflects the centrality given women in *A Vol d'oiseau*.

Tadjo's characters are generally nameless and often defined simply by their actions or function. The only exception to this is Akissi, and this is significant because Akissi is a woman, and she is going through an experience that affects women in the deepest way: an unwanted pregnancy and an illegal abortion.[16] Here, the use of a personal name specifies and makes intimate the vignette's action. In less than a page and with the economy of language characteristic of Tadjo's writing, the wide range of feelings agitating Akissi is evoked. Her unwillingness to accept this pregnancy is evident in her reaction to the transformations her body undergoes: "Jour après jour, elle sent ses seins gonfler. Son corps entier se transforme. Ele se voit devenir une autre. Elle ne comprend pas cette vie qui est entrée en elle et qui lui bouffe toutes ses forces. Elle n'est pas prête" [Day after day, she feels the swelling of her breasts. Her entire body is changing. She sees herself become another person. She does not understand the life that has slipped into her and is devouring all of her strength. She is not ready] (12).

In Akissi's case, pregnancy does not mean only a physical burden. It has serious psychological, emotional, and financial ramifications. The decision to terminate the pregnancy is in itself emotionally draining, all the more so because Akissi is forced into the back alleys filled with other women wanting to undergo the same operation. Like Ken Bugul in *The*

Abandoned Baobab, Tadjo shows the common fate shared by all these women patiently waiting for their turn, alone (except for the man performing the abortion, men are conspicuously absent from the scene), turned into masks of stone, walled in by silence. And Tadjo makes this silence resound with unspeakable feelings generated by fear, by the anticipation of pain both physical and psychological, in an indifferent environment where no words are exchanged. Not the slightest sign of caring is shown here. On the contrary, it is a mere financial transaction, quick, cold, impersonal, made even more poignant as Akissi has to borrow the money for the operation. Tadjo does not speak directly for or against abortion. She simply presents a brief dramatization of a woman's experience that works very effectively to indict the laws of the land.

In other vignettes Tadjo describes more aggressively how the female body is constantly violated, even in public places. For the narrator, it happens in a movie theater where a fast and deft hand fondles her, painfully reminding her of a deeper wound—here again described with so few words as to heighten the drama: "Une main dans la pénombre d'un cinéma. Une main que je n'avais pas comprise. Une main qui prend la mienne. Brusquement, avec la musique du film, les paroles et le noir. Un pénis moite. Un homme qui se sauve. Une sensation irréparable" [A hand in the shadowy light of a theater. A hand that I did not understand. A hand taking mine. Suddenly with the music of the film, its words, the darkness. A wet penis. A man running away. An irreparable violation] (61).

The passage is spare but direct, disclosing clearly yet with calculated restraint how subject women are to casual molestation. The end of the vignette pinpoints the consequences of such acts for women: "an irreparable violation"; irreparable in the sense that it remains indelible. It can never be erased, only pushed into the recesses of memory, with the added agony that any similar occurrence may trigger the memory and make the woman live through the experience all over again, in pain and such rage that she is filled with the desire "de frapper, de casser un corps, d'anéantir une tête malade" [to hit, to smash a body, to destroy a sick mind] (61).

Worse still, the female body is violated irrespective of age or social competence. Even female children who are still too innocent to understand what is happening to them are the victims of such defilement, as Tadjo illustrates in the story of an older man and a girl still wearing a white and blue grade school uniform. Tadjo has the man entice the girl with candy, a double symbol of childhood and eroticism that he reinforces with sexual discourse: "Tiens, suce ce bonbon et ensuite embrasse moi" [Here, suck this candy and then kiss me] (32). His words and his actions leave no doubt that he is the seducer, yet in a cowardly reversal, while caressing her hair he compares her to Mamy Wata, the water goddess who in African mythology is the fatal seductress par excellence.[17] Identifying her in this way he shifts the responsibility for his actions onto the female child. In the end, however, after he asks her to take her clothes off and as she lies naked, he finds he cannot go through with the act. He redeems himself at least slightly by saying: "Je ne peux pas. Tu es encore trop jeune" [I can't, you are still too young] (32). The girl's innocence is again transparent in her reply: "Trop jeune, pour quoi faire? . . . Pour quoi faire?" [Too young to do what? To do what?] (32).

Tadjo is clear that women must assert themselves, taking more control over their destiny, instead of being "des femmes repliées sur elles-mêmes, léchant leurs plaies . . . " [women withdrawn into themselves, licking their wounds . . .] (54). They must put an end to any relationship that debases and devalues them and refuse to suffer any outrage on account of their gender. Such empowered women will no longer tolerate abuse, be it physical or verbal, and will refuse to understand "ces hommes qui veulent déchirer et qui donnent des coups de pieds dans le ventre des femmes avec des mots méchants, des mots qui blessent en plein coeur" [those men who want to tear and kick women's stomachs with harsh words, wounding words that hurt right into the center of the heart] (54). By using phrases such as "to tear" or "to kick," Tadjo suggests that verbal violence is no less damaging than physical violence. These observations don't mean that Tadjo rejects men entirely: her point finally is to say that love does not need to be hurtful, physically or otherwise.

Véronique Tadjo's treatment of female-male relationships here is closely akin to Werewere Liking's concept of the misovire, who, it must be remembered, is a woman unable to find an admirable man. This theoretical admirable man can only be born out of the transformation of the social self. Indeed, faced with women's formidable determination, men will have to change their behavior, discern the difference between loving and destroying, and realize that destruction is no proof of manhood.

To make sure that this metamorphosis takes place, to help men as well as to protect themselves, Tadjo says women must also act: "Il faut leur dire d'arrêter. Les tenir à bout de bras et leur réapprendre l'alphabet" [We must tell them to stop. We must hold them at arm's length and teach them the alphabet all over again] (54). Reteaching the alphabet involves serious work on the part of both the teacher and the learner, but the work holds the promise of a new beginning, a new understanding, a new form of relationship between men and women. Women will not give up on the possibility of love. That is why Tadjo combines a resolute refusal to be abused in the name of love (or for any reason, for that matter) with an ardent desire for love, sensuality, and sexual fulfillment.

Writing has allowed women to speak the unspeakable, to utter words, ideas, concepts that are forbidden to them within the conventions laid out by patriarchal society. Sex, desire, passion, and love are topics that women are expected to pass over in silence. By transgressing these taboos through the medium of literature, writers such as Calixthe Beyala, Ken Bugul, Werewere Liking, and Véronique Tadjo break the unwritten conventions while still accepting, as positive value, the topology that regards women as emotionally sensitive; thus they reclaim the right to express their feelings. In *A Vol d'oiseau*, the protagonist admits to living through her skin. She does not hesitate to speak of the body as a seat of enjoyable sensations. She talks freely about everything from the tickle of water running on her skin in the shower to the intense pleasures of orgasm. The erotic sensuality of the following passage shows no recognition of the usual taboos that regulate the parameters of African women's discourse: "Je m'enveloppe de son odeur, mouille mon visage de sa sueur, touche sa peau, mords son épaule, avale son désir, ferme les yeux, tends mon corps, l'appelle et le rejette" [I wrap myself in his smell, wet my face with his sweat, touch his skin, bite his shoulder, swallow his desire, close my eyes, stretch my body, call and expel him] (80).

The quest for love is so central for Tadjo that she invents yet another story, which begins realistically and ends as a legend. The opening depicts a love between a sick woman and a man who shares her pain so deeply that "il aurait voulu hurler, transpercer les murs d'un son si puissant que la ville se serait tue et que le temps aurait reculé. Il aurait voulu

vivre la même souffrance—dans sa chair, la douleur qui aujourd'hui rem-
plaçait le plaisir" [he wished he could scream, pierce walls with a sound
so powerful that the city would become silent and time would recede.
He wished he could experience the same pain—in his flesh, experience the
pain which today was replacing pleasure] (39). To save his beloved he attempts to pray, but finds he no longer knows how. He then makes the only
choice he finds acceptable: "J'irai avec toi jusqu'à la mort.... je veux
t'aimer jusqu'au bout de ta souffrance" [I will travel with you until death
comes.... I want to love you to the limits of your suffering] (40).

At this point the realistic setting is left behind and the story's action
is transformed into myth. The lover takes the woman in his arms and
crosses thousands of miles, finally arriving at the sea. She expresses the
desire to die there and be buried by the waters, but he will not hear of it
and resumes his journey, traveling until he reaches a white mountain.
She expresses the desire to die there in a place peaceful, cold, and pure.
Again he refuses, and resumes his journeying until he reaches a desert,
where: "Ils surent ... qu'ils avaient atteint le bout du monde et qu'il ne
leur restait nulle part où aller" [They realized ... that they had reached
the end of the earth and there was no place else to go to] (41). The woman
expresses her desire to die in the desert; having no choice, the man asks
to make love to her for the last time, "et c'est là qu'entre ciel et terre ils
s'aimèrent si fort que le soleil fit une éclipse et qu'un vent de fraîcheur
balaya leurs corps" [and it is there, between sky and earth, that they
loved each other so intensely that the sun was eclipsed and a cool breeze
swept over their bodies] (41).[18]

This sad but beautiful story features a loving, compassionate com-
panion, the very essence of the new man sought for by the misovire. So
the greatest love story of the book is in the form of a mythological tale,
the most compassionate man is a character in a tale, the woman who enjoys such compassion is on the verge of dying. Tadjo seems to suggest this
conjunction of events might be possible only in an imaginary world; or
she might mean that the power of imagination can be towering enough
to accomplish the miracle of love. Yet love involves a wide array of relationships and the narrator extends it to her country as well as to individuals. She is connected to her country in an intimate manner, her
feelings even strengthened by her exile in the "stone country"—an un-

named Western nation. In a three-line vignette (LV), she conveys this attachment with an exquisitely unexpected love metaphor: "Je songe à mon pays qui m'obsède chaque fois. Je le porte en moi, le jour. La nuit, il s'allonge à mes côtés et me fait l'amour" [I think of my country which, for me, has become a constant obsession. In the daytime I carry my country inside me. At night my country lies beside me and makes love to me] (64). It is easy to understand, then, the suffering she feels when confronting the ills of her society. Its problems are so glaringly present that they impose themselves on all the senses: "Faut-il être aveugle pour ne pas voir? / Sourd pour ne pas entendre? / Muet pour ne pas crier?" [Should one be blind not to see? / Deaf not to hear? / Dumb not to shout?] (66).

What the narrator sees is a society characterized by a profound sense of malaise, one she describes with phrases of disjunction: "la vie a dû rater une marche" [Life must have missed one step] (8); "on doit vivre un siècle crasseux" [we must be living in a filthy time] (21); "on doit vivre un monde sans queue ni tête" [we must be living in a senseless world] (29); "c'est vraiment un siècle qui baisse la tête" [it is really a century that walks with its head down] (29). This social malaise needs to be overcome, of course, because there is an enormous amount of work to be done, and her sense of urgency in this is moved by the seriousness of the problems to be dealt with: "Il n'y a pas de quoi avoir la tête en l'air. Il n'y a pas de quoi rire et se croiser les bras" [This is no time to be absentminded. This is no time to laugh and sit around idly] (65). Tadjo's narrator cannot afford to laugh in the face of the social injustice she describes with evocative force: "Je dis les inégalités qui croissent comme des margouillats sous les ruines des taudis" [I speak of the inequalities that grow like lizards under the ruins of slums] (65). Starting her sentence with the declarative "I speak," the narrator performs an act of language that, assuming the responsibility of enunciation, makes the statement stronger and the concern more acute. Describing inequalities as "lizards" emphasizes the proliferation of these inequalities, and the image of the "ruins of slums" conveys the sense of a double destruction.

Even within the fictional mode in which *A Vol d'oiseau* is cast, there is a dialectical motion between the purely "imaginary" tales, such as the one about the dying woman, and the putatively "real" *histoires vécues*—stories lived, experienced by a character. Such an *histoire vécue* forms the background of chapter three, a long, first-person vignette. It tells the story of a young man who is at the same time the protagonist, focalizer, and narrator recounting his experiences as an actor. Within the story lies a depiction of the relationship that exists between intellectuals, politicians, and "ordinary" people. The young man is representative of the majority of the people as indicated by his modest background, his substandard living conditions, his speech patterns, his attitude toward education, and his aspirations. In fact, his representation of the people is doubled by the very role he acts within the play: "Je représente le peuple. Symboliquement. Je fais beaucoup de choses. Je cultive la terre. Je pêche. . . . Je danse. . . . Mes pas cadencés. Mon buste raidi. Mon cou cabré. Et puis 'Stop,' les bras en croix. Le héros se bat pour moi. Contre le monarque" [I represent the people. Symbolically. I do a lot of things. I till the land. I go fishing. . . . I dance. . . . In quick time. My chest stiffened. My neck taut. And then "Cut," arms in the form of the cross. The hero fights for me. Against the monarch] (15).

A variant of this speech is repeated at the end of the vignette: "Je représente le peuple. Symboliquement. J'ai les bras en croix. Le héros se bat pour moi. Contre le monarque" [I represent the people. Symbolically. My arms are in the form of the cross. The hero fights for me. Against the monarch] (20). Between this repeated quotation is Tadjo's generalized depiction of the state of African society. The young man simultaneously a representative of the people and representing them. Furthermore, his summary lines provide the reader with a vision of what life is like for the people he represents, an existence of hard labor that nonetheless finds some release in dance. Even that dance, though, is hampered by the strained positions of his body—positions symbolic of constraint and injustice. The phrase "my arms are in the form of a cross" suggests crucifixion, but the quotation goes on to describe a revolutionary mood personified by the "hero," who sides with the people, fighting with and for them against the monarch.

As there is a correlation between the "people" and the young man, a parallel can be drawn between the "hero" and the director of the theater company. The director represents an enlightened intellectual, one who turns ideas into action, and so commands the young man's admiration. He is intelligent, generous, and helpful in encouraging youngsters to use their creativity in acting. Creating a community of artists who can share all aspects of their lives, he develops a space where their talents can flourish. His home is opened to whoever needs a bed or food, and the visitor who happens to be there at lunch time is undoubtedly invited to share the meal.[19]

Not fully understanding the intricacies of the repressive system he is living in, the young man's innocent voice continuously makes remarks that are all the more powerful as they are understated. He laments the fact that arts are encouraged by neither politicians nor the public. At one performance there are only three rows of spectators, and, as participatory and encouraging as they are, the small audience points up the precariousness of artistic life in Africa. The young man observes: "Le théâtre, c'est pas un travail. Un jour on gagne, demain, on gagne rien. Ça me plaît, mais ce n'est vraiment pas un travail" [Acting is not a job. One day you earn some money, tomorrow, you earn nothing. I like acting, but really it is not a job] (18). In addition, theater is particularly censored because of its perceived potency. The director is constantly harassed by politicians, who see the plays as a threat, as again, the narrator ingenuously notes: "On dit qu'Il est un révolutionaire, que les pièces que nous on joue attaquent le gouvernement. Il y a toujours des problèmes" [They say He is a revolutionary, that the plays we perform are an attack against the government. We are always in trouble] (19).

One understands, then, why the people must have someone to fight for them, against the "monarch"—a living symbol of the oppressive political machinery.[20] It seems possible, however, that the people themselves will come to action because oppression cannot last for ever: "On en a tous marre de ce monarque qui s'assoit sur la tête de son peuple" [We are all fed up with this monarch who sits on his people's heads] (29). This image of sitting on someone's head, clearly an African idiom, takes on larger proportions because many African societies hold the belief that the head is the seat of life. Thus, to sit on people's heads is at worse to wish their death and at best to deprive them of all power. In search of inordinate power for himself, the monarch attempts to render his people powerless.

Powerlessness is also a characteristic of the poor, and poverty is personified by the mentally disturbed people who roam the streets, infested with lice, stinking so badly that their smell infests the whole city. The all-pervading stench shows that what happens to the "wretched of the earth" affects everybody. If those who exploit the people with detached indifference are blind to the crucial dimensions of human interdependency, violence will force them into such recognition. There will come a time when it will no longer be possible for them to count on their "lucky star." Their fat bank accounts and the endless privileges they enjoy will collapse with the rebellion of the down-trodden: "Vos jardins seront malmenés, vos autels sacrés assiégés et vos fétiches-idoles décapités. Vos demeures enfoncées. Vos livres jetés, vos maîtres à penser condamnés. Les traces de vos pas s'effaceront et sur une plage abandonnée, on transpercera vos poitrines de flèches empoisonnées" [Your gardens will be wrecked, your sacred shrines besieged and your fetish-idols will be beheaded. Your homes smashed in. Your books thrown away, your intellectual guides condemned. The traces of your steps will disappear and, on abandoned shores, your chests will be pierced with poisoned arrows] (66). If the exploiters retaliate, they will be unmasked by a mass media whose sophistication can now be used to the advantage of the voiceless majority: "Le monde entier verra les bouches tordues, le sang épaix et grotesque des corps aux derniers soubresauts" [The whole world will see the twisted mouths, and the thick, grotesque blood oozing out of bodies in their last convulsions] (66).

If her criticism of the sociopolitical structures and of the so-called leaders who maintain and enforce them is mordant, Tadjo still invites all individuals to work for a loftier ideal. That goal must be approached, not through complacency but through rigorous self-criticism: "Nous devons piétiner les mauvaises habitudes, déraciner les fausses théories et nous regarder face à face" [We must trample on bad habits, uproot false theories and look ourselves in the face] (65). All individuals have a responsibility both to themselves and to future generations, who eventually are going to ask: "Qu'avez-vous fait pour changer les choses?" [What have you done to change things?] (29). This is an interrogation that should spur the elders into reevaluating their acts, because "les actions que nous sculptons se cristallisent" [the actions that we take will crystalize] (65). And nothing would be more damaging than to crystallize the status quo for the younger generations.

Like Werewere Liking, Véronique Tadjo makes ancestral beliefs and rituals play an important role in the transformation of self and society.

At the personal level, when the narrator cannot make sense of her love life, when the pain of separation is no longer bearable, she longs to go back to her ancestors' belief systems. She would like to call the Gods, say incantations, assemble healers, sorcerers, and spirits, and resort to magic to annihilate her memory. But she strives not for escape, but for empowerment and a new beginning.

At the social level, Tadjo emphasizes the necessity to revive cultural survival rites, and advocates ritual on a large scale, both in the city and in the country: "Il nous faut procéder aux rites de pureté. Faire les sacrifices nécessaires. Il faut replanter nos grands arbres arrachés, nos forêts sacrées décimées" [We must perform cleansing rites. We must make the necessary sacrifices. We must plant again our tall uprooted trees, our decimated sacred forests] (67). Tadjo puts ritual into a twofold play, making it perform its traditional function and serve as a cure for modern problems. The sacrifices refer to both ritual and the renunciation necessary to become agents of change. In the same way, the act of replanting trees constitutes at once a genealogical and ecological symbol, emphasizing a cultural continuum. On the other hand, it serves as a means to solve the urgent problem of deforestation facing the continent.

Also, because ritual valorizes speech and is articulated through speech, however esoteric, it will be possible to rediscover the significance of the word in "la parole complète. Celle qui est à la fois silence et verbe, action et inertie. Celle que seuls les grands initiés possèdent" [the completeness of the word that is both silence and speech, action and inertia. The word that only the great initiates possessed] (67). Thus, ritual can constitute the mediating process for a judicious balance between speech and action.

The novelists studied here believe in a new sociopolitical order. Mostly, however, their fictions make it clear that *a new moral order* is desperately needed. Without it all other construction remains without foundation. The fictions also attest to the fact that this new moral order can only be turned into reality through individual commitment.

CONCLUSION

"It will take a long time,
but the story must be told."
Leslie Marmon Silko

When I began the study of Francophone women's writing, it quickly became clear that I would need to place their literary production in a framework that would allow for a coherent discussion. The works under study, therefore, were approached through an artificial hierarchy of social categories, beginning with a representation of the self, moving to women's position within the family, and finally concluding with the writer's concerns for society as a whole. In my introduction I illustrated these categories through diagram 1 (p. 25), made up of three concentric circles representing the self, the family, and the society. This structure enabled me to organize the analysis of a literature written by women from different backgrounds, coming from different countries, belonging to different social classes, using an array of literary styles and producing a body of literature that is in a state of constant flux because it is still in the making.

But, as I suggested earlier, it is useful to critique one's own categories and rules at some point, in order to discover what may have been left out or evaded in the analysis. Thus, in addition to the differences mentioned above, it should be noted that the female writers I examine here are of different ages, and therefore belong to different generations, even though, due to the historical reasons discussed earlier, they belong to the same literary generation.[1] There is also considerable difference in the "quality of the page" and in the "merit" of the various works I look at. Nafissatou Diallo's style is very simple, lacking the sophistication of Calixthe Beyala's writing, for instance; additionally, the pitfalls of translation obscure the instances in which Diallo's language becomes poetic and melodious, making it difficult for a non-French speaker to value her.[2] The most problematic book of all those I have discussed is certainly that of Angèle Rawiri. *Fureurs et cris de femmes* is incredibly melodramatic, relying on a scenario that suggests badly digested soap opera, with annoyingly flat characters and plot turnabouts that are very arbitrary (for example, the novel's lesbian episode). Yet the narrative structure remains strong, Rawiri manages to maintain a well-controlled suspense until the end of the novel, and, most important, her themes and situations represent fundamental problems that confront women in their daily lives.

Yet other differences emerge from the fact that all of these writers are not writing "out of Africa" or in their own country of origin. The Cameroonian Werewere Liking has been living and working in Côte d'Ivoire for more than a decade, Calixthe Beyala is now living in France, and their work will necessarily bear the mark of their exile. This mark is already visible in Beyala's fourth novel, *Le Petit Prince de Belleville,* her title recalling intertextually the Saint-Exupéry classic, but also referring to Belleville, a Paris suburb that is the new "home" of an increasing number of African immigrants, who live there in sordid conditions. Beyond the many differences, however, all the writers I discuss are linked by gender, a shared language, the very fact of writing, and their commitment to the self, society, and female issues within society. They all function as modern griottes who have broken open the exclusively male preserve of writing. Putting these women's works into the framework of diagram 1, therefore, made it possible, despite their many differences, to find an organizing principle for the three chapters that form the core of *Francophone African Women Writers: Destroying the Emptiness of Silence.*

Although I thought that the framework established by diagram 1 would be a useful analytical tool (as I believe it has proven to be), I also was aware of the arbitrariness of such a construct, and as a corrective I added diagram 2 (p. 26), showing the self / family / society circles no longer in a concentric position, but in a relation of intersections. Roughly, diagram 1 represents the outlook of a "traditional" society, where social entities are clearly delineated, whereas diagram 2, which depicts how the first diagram is deceptively simple, can be seen as the perspective on a "modern" society where nothing is clear-cut or smoothly connected. If no actual society can be fit to either diagram, the sketches at least suggest a continuum for social possibilities and the conflicts likely to emerge when opposing models meet. This meeting has certainly been taking place in African nations, and it has manifested itself in changing gender roles. Indeed, the intersected circles of diagram 2 show that there are contact points and areas of penumbra where the three "stages" of women's writing feed into each other, creating sectors of fusion, or of tension.

This intersection was evident in the very chapter dealing with autobiography. Although ostensibly centered around the presentation of self, in the accounts of all three autobiographers, Nafissatou Diallo, Ken Bugul, and Andrée Blouin, the self, of course, could never be dissociated from family or society. Indeed, Nafissatou Diallo is concerned with the self, but she also deals critically with Muslim society; Ken Bugul's journey to self-discovery is inseparable from her social background and the political forces—primarily colonization—that forged her ideological consciousness; Andrée Blouin's autobiography develops in the light of her coming to terms with her situation as a métisse, a situation that exists because of the colonial enterprise. And Blouin's autobiography is also a political history of several African nations on the eve of independence.

In the same way, Calixthe Beyala was placed in the circle of the family because the whole process of growing up as a woman is played out within the family. Yet the social and political criticism contained in *Tu t'appelleras Tanga* is as caustic as the satirical songs composed by women in the oral traditions. The same thing can be said of Mariama Bâ, whose *Scarlet Song* is, beyond posing problems faced by women of all races, an indictment of Senegalese society. Similarly, Werewere Liking, Aminata Sow Fall, and Véronique Tadjo's works are studied as social criticism, but they all have important sections dealing with self-identity and the connections with family structures.

171

The arbitrary nature of the analytical frame creates fusions and tensions all through my analyses, which reflect the fusions and tensions present in the texts themselves; but the presence of these conflicting elements, far from being a negative aspect of women's writing, enhances that writing and increases its richness and complexity. I would like to look briefly at this useful conflict in terms of specific examples, first as a fusion of social differences and then as a tension. The fusion has to do superficially with style, where strong elements of traditional culture, in this case orature, are used to help come to terms with contemporary social conditions. The tension has to do with how women who want to destroy their condition of silence need to approach this project with caution, through a balancing act that, in Africa, characterizes gender relations, and that here becomes a literary strategy as well.

I have already mentioned that most female writers acknowledge the role of their mothers or grandmothers as the storytellers who shaped their sense of orature. There is, among all the writers studied here, in all their diverse forms of writing, a strong inscription of orature, from words and expressions in African languages to the use of proverbs and folk stories, to the organization of narrative structures. This use of orature is not at all a decorative ploy, a way of creating a certain *couleur locale.* It is, in some instances, a narrative strategy, a structural device, as in Ken Bugul's *Abandoned Baobab.* As we have seen, the autobiography starts with a few pages entitled "Ken's Prehistory," which functions as a mythical tale of origin. The autobiography itself constitutes a lengthy second part entitled "Ken's History," preceded by two pages in italics, a veritable prelude that forms the linkage between Ken's prehistory and her life history. This narrative form, then, can be seen as a structural rendition in literature of an important element of orature—namely a genealogy—that situates the individual in time and space and in relation to ancestors as well as the present community.[3]

Véronique Tadjo's *A Vol d'oiseau* is another instance of successful integration of orature into literature. The passage from one to the other is very smoothly, almost effortlessly, executed, for even though written, Tadjo's style has a simple but eloquent poetic fluidity often found in orality. Her vignettes, which give the impression of being occasional knowledge, casual reminiscence, actually function as stories—and some are indeed modern tales—that could be told in the evening, around the palaver tree in the same way that stories used to be told when the village assembled in the moonlight. Yet through the very act of writing, Tadjo makes permanent something that could be ephemeral in an Africa where the performance and retention of orature is no longer what it used to be, particularly in urban settings.

Nafissatou Diallo uses orature in yet a different manner. She remembers with joy the stories her grandmother once told her, and she reproduces the opening formulas that used to delight her and create an exhilarating sense of anticipation. Andrée Blouin shares the same kind of memories. In *Scarlet Song*, Mariama Bâ builds her story line around a proverb that is at the core of the novel, both as narrative construct and as meaning-making device. The novel is enriched by a series of pithy proverbs appropriately used to illustrate a point or make it more powerful. To Yaye Khady, who is making a hasty judgement, her husband Djibril Guéye says, "Before you stop the mouth of the shepherd, first recognize the tune he is whistling" (55); the same character speaking of old age and of the necessity to accept one's passing says, "When a tree has borne fruit, it need have no regret at being cut down" (55). In her attempts to initiate Mireille into Senegalese culture, Rosalie tells her to present her in-laws with delicately cooked meals on occasion because, as she puts it, "The mouth that chews is always grateful to the hand that provides" (96). Some of these proverbs are given in Wolof, with a translation that is well integrated into the text: "Allah, Allah, *Bèye sa tôle.* Cultivate your own field. God helps those who help themselves" (111), or again, "Nit, nit modi garabam! Man, man is his own remedy" (165).

Aminata Sow Fall acknowledges orature as an important component of her art when she says: "Je suis tout à fait consciente que mes romans sont des romans, mais ce sont des romans qui portent un héritage de la tradition, des contes, des histoires, des légendes" [I am fully aware that my novels are novels, but they are novels that carry the heritage of tradition, tales, stories, legends] ("An interview," 25). I have shown how Werewere Liking uses ritual in her works, and she too recognizes the fecund fusion of orature and literature: "Nous nous inspirons des mécanismes et techniques de communication des rituels traditionnels. Mon théâtre et mes autres oeuvres puisent à cette même source. Mais la littérature orale n'influence que la forme de ces oeuvres . . . la thématique quant à elle, est plutôt moderne . . . " [We take our inspiration from methods and techniques of communication derived from traditional ritual. My theater and my other works draw from this same source. But the oral literature only influences the form of these works . . . the themes are quite modern . . .] ("Werewere Liking: Créatrice," 595).

For Liking, orature is the inspiration that gives form to modern content, an approach that parallels her belief that Africans should return to tradition because it contains basic, primordial, and fundamental values that may help to salvage contemporary Africa. The predilection revealed here for the fusion of orature and literature is not accidental. It marks the distinctiveness of African cultural expression, a frame in which women writers can use orature to produce a literary culture, thus ensuring a continuum between the old and the new and revitalizing the role that their female ancestors played in orature.

This revitalization, however, is not without its own dilemmas. I mentioned earlier that there was a "silence in print," one that women felt the need and indeed the duty to break. This silence imposed by patriarchal rule had to be dealt with in a way that would be firm enough to be effective and yet not alienate men, who are part and parcel of the new society women hope will evolve from the chaotic confusion of values in contemporary Africa. So there is for women a difficult double identification, with the self and with the society without which the self is not conceivable. Yet to destroy silence this society must be confronted, and the tension involved in this confrontation inevitably marks the written works. It is reflected in the invention by Werewere Liking of the word *misovire*, which she defines by rejecting its nominal meaning of "man-hater" for a new exegesis: "a woman who cannot find an admirable man." The same tension is found in Nafissatou Diallo, who resorts to the in-passing discourse to make her point, or in *Fureurs et cris de femmes*, where Rawiri develops "liberated" protagonists who are still too enmeshed in cultural codes to break away from the gender roles delineated by traditional principles within society.

Many female writers, then, go through what I have called elsewhere a "forward-backward motion."[4] Yet if they are making two steps forward only to make one step back, women are still moving ahead; even within this cautious, controlled mode, women question and denounce the patriarchal forces that limit their agency. Rejecting labels others assign them, moving away from the manner in which they are perceived and represented, women's self-representation involves a self-redefinition that emerges clearly and forcefully throughout their writing. Indeed, a woman is not a womb (Rawiri), a woman is not a sex object (Beyala, Tadjo), a woman is not a prisoner to be trapped physically or emotionally (Blouin, Beyala, Fall, Rawiri), a woman is not mute (Fall, Bâ). The negation of all these false attributes is part of the oppositional spirit that animates Francophone women writers and their works, and part of the whole process of inventing femino-centric paradigms for themselves.

There is no camouflage here. The inscription of gender is very strong, even with writers who, like Aminata Sow Fall, refuse to be labeled "feminists." Her treatment of Yandé as a victimized woman who seizes her own destiny in *L'Ex-père de la nation*, in particular, would negate all her pronouncements denying feminist intentions, because it is a testimony too eloquent to deny.[5] If writing is the vehicle that makes it possible to articulate society's salient issues, these women's poetics are inseparable from their interest in and commitment to the female condition. They realize that all women have the same fate, which is why, at the heart of their writing, there is recognition of the importance of a community of women belonging to all classes and all races, within and outside Africa.

The dilemmas and tensions described above are not faced only by writers of poetry or fiction. They also must be addressed by critics like myself who are, as Carole Boyce Davies says in *Out of the Kumbla*, "insiders" *and* "outsiders" vis-à-vis their own culture, or who are, as Gloria Andalzua puts its, at the "border," a situation that is a prime locus for ambiguity and contradiction, but that can also be a vantage point. Such individuals can be viewed as "monsters" who, as in African folk tales, have a "normal" pair of eyes on the face and another pair of eyes in the nape of their neck. This "monstrosity" can be an advantage, making it possible to see in two directions at once, toward one's culture of origin and toward one's culture of exile. Ideally, this dual vision produces what Edward Said calls the "syncretic border intellectual," but realistically such an ideal individual will not come into being without a prolonged conflict and internal debate.[6] This conflict is reflected in my own discussion of an African feminism and in my battles with the terrorism of a Western theory that seeks to impose on all peoples a Eurocentric view, elevated to the status of what the sociolinguist William Labov calls a "prestige dialect."

I might illustrate this locus of contradiction, ambiguity, dilemma, tension, and fusion with two proverbs epitomizing the position of an increasing number of so-called Third-World people now in exile in Europe and North America. The first proverb is borrowed from Andalzua: "I am a turtle, wherever I go I carry 'home' on my back." The second, which I have quoted earlier, comes out of Mariama Bâ's *Scarlet Song:* "When you abandon your hill, any hill you climb will crumble." Both proverbs are relevant for today's world of "nomads." The first expresses the irreducibility of identity, the second poses the contradictory desires to be open to the world while preserving one's identity. To return to my image of the monster with four eyes, that poor beast is in the uncomfortable position of having a foot on each hill. The question is whether one can indeed stand with a foot on each hill. Or the question is, with a foot on each hill, does one have any other choice?

At the end of this exploration of African women's writing can it be said that the emptiness of silence has been destroyed? It would be premature to say so. Yet as writing becomes a key to self-representation, self-redefinition, a means of proposing an alternative way of knowing, of doing, and of being in the world, women fill some of the pages that formerly were blank. Writing is a means of transgression, of resistance, of exposure. Indeed, women challenge the social and political structures, they assert their opinion and their position, they emphasize the need for a reformation of society that goes beyond individual responsibility and individual transformation. They demand *a new moral order.* And writing is also catharsis and celebration. The prise d'écriture, therefore, is a total commitment. "It will take a long time, but the story must be told," even if it is only to reflect a particular reality. If all representations are indeed constructions, the constructions must correspond to what women view *themselves* to be: full human beings who may know who and what they are. What is left to be done is to make sure that this view is acknowledged and accepted. Of course what women represent is in fact much larger than any representation, as astutely observed by

Catherine N'Diaye: "Il convient d'abord de distinguer—et même de dissocier—l'image de la femme dans la sphère des représentations et son rôle effectif. Ainsi, il se peut que le role effectif de la femme excède largement la représentation qu'on en a" [It is important to distinguish—and even to dissociate—the image of the woman in the realm of representations from her actual role. It may well be that the actual role of the woman far exceeds the representation that we have of it] (25).

The surge of Francophone women's writing empowers women and gives them a forum, a collective voice to discuss their own lives, to take a critical look at society and offer alternatives. Women as producers of texts offer a social vision that African society will find nowhere else. That vision promises a social understanding that is an invaluable resource, for nations and, equally important, for individuals. It is true for communities as well as for individuals that if the story is told, the silence, and its emptiness, may be destroyed.

NOTES

Introduction

1. It is the institution of the rule of the tribe or family by men that inspired feminist theorists to apply the term *patriarchy* in a metaphorical sense to signify male domination. It is also in that metaphorical sense that I speak of patriarchy as a formidable institution. Adrienne Rich provides a more specific definition of patriarchy as "the power of the fathers: a familial-social, ideological, political system in which men—by force, direct pressure, or through ritual, tradition, law, language, customs, etiquette, education, and the division of labor, determine what part women shall or shall not play" (*Of Woman Born*, 59).

2. Quoted in the preface of Grewal et al., *Charting the Journey*, 4–5.

3. See Davies and Graves, *Ngambika*. See also Borgomano, *Voix et visages de femmes*. *Orature* is a word coined by the Kenyan writer Ngugi wa Thiong'o and formed by the juxtaposition of the words *orality* and *literature*. In the same way that literature is the body of written works, orature is the body of oral artistic modes. The word *orature* is a necessary substitution for the term *oral literature*, which is anachronistic and subordinates orality to writing.

4. A *griot* (male) or a *griotte* (female) can be defined as: (1) a poet, and often musician, trained in the art of eloquence; (2) an individual entrusted with the memorization, recitation, and passing on of oral history from one generation to the next; (3) a professional praise and criticism singer and social commentator.

5. See Barber, *I Could Speak Until Tomorrow*. Barber provides the following definition: "*Oriki* are a genre of Yoruba poetry that could be described as attributions or appellations: collection of epithets, pithy or elaborated, which are addressed to a subject" (1). She also notes that "though *oriki* are often called 'praise poetry' [they] are [not] wholly flattering to their subjects" (13).

6. See Diallo, *De Tilène au Plateau*; Keïta, *Femme d'Afrique*; Barry, *Kesso, Princesse peuhle*.

7. This is an important departure from characterization by male writers who, with very few exceptions, always cast the *griot* as male. See, in particular, Bâ,

Une si longue lettre, and Ka, *"La Voie du salut" suivi de "Le Miroir de la vie."*
Another important departure made by women is the introduction of female healers; for instance, Ka in *La Voie,* Dooh-Bunya in *La Brise du jour,* and Rawiri in
Fureurs et cris de femmes. As for the exceptions in fiction written by men, in *Les
Bouts de bois de Dieu [God's Bits of Wood],* Sembène Ousmane describes Ramatoulaye in the following terms: "She knew . . . the bloodline of all the men for
generations back. She was, in fact a walking encyclopedia of every family in the
district" (40). One must note that although she is described as such, Ramatoulaye is not seen to function as a *griotte* in this novel. There is, however, a reference to a *griotte* in Ahmadou Kourouma's *Les Soleils des Indépendances.*

8. See also Adrienne Rich in her evocation of silence as a sign of strategic presence in "Cartographies of Silence."

9. Even though most critical works date the beginning of Francophone African
literature from the 1930s, at least four novelists published their first works in the
1920s. They are: Diagne, *Trois Volontés de Malic;* Diop, *Réprouvé;* Diallo, *Force-
Bonté;* and Couchoro, *L'Esclave.*

The history of Francophone African literature does not fall in the scope of the
present work. Numerous studies devoted to the genesis and development of this
body of writing are available. Among the important ones, interested readers
should consult: Blair, *African Literature in French;* Chevrier, *Littérature nègre;*
Cornevin, *Littérature d'Afrique noire de langue française;* Kane, *Roman africain
et tradition;* Kesteloot, *Ecrivains noirs de langue française;* Kimoni, *Destin de
la littérature négro-africaine;* Makouta Mboukou, *Introduction à la littérature
noire;* Midiohouan, *L'Idéologie;* and Nkashama, *Comprendre la Littérature
africaine écrite.*

10. The question of dates is important in an effort to redress women's literary
history. Indeed, most critical books claim that Aminata Sow Fall is the first Francophone female writer to publish a book; her first novel, *Le Revenant,* appeared
in 1976. Before that date, however, two autobiographies appeared, both in 1975:
Diallo's *De Tilène au Plateau* and Keita's *Femme d'Afrique: La vie d'Aoua Keita
racontée par elle-même.* But most significantly, it may turn out that the first
Francophone female writer is Thérèse Kuoh-Moukouri from Cameroon, who
produced a novel, *Rencontres essentielles,* in 1969. In most bibliographies, this
work is dated 1981, the publication date of the edition by L'Harmattan (Paris),
which does not mention the existence of any previous edition. However, I found
two sources giving 1969 as the first date of publication. In Ambroise Kom's *Dictionnaire* (1983) it is listed as follows: "Thérèse Kuoh-Moukouri. *Rencontres Essentielles.* Paris, Imprimerie Edgard, 1969, 127p."; in Christine H. Guyonneau's
"Francophone Women Writers" (1985): "Thérèse Kuoh-Moukouri. *Rencontres
Essentielles.* Adamawa: Chez l'auteur et Paris: Imprimerie Edgard, 1969, 125p."

There is a discrepancy in the location of the publishing house, although the book might have been simultaneously issued in Cameroon and in France. Both sources, however, cite the same date, 1969. The fact that Kuoh-Moukouri's autobiographical novel was produced by a small local publishing house (or perhaps was privately printed) is related to the neglect of that work, a situation that says a great deal about the politics of publication and distribution. It should also be noted that Francophone African women published poetry at least a decade before they produced fiction.

11. It is well known that the reading public is rather limited in most African countries. However, one of the most popular novels written by a woman—*Une si longue lettre* by Mariama Bâ—has been converted into a play and then into a six-part television series in Wolof, the main language spoken in Senegal. Also, as Aminata Sow Fall mentions in an interview by Françoise Pfaff ("Aminata Sow Fall," 135), it is not unusual that literate people read novels and then recount them to their unlettered friends and relatives. This is an interesting reversal of the usual passage from the oral to the written tradition.

12. Ambroise Kom is currently preparing a second dictionary, which will study African literary works of the last decade, and judging from recent literary output by women, the difference in the numbers of female writers will be substantial.

13. For a detailed discussion of colonial educational policies and goals as they related to women, see Diane Barthel's revealing study of the Senegalese case in "Women's Educational Experience under colonialism: Toward a Diachronic Model," *Signs: Journal of Women in Culture and Society* 11, no. 1 (1985): 137–54.

14. However, we must not assume that the West introduced written literature in Africa. There were, as Jean Boyd shows in *The Caliph's Sister*, literate traditions in which women excelled in Islamized West Africa.

15. Julien adds: "John Johnson notes, for example, that women bards in the Mande traditions do not narrate epics as do men, although a woman may accompany her husband by reciting the epics as he plays a musical instrument" (162). However, it seems to me that we must question the assumption that the epic was a "hierarchic form" to be classified in "high" orature as it were—an assumption that comes no doubt from Western paradigms influenced by ancient Greek values. Indeed, how "popular" was the epic and what was its distribution in African societies? An investigation into indigenous genre classification could reveal whether or not societies with epic traditions viewed this genre as "great" orature.

16. Brenda F. Berrian is one of the pioneers in efforts to recover forgotten or neglected women writers from Africa and the Caribbean. She compiled a number of important bibliographies for articles, such as "Bibliographies of Nine Anglophone Women Writers" and "An Update." She also produced two books: *Bibli-*

ography of African Women Writers and Journalists and *Bibliography of Women Writers from the Caribbean.*

17. Audre Lorde, "The Transformation of Silence into Language and Action," in *Sister Outsider.*

18. Of course, a hypothesis that might be tested is that perhaps the *prise d'écriture* in fiction and poetry does not constitute a radical change but a gradual process, prepared by the work of women in journalism for instance or other areas not traditionally referred to as "literature."

19. Several works have emphasized this idealization of women: Lippert, "Changing Role of Women"; Lee, "L'image de la femme"; Chemain-Degrange, *Emancipation féminine et roman africain.* See also the introduction to Brown, *Women Writers in Black Africa.* Women are now revising and even rejecting this idealized representation in their fiction.

20. N'Diaye proceeds to explain in a footnote fully reproduced here the fundamental distinction she makes between desire and need: "Le désir ne s'oppose pas tant au besoin parce qu'il est fantasmatique et que le besoin s'adresse au réel—mais c'est surtout que le besoin est grégaire, collectif, commun, tandis que le désir est unique, singulier. Cette opposition conduit à celle de la langue et du style. La langue du besoin, c'est la langue de tout le monde, la langue commune; elle n'a rien à voir avec le style, c'est-à-dire l'invention d'une écriture qui fait le véritable métier d'écrivain . . . car ce n'est jamais qu'un métier. Les professions de foi et les recueils d'anecdotes ne sont donc pas de la littérature" [Desire differs from need, not so much because it is phantasmic whereas need deals with reality, but mainly because need is gregarious, collective, common, whereas desire is unique, singular. This opposition leads to that between language and style. The language of need is everybody's language, the common language; it has nothing to do with style, that is, with the invention of a way of writing that constitutes the writer's true metier . . . because it is never anything but a metier. Therefore, professions of faith and collections of anecdotes are not literature] (159–60).

21. For a general overview, see Houéto, "La Femme," 51–66; and Keller and Bay, "African Women and Problems of Modernization." For the role of women in the economy, see Boserup, *Women's Role in Economic Development;* Awe, "The Economic Role of Women"; and Obbo, *African Women.* For women's involvement in politics, see Lebeuf, "Role of Women"; Aidoo, "Asante Queen Mothers"; and Okonjo, "Women's Political Participation in Nigeria."

22. Esther Fuchs makes the same remark as Mohanty when speaking of the ambivalence shown by Israeli women when confronted with the term *feminism.* See her *Israeli Mythogynies.* Dorinne K. Kondo discusses the same issue in the context of Japanese women in *Crafting Selves.*

23. See Ogunyemi, "Womanism."

24. Cleonora Hudson-Weems introduced the term *Africana Womanism* at the National council for Black Studies Conference in March 1988. She expanded on the concept with a definition of Africana as "people of African descent . . . African-American, African-Caribbean, and continental Africans" (189), a critique of the term *black feminism* and of bell hook's position on the question. See "Cultural and Agenda Conflicts in Academia."

Of *Afrofemcentrism*, Freida High W. Tesfagiorgis says: "I coined this term in 1984 to designate what I see as a unique assertiveness-consciousness in Afro-American women—'black feminism' appearing much too incomplete" ("Afro-femcentrism and Its Fruition," 485). See also Sherley Anne Williams, "Some Implications of Womanist Theory."

25. See, in particular, "African Women, Culture and Another Development"; "Not Spinning on the Axis of Maleness"; and "Female Writer and Her Commitment."

26. As illustrated by Lauretta Ngcobo ("African Motherhood"), this is a recurrent concern among African women: "It is . . . undeniable that the movement in the West enlivens our own consciousness. . . . So we recognize the possibilities in the feminist movement and whilst we disagree on certain points we are not denigrating feminism" (184–85).

27. In fact, Filomina C. Steady is also of the opinion that "some African traditional institutions facilitated the development of a self-reliant ideology among women. Ironically polygyny . . . in many ways contributed to the development of this ideology" (*Black Woman*, 16).

28. As this program of action suggests, women in Senegal have organized themselves to form a feminist movement. In socialist countries or countries that underwent nationalist struggles, women were organized politically, but the progressive movements they belonged to rarely addressed the problems women had *as women*. (See, for instance, Hale, "Sudanese Women.") In other countries, such as Benin, there is, at present, no formal feminist movement, though women are using their professional organizations to fight for their rights. On the initiative of its president, Grâce d'Almeida Adamon, the Association of Women Lawyers of Benin put together a booklet (114 pages) entitled *Guide juridique de la femme béninoise*. This is another instance of the goal-oriented, practical perspective that women, working with other women in Africa, have. The opening words of the preamble make this point: "L'Association des Femmes Juristes du Bénin en prenant l'initiative d'élaborer ce guide a voulu, en se servant des textes de Loi existants au Bénin donner quelques rudiments juridiques à la femme pour qu'elle puisse améliorer ses conditions de vie par des moyens légaux" [In taking the ini-

tiative for making this guide available to women, the Association of Women Lawyers' goal was to provide Benin's women with a few basic legal procedures— based on the legal texts that govern the country—to help them better their lives through legal means]. The *Guide juridique* was translated in Fon and Batonou, two major languages spoken in Benin, to enable a wider access to women who do not speak or read French.

29. The arrogance of the dominant discourse is obvious here. Starting with language, with terminology, it extends to behavior. When Buchi Emecheta gives one of her chapters in *The Joys of Motherhood* the title "A Man is Never Ugly," she describes in behavioral terms that arrogance also stressed by Liking: "A-t-on jamais vu un mâle se juger indigne d'un morceau de roi? Le plus laid le plus vulgaire et le plus démuni stupide ne s'inquiète pas de faire des avances à la meilleure des femmes à la déesse elle-même et ne se demande jamais ce qu'il peut proposer apporter dans ce dialogue. Sans doute parce que les hommes s'imaginent que leur phallus suffit à tout compenser" [Have you ever seen a male think he is unworthy of a prize fit for a king? The ugliest the most vulgar the most impoverished stupid has no qualms about making advances to the best of women to the goddess herself and he never worries about what he can bring to the dialogue. Probably because men believe that their phallus alone is enough to compensate for everything] (*Elle sera de jaspe*, 150).

30. In the French context, Monique Wittig has invented the word *misandre*, which, etymologically, has the same meaning as *misovire*.

31. Again, Filomina C. Steady characterizes black feminism as being "less antagonistic" (*Black Woman*, 23).

32. This idea seems to be a consensus among black women who have explored alternative feminisms. For instance, Cleonora Hudson-Weems is of the same opinion in her analysis of Africana people vis-à-vis feminism: "Instead of alienating the Africana male sector from the struggle today, Africanans must call for a renegotiation of Africanan male-female roles in society. In so doing, there must be a call to halt once and for all female subjugation, while continuing the crucial struggle for the liberation of Africana people the world over" (188).

33. Similarly, Filomina C. Steady speaks of a "humanistic feminism." Her point is slightly different, however. She sees this "African feminism" as "inclusive," combining racial, sexual, class, and cultural dimensions to form a "feminism through which women are viewed first and foremost as *human*, rather than sexual beings" ("African Feminism," 4).

34. See, in particular, Christiane Makward and Odile Cazenave, "The Others' Others: 'Francophone' Women and writing," *Yale French Studies* 19 (Fall 1988): 404–6.

35. *Third World* is a term to which I strongly object, partly because it betrays the unhappy habit, so frequent in the West, of naming others, labeling them or grouping them inappropriately, and of course because Africans were never involved in this ordering of reality. I recognize the fact that it is, in some ways, a convenient—perhaps too convenient—term to use, and in the absence of an adequate substitute I always speak of a "so-called Third World." Of special interest in that respect is Kumkum Sangari's analysis of the phrase *Third World* as a "term that both signifies and blurs the functioning of an economic, political and imaginary geography able to unite vast and vastly differentiated areas of the world into 'underdeveloped' terrain." "The Politics of the Possible," in *The Nature and Context of Minority Discourse*, ed. Abdul R. JanMohamed and David Lloyd (Oxford: Oxford University Press, 1990), 217.

36. The phrase "from margin to center" is borrowed from bell hooks, who in her *Feminist Theory from Margin to Center* problematizes the positionality of black women by challenging the very concept of "margin" and "center."

37. It is the same thinking that informs Aminata Sow Fall, who maintains that the country she describes in her fourth novel, *L'Ex-père de la nation*, is not a specific African country, and certainly not Senegal: "La République africaine dont mon personnage principal est le président est une synthèse de plusieurs pays africains" [The African Republic my main character is the president of, is a synthesis of several African countries] ("Entretiens," 25).

38. For further discussion on *francophonie*, see: Léger, *Francophonie*; and Tétu, *Francophonie*.

39. For an analysis of the concept of *francophonie* as a problematic one for Africans, see Traoré, *Questions africaines*; Mwayila, *Francophonie et géopolitique africaine*; and Midiohouan, *L'Idéologie*, 21–22.

40. One of the first African critics to discuss the dangers of an African literature written in Western languages was Obi Wali in "Dead End of African Literature." One of the most vocal writers on the question has been Ngugi wa Thiong'o, who not only criticized the widespread acceptance of Western languages but also stopped writing in English altogether to write in Kikuyu, his native tongue. See, in particular, Ngugi's *Writers in Politics*, 4–33, and *Decolonizing the Mind*, 63–86. For an elaboration of the language question as it relates to African fiction, see d'Almeida, "Language of African Fiction"; Amuta, *Theory of African Literature*; and Ngara's *Stylistic Criticism and the African Novel* and *Art and Ideology in the Novel*.

41. These two diagrams first appeared in "L'écriture féminine en Afrique Noire Francophone" [Women's writing in Francophone Africa], an article I wrote in collaboration with Sion Hamou.

42. Soyinka rightly points out that neither writers nor critics come out of a vacuum. This fact, he argues, is too often overlooked when dealing with the African critic. He notes: "To my knowledge very few attempts have been made to study the critic as a socially situated producer, and therefore as a creature of social conditioning" ("Critic and Society," 28–29).

43. This essay was in fact a paper presented at a symposium on "The Function of the Modern Literatures of Black Africa" held in Frankfurt in October 1980 and reproduced in extenso in *Ecriture française dans le monde.*

44. An impressive number of male writers and critics in both the Francophone and Anglophone worlds have abundantly and eloquently made that point. For an elaboration of this, see my dissertation, "Making of an African Literary-Critical Tradition," especially the sociological and Marxist approaches (134–254).

45. I am mostly interested in narratology as defined and explained by Gérard Genette and expanded on by female narratologists such as Mieke Bal (1985) and Sholmith Rimmon-Kenan (1983). One of the reasons I am increasingly attracted to narratology is that it is a theory that cuts across cultures and thus does not affect the specificity of African literature, which is greatly influenced by the oral tradition—"one of its major impulses," as Emmanuel Obiechina pointed out (26).

46. I am not suggesting that all texts are born equal, nor do I equate "canonization" with "selection." I am referring here to the *politics* of canonization, in which individual "selection" may well be determined by extraliterary criteria, e.g., the geography or economics of publishing, racial or gender discrimination, and so forth. I am also questioning the authoritarianism of a literary "canon" in the same way as does Culley ("Women's Vernacular Literature," 13), who affirms: "What feminist scholars must be done with if they are to replace dead leaves with radical restructuring of literary studies is the exclusive allegiance to the idea of canonicity itself."

1. The Self: Autobiography as *De/couvérte*

1. Other autobiographies by Francophone women are: Keita, *Femme d'Afrique;* Kaya, *Les Danseuses d'Impe-Eya;* N'Diaye, *Collier de cheville;* and Barry, *Kesso, Princesse peuhle.*

2. I am aware that the claims to an "ordinary life" are also a common topos of modesty in autobiographical writing by men. This claim can be found in Montaigne and Rousseau, for instance. Yet it is possible to wonder if this is not simply a case of "fausse modestie" on men's part. It seems that women, on the contrary, socially conditioned as they often are, genuinely believe that their lives

as women are not important enough to be written down. Smith (*Poetics of Women's Autobiography*, 10) notes that St. Teresa of Avila was an "unwilling author" who "consistently insists that as an unlearned woman she ought not to be writing." In "Feminism with a small 'f'!" Emecheta is extremely apologetic about her fictional writing. She claims: "I am just an ordinary writer, an ordinary writer who has to write" (173). She goes on to say: "I don't deal with great ideological issues. I write about little happenings of everyday life" (175).

3. Annette Mbaye d'Erneville in an unpublished interview recorded by Anne Adams, 1989.

4. Philippe Lejeune explores this question in *Pacte autobiographique* and in *Je est un autre*. See also Beaujour, *Miroirs d'encre*; Gunn, *Autobiography*; Jelinek, *Women's Autobiography*; Lionnet, *Autobiographical Voices*; May, *L'Autobiographie*; Olney, *Autobiography*; Smith, *Poetics of Women's Autobiography*; and Stanton and Plottel, *Female Autograph*.

5. Lejeune, *On Autobiography*.

6. See, in particular, Stanton and Plottel, *Female Autograph*.

7. In her study of black women in the United States, Blackburn ("In Search of the Black Female Self") makes the same point. She argues that even though black women share a common experience of racism and sexism, they do not lend themselves to easy generalizations. She goes on to say that "it is a mistake to study African-American women only as a group" (133).

8. Mbye B. Cham identifies several creative responses to Islam taken by Senegalese artists who can be (1) traditional promoters, (2) modern promoters, (3) irreverents, (4) iconoclasts, or (5) apostates. See "Islam in Senegalese Literature and Film," in *Faces of Islam in African Literature*, ed. Kenneth W. Harrow, 163–86 (Portsmouth, N.H.: Heinemann, 1991).

9. Barry goes on to say that men know only too well why excision is still performed, but they choose to be silent on this issue, covering it with the cloth of tradition (*Kesso, Princesse peuhle*, 111–12). It has become very fashionable to speak of excision in the West and to offer a critique of it. But it must be noted that long before the West took this subject and made it a crusade, Francophone African women writers themselves had been addressing and denouncing this practice. Kesso Barry, Calixthe Beyala, and Aminata Maïga Ka (as well as Ama Ata Aidoo in the Anglophone world) have all written against excision, and with an understanding of cultural and patriarchal contexts that is sadly lacking in a work like Alice Walker's *Possessing the Secret of Joy*. Walker's novel manages to demonize African women who perform excisions, an effect even more noticeable in her documentary film *Warrior Marks*, which she made in collaboration with Pratibha Parmar.

10. For an elaboration of the caste system in Senegal, see Diop, *La Société Wolof.*

11. See her very insightful "Poetics of Exile and Errancy." See also Borgomano, who, in *Voix et visages de femmes*, uses, among other things, musical analogies to make an excellent analysis of the structure of *Le Baobab fou.* See, in particular, 55–60.

12. One could perhaps object that skin color *is* an issue for some Africans, given the phenomenon of attempting to lighten one's skin by means of cosmetics (cosmetics which, incidentally, are imported from the West). This bleaching practice, known as *Xeesal* in Senegal and *Gbodju* in Benin, is a recent development in Africa. I recall my grandmother telling me that in the old times when a child was born with a light skin there were medicinal plants and tree barks that women boiled to obtain a very dark concoction. The child was then literally soaked in that solution to make it blacker, for deep blackness was indeed a sign of beauty. This practice appears in a different form in Alex Haley's *Roots*, where Kunta Kinte asks why Binta, his mother, blackens her hands and feet with *hene.* His father Omoro explains: "The more blackness a woman has, the more beautiful she is" (46). I would suggests that in contemporary Africa the people who use whitening cosmetics (and most are women) are not trying to become white, they are trying to become more beautiful, just as whites do when they use cosmetics or sit in the sun for hours to get a "tan." Let's note in passing that when whites want a tan, nobody thinks that they want to become black!

13. See, for instance, Diop (*Les Contes d'Amadou Koumba*), who dedicates his folk stories to his children: "A mes filles . . . pour qu'elles apprennent et n'oublient pas que l'arbre ne s'élève qu'en enfonçant ses racines dans la Terre nourricière" [To my daughters . . . so that they learn and not forget that the tree only grows by pushing its roots into the nourishing Soil].

14. See "Ken Bugul," 152 (interview by Bernard Magnier).

15. In certain countries, for instance Senegal, the French had policies that separated the blacks from the *métisses*, in the towns of Saint Louis and Gorée, in particular. However, this example of orphanages for mixed-blood children seems to be a characteristic of the Congo, a country where indigenous people were notoriously abused.

16. In fact there were no differences between black and *métisse* women in terms of how they were treated by white colonialists—as concubines and mistresses to be hidden from other whites. See, for instance, the character of Sophie in Oyono's *Vie de boy.*

17. The Ecole Polytechnique is one of the prestigious grandes écoles that in the French system train the technocrats who manage the Civil Service. The closest

American equivalent to this specific school might be the Massachusetts Institute of Technology.

18. There are very few *métisse* women who have treated the *métisse* question from their own point of view. To my knowledge, Blouin remained the only one until 1990, when Marie Ndiaye published *En Famille.*

19. See Cazenave, "Marginalisation et identité." See also Madubuike, *Senegalese Novel.*

20. The name Black Pasionaria was given to Andrée Blouin by Pierre Davister, a Belgian reporter for the newspaper *Pourquoi pas!* Davister wrote an article about Blouin's expulsion from the Congo and likened her to Dolores Ibarruri, one of the most famous and controversial figures in Spain during the Spanish Civil War. A political leader popularly known as La Pasionaria (the Passion Flower) because she published articles under that pen name, Ibarruri was expelled from Spain and spent most of the rest of her life in the Soviet Union.

21. In the same way, it can be said that Keita's autobiography, *Femme d'Afrique,* which offers significant parallels with Andrée Blouin's, is also a political history of the French Sudan, now Mali. Keita displays that period of history through the depiction of her own political involvement, which lasted about thirty years, from 1931 to 1960. During that time she was militant in the Union Soudanaise, which became the local branch of the RDA (Rassemblement Démocratique Africain) in 1946, and finally she relates how, with other women, she helped shape the political orientation of her country on the eve of independence.

22. For an interesting discussion of this matter, see Edmondson, "Black Aesthetics, Feminist Aesthetics."

23. See Domna C. Stanton, "Autobiography: Is the Subject Different?" in *The Female Autograph,* 5–22.

2. Speaking Up, Disclosing Family Life

1. See "Ken Bugul," 154 (interview by Bernard Magnier).

2. The title has been taken from the first song of Song of Solomon, and the biblical translation should be: "The sun hath looked upon me." I have chosen to translate the title as "it is the sun that burnt me" because the actual burning of the sun on the main protagonist of the novel has important symbolic value.

3. After *Tu t'appelleras Tanga,* Beyala wrote three other novels: *Seul le Diable le savait* [Only the devil knew it] (Paris: Le Pré aux Clercs, 1990), *Le Petit Prince de Belleville* [The little prince of Belleville] (Paris: Albin Michel, 1992), and *Maman a un amant* [Mother has a lover] (Paris: Albin Michel, 1993).

4. For greater detail on naming customs and rituals, see Mbiti, *African Religions and Philosophy,* 154–57.

5. Ayi Kwei Armah, *The Beautyful Ones Are Not Yet Born* (London: Heinemann Educational Books, 1968).

6. Of course, this observation needs to be qualified: obviously it is not true of autobiographies or autobiographical novels written by men. And there are exceptions among male writers; for instance, Sembène Ousmane places children in his novels, and Ahmed Tidjani Cissé dedicates his book of poems to children with these words: "Aux enfants de mon pays dont on a brisé la modeste calebasse de bonheur à coup de cruauté. A tous les enfants à qui on a confisqué leur part de rire" [For my country's children whose modest calabash of happiness has been cruelly smashed to pieces. For all the children whose share of laughter has been confiscated]. From *Quand les Graines éclosent* [When the seeds bud] (Paris: Nubia, 1984).

7. The way Beyala describes this relationship is reminiscent of Wade-Gayles's description of how African-American women also write about the mother-daughter relationship in terms "of anger and love, suspicion and trust, conflict and understanding, estrangement and bonding" ("The Truths of Our Mother's Lives," 9).

8. The fear of madness and death Tanga associates with her mother is very reminiscent of Marie Cardinal's relationship with her own mother. Cardinal depicts this relationship in her autobiographical novel, *The Words to Say It,* trans. Pat Goodheart (Cambridge, Mass.: VanVactor and Goodheart, 1983); originally published as *Les Mots pour le dire* (Paris: Editions Grassets and Fasquelle, 1975).

9. Tanga is attracted to the crippled and outcasts in society. One of her lovers is named Cul-de-jatte and is in fact a *cul-de-jatte,* a legless cripple. Also, the abandoned children have names like Pieds-de-cochon (Pig's Feet) and Pieds-de-poulet (Chicken's Feet), and Ningue is described as having "rotten teeth." Their different physical ailments have been caused by material and emotional neglect.

10. There is, of course, a degree of exaggeration in the portrayal of Iningué, enough to make the critic Doumbi-Fakoly say that Beyala's is a "futuristic vision of Africa." Doumbi-Fakoly is concerned that this kind of literature will provide yet another weapon to the detractors of Africa (148). However, mediated by the creative process, Beyala's depiction of Africa is a fiction used to demystify old, irrelevant myths.

11. To be fair, it must be said that because children are so extremely valued in society, men who have no children are *also* stigmatized. In many instances, however, a man's infertility can be "masked" by "giving" his wife to another man in secrecy for the sole purpose of impregnating her. A child thus conceived belongs to the woman's husband.

12. In the Anglophone world, two classics on the topic are Nwapa's *Efuru* and Emecheta's *Joys of Motherhood.*

13. The crucial nature of childbearing is powerfully demonstrated in *Voie du salut,* a novella by Aminata Maïga Ka. When the heroine, Rokhaya, does not become pregnant for a long time after her wedding, her brother-in-law, jealous of her comfort and material riches, remarks devastatingly: "Depuis deux ans que mon frère t'a épousée, tu es incapable de lui donner un enfant! Tu ne connaîtra jamais l'amour maternel, femme stérile que tu es" [It has been two years since my brother married you, and yet you are unable to give him a child. Never will you know what motherly love is, you barren woman!] (44).

14. Rawiri, *Fureurs et cris de femmes.* Angèle Rawiri, also known as Ntyug-wetondo Rawiri, has written two other novels: *Elonga* and *G'Amérakano—Au carrefour.*

15. Childbearing goes hand-in-hand with marriage, which is also an institution of primary importance in African societies. Whether arranged or voluntary, marriage is expected of women. That is why in most households girls are raised to become wives. Kesso Barry recounts how, because she was rebellious in her youth and had a will of her own, her father's friends were worried that she would never be married. See Barry, *Kesso, Princesse peuhle,* 72–73. Also, in *Voie du salut,* Rokhaya insists that "le mariage est la seule gloire de la femme. Quels que puissent être sa richesse et son savoir, elle ne trouve sa plénitude que dans le mariage" [marriage is a woman's sole glory. Whatever riches or knowledge she may have, it is only within marriage that she will be fulfilled] (70). This theme is also explored by Dooh-Bunya in *Brise du jour.*

16. In this novel, although the husband does not practice polygamy, he does have a *deuxième bureau* (second office), a term originating in Zaire and referring to a kept mistress. The practice is called deuxième bureau because a man's excuse to leave home and visit his mistress was often that he was going to the office.

The new vision of the couple is also evident in Bâ's two novels, *Une si longue lettre* and *Chant écarlate;* in *Brise du jour* by Dooh-Bunya; in *Voie du salut* and *Miroir de la vie* by Ka; and several others.

17. The metaphor of the marital space as prison is recurrent in African women's fiction. The claustrophobic confinement to a room can also be seen in Myriam Warner-Vieyra's *Juletane* (Paris: Présence Africaine, 1982).

18. This proverb is quoted in French by Adiaffi in her novel *Vie hypothéquée:* "La rebellion d'une femme est comparable à un verre d'eau chaude. Il suffit de la laisser refroidir" (125).

19. In an excellent article entitled "Rewriting History," Andrade specifically notes the existence of blind spots concerning motherhood in Flora Nwapa's writing: "Nwapa's tribute to women's independence notwithstanding, the narrative manifests a blindspot about the ideology of motherhood. Although the novel moves toward a celebration of Efuru's independence, economic success and goodness, there is a constant undercurrent of doubt about the ability of a woman without children to be happy" (100).

20. Bâ, *Scarlet Song*, trans. Blair. All quotations are made from this edition and page numbers are indicated parenthetically within the text.

21. Ogundipe-Leslie, "Not Spinning," 498–504.

22. Genette defines an *amorce* as a " 'germe insigifiant' et même imperceptible, dont la valeur de germe ne sera reconnue que plus tard, et de façon rétrospective" [an indicator, or "insignificant germ" that is almost imperceptible and whose germinating value will only be recognized later and in retrospect] (113).

23. On this score I take issue with Dorothy Blair when she claims that "the plot and structure of *Un Chant écarlate* lack the originality of Mariama Ba's first novel. There are superficialities and inconsistencies in the characterization of the main protagonists who act out a set drama arising from the exigencies of the situation and its message, rather than as a product of their own intrinsic personalities" (*Senegalese Literature*, 140). My analysis showing the strengths of *Un Chant écarlate* fully concurs with Nnaemeka's findings in "Mariama Bâ."

24. In the original French version, Monsieur de la Vallée's words are: "Connais-tu 'Ça' "? (40). "Ça" is even more insulting than "that object," because "Ça" is not only an object but also a nondescript thing that can have no human attributes whatsoever, thus connoting an even greater contempt than the English translation "this object" expresses.

25. Traoré defines neocolonialism as "un système de mesures politiques, économiques, financières, commerciales, militaires, stratégiques, culturelles et idéologiques, qui restaurent l'ancien colonialisme sous de nouvelles formes, perpétuant la domination et l'exploitation impérialistes dans des Etats formellement indépendants" [a system of political, economic, financial, commercial, military, strategic, cultural and ideological measures perpetuating imperialist domination and exploitation in Nations having a nominal independence] (*Questions africaines*, 10).

26. The force of this pivotal proverb is better rendered as: "When you abandon your hill, any hill you climb will crumble."

27. *Turn:* "In a polygamous Islamic marriage, the period when a wife can expect her husband to sleep with her and during which she is responsible for cooking for the household and doing his washing" (171; translator's note).

28. For a better understanding of the mother-in-law / daughter-in-law relationship in Islamic countries, see Mernissi, *Sexe, Idéologie, Islam,* 133–52.

29. *Djité laye:* "A very short loin-cloth or *pagne* women wear as an underpetticoat; often combined with strings of beads around the hip for sexual titillation" (171; translator's note).

30. This confusion, which I've discussed in a previous section, is related to the mission the men of the negritude movement assumed, a mission Mariama Bâ herself has criticized.

31. Here again, the comparison with Juletane in Warner-Vieyra's *Juletane* is striking. Juletane too burnt all bridges, and she too ended in madness.

32. See Cham, "Female Condition," 45–46.

33. See Bâ, "Mariama Bâ," 209–14.

3. W/Riting Change: Women as Social Critics

1. Werewere Liking is one of the most prolific female writers in French-speaking West Africa. Some of her works include: *On ne raisonne pas le venin* [One does not reason venom], poems (Paris: Saint Germain-des-Prés, 1977); *Orphée-Dafric,* novel, followed by *Orphée d'Afrique,* ritual theater by Manuna Ma Njock; *Elle sera de jaspe,* a song-novel; and *L'Amour cent-vies.* As a playwright, she published *La Puissance de Um* [Um's power] (Abidjan: CEDA, 1979); "La Queue du diable" [The devil's tail] in *Du Rituel à la scène chez les Bassa du Cameroun* [From ritual to the stage among the Bassa of Cameroun] (Paris: Nizet, 1979); *Une nouvelle terre* [A new land] followed by *Du Sommeil d'injuste* [Unjust sleep] (Dakar: Nouvelles Editions Africaines, 1980). Many other plays, not yet published, have been produced on stage.

Liking has also written essays of literary criticism and monographs, such as *La Vision de Kaydara d'Hamadou Hampaté Bâ* [Perspectives on Hamadou Hampaté Bâ's *Kaydara*] (Dakar: Nouvelles Editions Africaines, 1984), and an art history book, *Statues colons* [Statues of colonialists] (Paris: NEA-ARHIS, 1987).

2. Liking provides this explanation in an interview by Christine Pillot, " 'Vivre vrai,' de Werewere Liking" [Werewere Liking's "Living authentically"] *Notre Librairie* 102 (July-August 1990):54–58. To a Western reader it may seem Liking's community of artists would contradict the traditional position of the African artist within the society. In fact, Villa Ki-Yi tries to maintain or restore that communal relation in the face of changing social structures in Africa. The phenomena of urbanization have been especially destructive of the old support relations between artist and community, and Liking would like to discover the means by which those relations might be renewed.

3. The two women's collaboration was extremely fruitful. In addition to the book under study and *From Ritual*, they published together *Liboy li Nkundung, an Initiation Tale* (Paris: Classiques Africains, 1980); *A la Rencontre de; Contes d'initiation féminine du pays Bassa* [Female initiation tales of the Bassa] (Yaoundé: St. Paul, 1984); and *Les Spectacles rituels* [Ritual plays] Dakar: Nouvelles Editions Africaines, 1987. They also wrote essays such as "Les vestiges d'un Kotéba," *Revue de Littérature et d'ésthétique négro-africaine* 3 (1981): 35–50.

4. Note the spelling of *Orphée-Dafric*, which is not a mistake but a deliberate choice of the novelist's. Werewere Liking enjoys playing with words and is extremely creative with language. In an article entitled "Echoes of Orpheus in Werewere Liking's *Orphée-Dafric* and Wole Soyinka's *Season of Anomy*," in *Comparative Literature Studies*, 31, no. 1 (1994):52–71, I show how Liking and Soyinka have taken the myth of Orpheus as a metaphorical and archetypal foundation and have remade it into an African narrative. The article deals primarily with these novels, but it might be noted that in African literature, the myth of Orpheus has also been used in drama and in poetry, notably in *L'enfer c'est Orphéo*, a play by Martial Malinda (Paris:ORTF/DAEC, 1971), and in *Orphée rebelle*, a collection of poems by Lisembe P. Elebe (Paris: Saint-Germain-des-Près, 1972). Also, some African novels that do not specifically deal with the Orpheus myth but have a strong quest motif can be read as Orphic; one such novel is M. a M. Ngal's *L'Errance* (Yaoundé: CLE, 1979). Finally, in 1957 Ulli Beier founded a cultural journal in Nigeria entitled *Black Orpheus*. The title was borrowed from Sartre's well-known introduction to Senghor's anthology of poems. For a history of the foundation of *Black Orpheus* and for its impact on African arts and letters, see Peter Benson's "Border Operators: *Black Orpheus* and the genesis of Modern African Arts and Literature," *Research in African Literatures* 14, no. 4 (Winter 1983): 431–73.

5. Senghor expounded his concept of "African humanism" in numerous speeches and essays. See in particular, *Liberté III. Négritude et Civilisation de l'Universel* (Paris: Seuil, 1977). The use of intertextual material concerning Léopold Sédar Senghor's ideas is much more explicit in *Elle sera de jaspe*, where mention is often made of a philosopher named Ségar, a slight alteration of Sédar, Senghor's middle name. I explore this theme further in an article entitled "The Intertext: Werewere Liking's Tool for Transformation and Renewal," to be published in *Beyond the Hexagon: Women Writing in French*, edited by Karen Gould, Mary-Jean Green, and Micheline Rice-Maximin (University of Minnesota Press).

6. The criticism of women is even stronger in *Elle sera de jaspe*, in which Liking, using elements of orature, invents a mythical story to allegorize how women have lost their original knowledge and given up their primordial way of being-in-the-world. See, in particular, pages 74–81.

7. This word has a double connotation. It refers to the one party system imposed by many political regimes in Africa while satirizing its adherents who have no sense of personal direction and behave like sheep following one another.

8. Aminata Sow Fall's earlier novels are: *Le Revenant, La Grève des battu,* and *L'Appel des arènes;* her latest to date is *Le Jujubier du Patriarche.*

9. Tadjo's *Latérite* won the Agence de Coopération Culturelle et Technique prize in 1983. She wrote *Chanson de la vie* and *Lord of the Dance,* self-illustrated books of stories (some in prose, others in poetry) for children, inspired by African orature. Tadjo has also produced two novels: *A Vol d'oiseau* and *Le Royaume aveugle.*

10. My comparison of Tadjo's text as texture / textile is not meant to erase the writing subject in order to privilege the process of writing, as Nancy Miller's critique of Barthes's *Pleasure of the Text* suggests he does. (See "Arachnelogies: The Woman, the Text and the Critic," in Miller, *Poetics of Gender.*) My comparison is no doubt made in relation to etymology, but more so from a cultural standpoint that does not emphasize gender—the metaphor of weaving has been used by male and female writers alike. Charlotte H. Bruner entitles a book *Unwinding Threads,* an image borrowed from the Kabyle folk singers in the Algerian mountains who always begin their tales with the following formulaic phrase: "Que mon conte soit beau et se déroule comme un long fil . . ." [May my story be beautiful and unwind like a long thread . . .]. Also, in *Contes d'Amadou Koumba,* Diop describes himself as a weaver using threads to make a *pagne,* that is, a "cloth" or "wrapper" (12). Using the same metaphor, Dadié entitles his collection of folk stories *Le Pagne noir.*

11. For a discussion of chronology in fiction and as fiction, see Kermode's masterful analyses in *Sense of an Ending.*

12. The phatic function is also visible in the narrator's numerous interventions. For instance, after recounting the story of a woman who died in her bathroom because of poor construction caused by a dishonest architect, she says: "On m'a raconté cette histoire et c'est ainsi que je vous la livre" [I was told this story and I am passing it on to you as it was told to me] (22). Further along, making a distinction between the leper who "licks the ground" and the fighter who, instead, has great pride, she tells the reader: "Ce n'est pas moi qui le dis. Je l'ai lu quelque part" [I am not the one who says so. I read that somewhere] (38). Also, speaking of the violence that men inflict on women she says: "Mais oublions tout cela et laissez-moi vous parler d'autre chose" [But let us forget all this and let me tell you about something else] (54).

13. Lafont and Gardès-Madray (*Introduction à l'analyse textuelle,* 93) analyze the dialectics of the *Je* / I and the *tu* / you in terms of temporality, which is not my purpose here. It is interesting, though, that they go on to say: "Il y a donc

dans le mouvement par lequel *tu* devient *je* . . . un passage de l'éventualité à la réalité. Mais dans ce même mouvement, le *je* précédent devient un *tu*. Si l'on considère ce movement dans la fluence temporelle, on voit que *tu* est à la fois l'avenir et le passé du *je*" [Therefore, there exists in the motion through which *I* becomes *you* . . . a passage from a possibility to a reality. Yet, in the same motion, the preceding *I* becomes a *you*. If one considers the temporal flow in this motion, one sees that *you* is at once the future and the past of *I*].

14. The pronominal interpretation is further extended in the course of the narrative to include the third person, more often "she" than "he," and also a collective "we."

15. This is the only instance in which Tadjo uses the metaphor of silence for an act of "silencing." However, she often explores various aspects of silence, stressing the importance of silence and speech in human relationships. She muses over the potency of the word that, bringing to life that which is not, makes the difference between being and nothingness.

16. The name Akissi must have a special significance for Tadjo: Akissi is found in *Latérite* and also in *Le Royaume aveugle*, where she is King Ato V's rebellious daughter.

17. Mamy Wata, or Mami Wata, the water goddess or water spirit, is worshipped by many riverside communities in West Africa. She is said to attract men with her legendary beauty and bury them in the waters. She is mentioned in passing in Achebe's short story "Sacrificial Egg" and in Emecheta's *Joys of Motherhood*. Mamy Wata is central to Nwapa's *Efuru* and to Amadi's *Concubine*.

18. The end of this vignette is very reminiscent of one of the myths of creation among the Fon of Benin: "The Fon of Abomey . . . . speak of a supreme god (Mawu) and many other beings related to him. But Mawu is sometimes called male and sometimes female; Mawu has a partner called Lisa, and they may be spoken of as twins. One myth says that these twins were born from a primordial mother, Nana Buluku, who created the world and then retired. Mawu was the moon and female, controlling the night and dwelling in the west. Lisa was male, the sun, and lived in the east. They had no children when they first took up their stations, but eventually they came together in an eclipse. Whenever there is an eclipse of the sun or moon it is said that Mawu and Lisa are making love" (Parrinder, *African Mythology*, 23).

19. The description of this director is very reminiscent of Werewere Liking, who is also a theater director and has created a community of artists in her Villa Ki-yi in Abidjan. The artists also share everything and the villa is open to all. I had the good fortune of spending a day in the villa, where, in addition to interviewing Liking, I was invited to share a meal and see the rehearsal of *Singue*

Mura: Considérant que la femme, a play that Liking was preparing for the Congrès de la Francophonie at Limoges, France. I also had the good fortune to see the play in its final form at Limoges in October 1990. It was a true spectacle, impressively presenting acting accompanied with song, dance, a display of living masks, and an epiphany of colorful and daring costume. The artistry of the cast was phenomenal.

20. Political oppression is for Tadjo a major preoccupation. She effectively denounces it in *Le Royaume aveugle* (meaning both "the kingdom of the blind" and "the blind kingdom"), an allegorical novel describing the iniquities of a totalitarian regime.

Conclusion

1. Thus, while Andrée Blouin was born in 1920, Véronique Tadjo was born only in 1955. However, Blouin's book came out in 1983, and Tadjo's first book was published in 1984.

2. The quality of the existing translations and of the original texts of African literature varies widely. For instance, Blair's translation of Bâ's *Chant écarlate* is fairly good, but her translation of *De Tilène au Plateau* much less successful. Although it is not often possible to translate the musicality of a language, some culture-specific words or expressions must be given close attention. In *De Tilène*, to see the Muslim community reciting the "rosary" is rather absurd. "Prayer beads" would have been a more accurate rendering. Further, even the French texts of some works are at times so badly edited as to hide the quality of the writing. In Bugul's *Baobab fou*, for example, the French text is full of errors, some of them typographical, and serious grammatical mistakes. The writer or her editors did a rather poor job of checking the manuscript before putting it into print. It required more than one reading for me to get beyond these flaws and discover the complexities of this text.

3. In *Pluie et vent*, Schwarz-Bart has a similar pattern. This novel has two parts. The first, comprising forty pages, is entitled "Présentation des miens" [Introducing my ancestry], and the second part, with the title "Histoire de ma vie" [The story of my life], forms the rest of the novel.

4. See d'Almeida, "Concept of Choice," 167.

5. Lucien Houédanou also notes how forcefully Fall cast her female characters. He quotes Fall as saying: "Moi, je n'écris pas du point de vue de la femme, mais plutôt du point de vue de la citoyenne. L'écrivain-femme n'a pas à choisir que des thèmes féminins. . . . Je ne pense pas que nous ayions une spécificité par rapport aux hommes" [*I* do not write from a woman's perspective but from the perspective of the citizen. The female writer does not have to choose only female

themes. . . . I do not believe that we have a specificity vis-à-vis men] ("Islam et Société," 163). But he also shows how some of Fall's other statements cannot move away from the female question. Also, I explore the reasons why African women often refuse to be labeled feminists when their discourse is highly feminist, in "Femme? Féministe? 'Misovire'? Les romancières africaines face au féminisme" [Woman? Feminist? 'Misovire?' Francophone African Women novelists' position vis-a-vis feminism]. This article is to be published by *Notre Librairie* (Fall 1994) in a special issue on African women writers.

6. I quote Said's phrase from a useful article by JanMohamed, "Worldiness-Without-World." My discussion of these questions is necessarily brief, but those interested in further readings might look at Anzaldua, *Borderlands / La Frontera*.

BIBLIOGRAPHY

Primary Sources

Bâ, Mariama. *Scarlet Song*. Translated by Dorothy Blair. London: Longman, 1986. Originally published as *Un Chant écarlate* (Dakar: NEA, 1981).

Beyala, Calixthe. *Tu t'appelleras Tanga* [Your name will be Tanga]. Paris: Stock, 1988.

Blouin, Andrée. *My Country, Africa: Autobiography of the Black Pasionaria*. New York: Praeger, 1983.

Bugul, Ken. *The Abandoned Baobab: The Autobiography of a Senegalese Woman*. Translated by Marjoliyn de Jager. New York: Lawrence Hill Books, 1991. Originally published as *Le Baobab fou* (Dakar: NEA, 1983).

Diallo, Nafissatou. *A Dakar Childhood*. Translated by Dorothy Blair. London: Longman, 1982. Originally published as *De Tiléne au Plateau: une enfance dakaroise* (Dakar: NEA, 1975).

Fall, Aminata Sow. *L'Ex-père de la nation* [The ex-father of the nation]. Paris: L'Harmattan, 1987.

Liking, Werewere, and Manuna Ma-Njock. *"Orphée-Dafric" roman suivi de "Orphée d'Afrique."* Paris: L'Harmattan, 1981.

Rawiri, Angèle. *Fureurs et cris de femmes* [Cries and fury of women]. Paris: L'Harmattan, 1989.

Tadjo, Véronique. *A Vol d'oiseau* [As the crow flies]. Paris: Editions Nathan, 1986.

Secondary Sources

Achebe, Chinua. "The Sacrificial Egg." In *Girls at War*. London: Heinemann, 1972.

Adiaffi, Anne-Marie. *Une Vie hypothéquée* [A mortgaged life]. Abidjan: NEA, 1984.

———. *La Ligne brisée* [The broken line]. Abidjan: NEA, 1989.

Amadi, Elechi. *The Concubine.* London: Heinemann, 1966.

Armah, Ayi Kwei. *The Beautyful Ones Are Not Yet Born.* London: Heinemann, 1968.

Bâ, Mariama. *So Long a Letter.* Translated by Dupe Bode-Thomas. London: Heinemann 1981. Originally published as *Une si longue lettre* (Dakar: NEA, 1979).

Barry, Kesso. *Kesso, Princesse peuhle* [Kesso, the Peuhl princess]. Paris: Seghers, 1988.

Beyala, Calixthe. *C'est le Soleil qui m'a brulée* [It is the sun that burnt me]. Paris: Stock, 1987.

———. *Maman a un amant.* [Mother has a lover]. Paris: Albin Michel, 1993.

———. *Le Petit Prince de Belleville.* Paris: Albin Michel, 1992.

———. *Seul le Diable le savait* [Only the devil knew it]. Paris: Le Pré aux Clercs, 1990.

Bolli, Fatou. *Djigbô.* Abidjan: CEDA, 1977.

Cardinal, Marie. *Les Mots pour le dire.* Paris: Editions Grasset & Fasquelle, 1975. Translated as *The Words to Say it* by Pat Goodheart. Cambridge: Mass., Van Vactor & Goodheart, 1983.

Couchoro, Felix. *L'Esclave.* Paris: La Dépêche Africaine, 1929.

Dadié, Bernard. *Le Pagne noir.* Paris: Présence Africaine, 1955.

Diagne, Ahmadou Mapaté. *Les Trois Volontés de Malic.* Paris: Larose, 1920.

Diallo, Bakary. *Force-Bonté.* Paris: Rieder, 1926.

Diallo, Nafissatou. *Fary, Princess of Tiali.* Translated by Ann Woollcombe. Washington, D.C., 1987. Originally published as *La Princesse de Tiali* (Dakar: NEA, 1987).

———. *Le Fort maudit.* Paris: Hatier, 1980.

Diop, Birago. *Tales of Amadou Koumba.* Translated by Dorothy S. Blair. London: Oxford University Press, 1966. Originally published as *Les Contes d'Amadou Koumba* (Paris: Présence Africaine, 1961).

Diop, Massyla. *Le Réprouvé.* Dakar: Revue Africaine Artistique et Littéraire, 6 July 1925.

Dooh-Bunya, Lydie. *La Brise du jour* [The morning breeze]. Yaoundé: Editions CLE, 1977.

Emecheta, Buchi. *The Joys of Motherhood.* New York: George Braziller, 1979.

Fall, Aminata Sow. *L'Appel des arènes* [The appeal of the wrestling fields]. Dakar: NEA, 1981.

———. *The Beggars' Strike, or the Dregs of Society.* Translated by Dorothy Blair. London: Longman, 1982. Originally published as *La Grève des battu ou les déchets humains* (Dakar: NEA, 1979).

————. *Le Jujubier du Patriarche* [The Patriarch's jujube tree]. Dakar: CAEC, Khoudia Editions, 1993.

————. *Le Revenant* [The ghost]. Dakar: NEA, 1976.

Ka, Aminata Maïga. *En Votre Nom et au mien* [On your behalf and on mine]. Abidjan: NEA, 1989.

————. *"La Voie du salut" suivi de "Le Miroir de la vie"* ["The path to salvation" followed by "The mirror of life"]. Paris: Présence Africaine, 1985.

Kaya, Simone. *Les Danseuses d'Impé-Eya, jeunes filles à Abidjan* [Impe-Eya dancers, young women in Abidjan]. Abidjan: INADES, 1976.

————. *Le Prix d'une vie* [The price of a life]. Abidjan: CEDA, 1984.

Keita, Aoua. *Femme d'Afrique: La vie d'Aoua Keita racontée par elle-même* [Woman of Africa: The life of Aoua Keita as told by herself]. Paris: Présence Africaine, 1975.

Kourouma, Ahmadou. *Les Soleils des Indépendances* [The suns of the Independence years]. Paris: Editions du Seuil, 1976.

Kuoh-Moukouri, Thérèse. *Rencontres essentielles.* Adamawa and Paris: Imprimerie Edgar, 1969. A later edition was published by L'Harmattan (Paris, 1981).

Liking, Werewere. *L'Amour-cent-vies* [One hundred years of love]. Paris: Publisud, 1989.

————. *Elle sera de jaspe et de corail: Journal d'une misovire . . .* [It will be of jasper and coral: Journal of a *misovire . . .*]. Paris: L'Harmattan, 1983.

————. *Une nouvelle terre* [A new land] followed by *Du sommeil d'injuste* [Unjust sleep]. Dakar: NEA, 1980.

————. *On ne raisonne pas le venin* [One does not reason venom]. Paris: Saint Germain-des-Prés, 1977.

————. *La puissance de Um* [Um's Power]. Abidjan: CEDA, 1979.

Liking, Werewere, and Marie-José Hourantier. *A la rencontre de . . .* [Meeting with . . .]. Dakar: NEA, 1980.

————. *Contes d'initiation féminine du pays bassa* [Tales of female initiation among the Bassa people]. Paris: Editions St. Paul, 1981.

————. *Liboy li nkundung.* Conte initiatique [Initiation tale]. Paris: Editions St. Paul, 1980.

————. *Les Spectacles rituels* [Ritual theater]. Dakar: NEA, 1987.

Liking, Werewere, Marie-José Hourantier, and Jacques Scherer. *Du rituel à la scène chez les Bassa du Cameroun* [From ritual to the stage among the Bassa of Cameroon]. Paris: Nizet, 1979.

Liking, Werewere, Bomou Mamadou, and Binda Ngazolo. *Singue Mura: Considérant que la femme . . .* [Singue Mura: Considering that woman . . .]. Abidjan: Eyo-Ki-yi Editions, 1990.

Mbacke, Mame Seck. *Le Froid et le piment: nous travailleurs émigrés* [Cold pepper: We emigrant workers]. Dakar: NEA, 1975.

N'Diaye, Adja Ndèye Boury. *Collier de cheville* [The anklet]. Dakar: NEA, 1983.

Ndiaye, Marie. *En Famille* [In the family]. Paris: Editions de Minuit, 1990.

Nwapa, Flora. *Efuru*. London: Heinemann, 1966.

Rawiri, Ntyugwetondon A. *Elonga*. Paris: Silex, 1986.

———. *G'amèrakano au carrefour* [G'amèrakano at crossroads]. Paris: Silex, 1988.

Sadji, Abdoulaye. *Nini, Mulâtresse du Sénégal* [Nini, a Senegalese mulatto] In *Trois Ecrivains noirs* [Three black writers], 291–426. Paris: Présence Africaine, 1954.

Schwarz-Bart, Simone. *Pluie et vent sur Télumée Miracle*. Paris: Editions du Seuil, 1972.

Sembène, Ousmane. *God's Bits of Wood*. Translated by Francis Price. London: Heinemann, 1976. Originally published as *Les Bouts de bois de Dieu* (Paris: Le Livre Contemporain, 1960).

———. *L'Harmattan*. Tome I. Référendum. Paris: Présence Africaine, 1964.

Tadjo, Véronique. *La Chanson de la vie et autres histoires* [The song of life and other stories]. Paris: Hatier, Collection Monde Noir Jeunesse, 1989.

———. *Latérite*. Paris: Hatier, 1984.

———. *Lord of the Dance: An African Retelling*. New York: Lipp Jr. Books (Harper Collins Children's Books), 1989.

———. *Le Royaume aveugle* [The kingdom of the blind]. Paris: L'Harmattan, 1990.

Walker, Alice. *Possessing the Secret of Joy*. New York: Harcourt Brace Jovanovich, 1992.

Warner-Vieyra, Myriam. *Juletane*. Paris: Présence Africaine, 1982.

Yaoui, Angèle. *Aihui Anka*. Dakar: NEA, 1988.

———. *Lezou Marie ou les écueils de la vie* [Lezou Marie or the snares of life]. Paris: EDICEF, 1982.

Critical Sources

Adams, Anne. "To W/rite a New language: Werewere Liking's Adaptation of Ritual to the Novel." *Callaloo* 16, no. 1 (Winter 1993): 153–86.

Aidoo, Akosua. "Asante Queen Mothers in Government and Politics." In *The Black Woman Cross-Culturally*, edited by Filomina Chioma Steady, 65–77. Cambridge, Mass.: Schenkman Publishing, 1981.

Amuta, Chidi. *The Theory of African Literature*. London: Zed Press, 1989.

Bibliography

Andrade, Susan Z. "Rewriting History, Motherhood, and Rebellion: Naming an African Woman's Literary Tradition." *Research in African Literatures* 21, no. 1 (Spring 1990): 91–110.

Anzaldua, Gloria. *Borderlands/La Frontera: The New Mestiza*. San Francisco: Spinster/Aunt Lute, 1987.

Awe, Bolanle. "The Economic Role of Women in a Traditional African Society: The Yoruba Example." In *La Civilisation de la femme dans la tradition africaine*, 259–74. Paris: Présence Africaine, 1975.

Bâ, Mariama. "Fonction politique des littératures africaines écrites." *Ecriture française dans le monde* 3, no. 5 (1981): 3–7.

———. "Mariama Bâ, Winner of the First Noma Award for Publishing in Africa." Interview by Barbara Harrell-Bond. *African Publishing Record* 6 (1980): 209–14.

Bal, Mieke. *Narratology: Introduction to the Theory of Narrative*. Translated by Christine van Boheemen. Toronto: University of Toronto Press, 1985. Originally published as *De Theorie van vertellen en verhalen* (Muiderberg: Coutinho, 1980).

Barber, Karin. *I Could Speak Until Tomorrow: Oriki, Women, and the Past in a Yoruba Town*. Edinburgh: Edinburgh University Press, 1991.

Beaujour, Michel. *Miroirs d'encre: Rhétorique de l'autoportrait*. Paris: Editions du Seuil, 1980.

Berrian, Brenda F. "Bibliographies of Nine Anglophone Women Writers." *Research in African Literatures* 12 (1981): 214–36.

———. *Bibliography of Women Writers from the Caribbean*. Washington, D.C.: Three Continents Press, 1989.

———. "An Update: Bibliography of Twelve African Women Writers." *Research in African Literatures* 19, no. 2 (Summer 1988): 206–31.

Berrian, Brenda F., and Aart Broek. *Bibliography of African Women Writers and Journalists: Ancient Egypt–1984*. Washington, D.C.: Three Continents Press, 1985.

Beyala, Calixthe. "Un nouveau roman de Calixthe Beyala" [A new novel by Calixthe Beyala]. Interview by Assiatou Bah Diallo. *Amina* 223 (November 1988): 85.

Blackburn, Regina. "In Search of the Black Female Self: African-American Women's Autobiographies and Ethnicity." In *Women's Autobiography. Essays in Criticism*, edited by Estelle C. Jelinek, 133–48. Bloomington: Indiana University Press, 1980.

Blair, Dorothy. *African Literature in French*. London: Cambridge University Press, 1976.

———. *Senegalese Literature: A Critical History.* Boston: G. K. Hall, 1984.

Borgomano, Madeleine. *Voix et visages de femmes dans les livres écrits par des femmes en Afrique francophone.* Abidjan: CEDA, 1989.

Boserup. *Women's Role in Economic Development.* London: Allen and Unwinn, 1970.

Boyd, Jean. *The Caliph's Sister: Nana Asma'u, 1793–1865, Teacher, Poet and Islamic Leader.* London: F. Cass, 1989.

Brown, Lloyd W. *Women Writers in Black Africa.* Westport, Conn.: Greenwood Press, 1981.

Bruner, Charlotte H. "First Novels of Girlhood." *College Language Association Journal* 31, no. 3 (March 1988): 324–38.

———. *Unwinding Threads: Writing by Women In Africa.* London: Heinemann, 1983.

Bugul, Ken. "Ken Bugul ou l'écriture thérapeutique." Interview by Bernard Magnier. *Notre Librairie* 81 (1985): 151–55.

Campbell, Joseph. *The Hero with a Thousand Faces.* Princeton, N.J.: Princeton University Press, 1949.

Cazenave, Odile. "Marginalisation et identité des personnages dans la littérature négro-africaine des années 80: L'image du Métis." *Présence francophone* 38 (1991): 111–32.

Cham, Mbye Boubacar. "The Female Condition in Africa: A Literary Exploration by Mariama Bâ." *Current Bibliography on African Affairs* 17, no. 1 (1984–85): 29–51.

Chemain-Degrange, Arlette. "L'écriture de Calixthe Beyala: Provocation ou révolte génereuse." *Notre Librairie* 99 (October–December 1989): 162–63.

———. *Emancipation féminine et roman africain.* Dakar: Nouvelles Editions Africaines, 1980.

Chevrier, Jacques. *Littérature nègre.* Paris: Armand Colin, 1974.

Christian, Barbara. "The Race for Theory." *Feminist Studies* 14, no. 1 (Spring 1988): 67–79.

Cocks, Joan E. *The Oppositional Imagination: Feminism Critique and Political Theory.* London: Routledge, Chapman and Hall, 1989.

Cornevin, Robert. *Littérature d'Afrique noire de langue française.* Paris: PUF, 1976.

Culley, Margo. "Women's Vernacular Literature: Teaching the Mother-Tongue." In *Women's Personal Narratives: Essays in Criticism and Pedagogy,* edited by Leonore Hoffman and Margo Culley, 9–17. New York: Modern Language Association of America, 1985.

Dabla, Séwanou. *Nouvelles écritures africaines. Romanciers de la seconde génération.* Paris: L'Harmattan, 1986.

d'Almeida Adamon, Grâce. Introduction to *Guide juridique de la femme Béninoise* [Legal guide for Benin's women]. Cotonou: Imprimerie Minute, 1992.

d'Almeida, Irène Assiba. "The Concept of Choice in Mariama Bâ's Fiction." In *Ngambika: Studies of Women in African Literature,* edited by Carole Boyce Davies and Anne Adams Graves, 161–71. Trenton, N.J.: Africa World Press, 1986.

———. "Echoes of Orpheus in Werewere Liking's *Orphée-Dafric* and Wole Soyinka's *Season of Anomy.*" *Comparative Literature Studies* 31, no. 1 (1994): 52–71.

———. "Femme? Féministe? 'Misovire'? Les romancières africaines face au féminisme" [Woman? Feminist? 'Misovire'?" Francophone African women novelists' position vis-à-vis feminism." Forthcoming in *Notre Librairie* (Fall 1994).

———. "The Intertext: Werewere Liking's Tool for Transformation and Renewal." Forthcoming in *Beyond the Hexagon: Women Writing in French,* edited by Karen Gould, Mary Jean Green, and Micheline Rice-Maximin. Minneapolis: University of Minnesota Press.

———. "The Language of African Fiction: Reflections on Ngugi's Advocacy of an Afro-African Literature." *Présence africaine* 120 (1981): 83–92.

———. "The Making of an African Literary-Critical Tradition." Ph.D. diss., Emory University, 1987.

d'Almeida, Irène Assiba, and Sion Hamou. "L'écriture féminine en Afrique Noire Francophone: Le temps du miroir" [Francophone African women writers: The stage of the mirror]. *Etudes Littéraires* 24, no. 2 (Fall 1991): 41–50.

Davies, Carole B., and Anne A. Graves, eds. *Ngambika. Studies of Women in African Literature.* Trenton, N.J.: Africa World Press, 1986.

Davies, Carole B., Anne A. Graves, and Elaine Savory Fido, eds. *Out of the Kumbla: Caribbean Women and Literature.* Trenton, N.J.: Africa World Press, 1990.

Deniau, Xavier. *La Francophonie.* Paris: Presses Universitaires de France, 1983.

Derrida, Jacques. "Sending: On Representation." *Social Research* 49, no. 2 (1982): 294–326.

Diop, Abdoulaye-Bara. *La Société Wolof: Tradition et changement; Les systèmes d'inégalité et de domination.* Paris: Editions Karthala, 1981.

Doumbi-Fakoly. Review of *Tu t'appelleras Tanga,* by Calixthe Beyala. *Présence africaine* 148 (1988): 147–48.

Edmondson, Belinda. "Black Aesthetics, Feminist Aesthetics and the Problems of Oppositional Discourse." *Cultural Critique* 22 (Fall 1992): 75–98.

Ekoto, Grâce Etonde. "La femme et la libération de l'Afrique: Quelques figures culturelles." *Présence africaine* 140 (1986): 140–53.

Emecheta, Buchi. "Feminism with a Small 'f.' " In *Criticism and Ideology*, edited by Kirsten Holst Peterson, 173–85. Second Writers's Conference, Stockholm, 1986. Nordiska afrikainstituted, 1988.

Fall, Aminata Sow. "Aminata Sow Fall: L'écriture au féminin." Interview by Françoise Pfaff. *Notre Librairie* 81 (1985): 135–38.

——. "Entretiens avec Aminata Sow Fall." Interview by Sonia Lee, Dakar, 1987. *African Literature Association Bulletin* 14, no. 4 (Fall 1988): 23–26.

——. "An Interview with Senegalese Novelist Aminata Sow Fall." By Peter Hawkins. *French Studies Bulletin: A Quarterly Supplement* 22 (Spring 1987): 19–21.

Fanon, Frantz. *Black Skin, White Masks.* Translated by Charles Lam Markmann. New York: Grove Press, 1967. Originally published as *Peau noire, masques blancs* (Paris: Editions du Seuil, 1952).

Fuchs, Esther. *Israeli Mythogynies: Women in Contemporary Fiction.* Albany: State University of New York, 1987.

Gates, Henry Louis, Jr., ed. *Black Literature and Literary Theory.* New York: Methuen, 1984.

——, ed. *Reading Black, Reading Feminist: A Critical Anthology.* New York: Penguin, 1990.

——. *The Signifying Monkey: A Theory of Afro-American Literary Criticism.* New York: Oxford University Press, 1988.

Genette, Gérard. *Figures III.* Paris: Seuil, 1972.

——. *Nouveau Discours du récit.* Paris: Seuil, 1983.

Grewal, Shabnam Grewal, Jackie Kay, Liliane Landor, Gail Lewis, and Pratibha Parmar, eds. *Charting the Journey: Writings by Black and Third World Women.* London: Sheba Feminist Publishers, 1988.

Gunn, Janet Varer. *Autobiography: Toward a Poetics of Experience.* Philadelphia: University of Pennsylvania Press, 1982.

Guyonneau, Christine H. "Francophone Women Writers from Sub-Saharan Africa." *Callaloo* 24 (1985): 453–78.

Hale, Sondra. "Sudanese Women and Revolutionary Parties: The Wing of the Patriarch." *Middle East Report* (January–February 1986): 25–30.

Haley, Alex . *Roots: The Saga of an American Family.* New York: Dell, 1976.

Harrell-Bond, Barbara. "Africa Asserts Its Identity. Part II: Transcending Cultural Boundaries through Fiction." *American Universities Field Staff Report* 10 (1981): 1–5.

Hewitt, Leah D. *Auto-bio-graph-ical Tight-ropes.* Lincoln: University of Nebraska Press, 1990.

Hill-Lubin, Mildred A. "The Grandmother in African and African American Literature: A Survivor of the African Extended Family." In *Ngambika. Studies of Women in African Literature*, edited by Carole B. Davies and Anne A. Graves, 257–70. Trenton, N.J.: Africa World Press, 1986.

hooks, bell. *Feminist Theory from Margin to Center*. Boston: South End Press, 1984.

Houédanou, Lucien. "Islam et Société dans la littérature féminine du Sénégal." *Nouvelles du sud* 7 (1987): 159–70.

Houéto, Colette. "La Femme, source de vie dans l'Afrique traditionnelle" [The woman, source of life in traditional Africa]. In *La Civilisation de la femme dans la tradition africaine*. Conference proceedings, Abidjan, Ivory Coast, July 3–8, 1972. Présence Africaine, 1975.

Hudson-Weems, Cleonora. "Cultural and Agenda Conflicts in Academia: Critical Issues for Africana Women's Studies." *Western Journal of Black Studies* 13, no. 4 (1989): 185–89.

Izevbaye, Dan. "Soyinka's Black Orpheus." In *Neo-African Literature and Culture*, edited by Bernth Lindfors and Ulla Schild. Mainz: Heyman, 1976.

Jahn, Janheinz, Ulla Schild, and Almut Nordmann. *Who's Who in African Literature: Biographies, Works, Commentaries*. Tubingen: Horst Erdmann, 1972.

JanMohammed, Abdul R. "Worldliness-Without-World, Homeless-As-Home: Toward a Definition of the Specular Border Intellectual." In *Edward Said: A Critical Reader*, edited by Michael Sprinker, 96–120. Cambridge, Mass.: Blackwell, 1992.

Jelinek, Estelle C., ed. *Women's Autobiography*. Bloomington: Indiana University Press, 1980.

Johnson, John, trans. *The Epic of Son-jara*. Bloomington: Indiana University Press, 1986.

Johnson-Odim, Cheryl. "Common Themes, Different Contexts: Third World Women and Feminism." In *Third World Women and the Politics of Feminism*, edited by Chandra Talpade Mohanty, Ann Russo, and Lourdes Torres, 314–27. Bloomington: Indiana University Press, 1991.

Julien, Eileen. *African Novels and the Question of Orality*. Bloomington: Indiana University Press, 1992.

Ka, Aminata Maïga. "L'écriture qui libère." In *Forces Littéraires d'Afrique: Points de repères et témoignages*, edited by Jean-Pierre Jacquemin and Monkassa-Bitumba, 123–26. Bruxelles: De boeck-Wesmael s.a., 1987.

———. "Ramatoulaye, Aissatou, Mireille, et . . . Mariama Bâ." *Notre Librairie* 81 (1985): 129–34.

Kane, Mohamadou. *Roman africain et tradition*. Dakar: Nouvelles Editions Africaines, 1982.

Keller, Bonnie, and Edna G. Bay. "African Women and Problems of Modernization." In *African Society, Culture and Politics: An Introduction*, edited by

C. C. Mojeku, V. C. Uchendu, and L. F. Van Hoey, 215–37. Washington, D.C.: University Press of America, 1977.

Kermode, Frank. *The Sense of an Ending: Studies in the Theory of Fiction*. London: Oxford University Press, 1966.

Kesteloot, Lilyan. *Les Ecrivains noirs de langue française: naissance d'une littérature*. Bruxelles: Institut Solvay, 1963.

Kimoni, Iyay. *Destin de la littérature négro-africaine ou problématique d'une culture*. Sherbrooke, Quebec: Editions Naaman, 1975.

Kom, Ambroise. *Dictionnaire des oeuvres littéraires négro-africaines de langue française; des origines à nos jours*. Sherbrooke, Quebec: Editions Naaman, Paris: Agence de Coopération Culturelle et Technique, 1983.

Kondo, Dorinne K. *Crafting Selves: Power, Gender and Discourses of Identity in a Japanese Workplace*. Chicago: Chicago University Press, 1990.

Kristeva, Julia. *Desire in Language. A Semiotic Approach to Literature and Art*. Edited by Leon S. Roudiez and translated by Thomas Gora, Alice Jardine, and Leon S. Roudier. New York: Columbia University Press, 1980.

Lafont, Robert, and Françoise Gardès-Madray. *Introduction à l'analyse textuelle*. Paris: Larousse, 1976.

Lebeuf, Annie M. D. "The Role of Women in the Political Organization of African Societies." In *Women of Tropical Africa*, translated by H. M. Right, 93–119. London: Routledge and Kegan Paul, 1963. Originally published as *Femmes d'Afrique noire*, edited by Denise Paulme. Paris: Mouton, 1960.

Lee, Sonia. "L'image de la femme dans le roman francophone de l'Afrique occidentale." Ph.D. diss., University of Massachusetts, 1974.

Léger, Jean-Marc Léger. *La Francophonie: grand dessein, grande ambiguïté*. Lasalle, Quebec: Editions Hurtubise HMM, 1987.

Lejeune, Philippe. *Je est un autre: L'autobiographie de la littérature aux médias*. Paris: Seuil, 1980.

———. *Le Pacte autobiographique*. Paris: Seuil, 1975. Selected parts in *On Autobiography*, translated by Katherine Leary with a foreword by Paul John Eakin. Minneapolis: University of Minnesota Press, 1989.

Liking, Werewere. "A la rencontre de . . . Werewere Liking." Interview by Bernard Magnier. *Notre Librairie* 79 (1985): 17–21.

———. "La femme par qui le scandale arrive." Interview by Sennen Andriamirado. *Jeune Afrique* 1172 (22 June 1983): 68–70.

———. *Marionnettes du Mali* [Puppets of Mali]. Dakar/Paris: NEA-Arhis, 1987.

———. *Statues colons* [Statues of colonialists]. Dakar/Paris: NEA-Arhis, 1987.

———. *La Vision de Kaydara d'Hamadou Hampaté Bâ* [The vision of Hamadou Hampaté Bâ's *Kaydara*]. Dakar: NEA, 1984.

————. "Le 'vivre vrai' de Werewere Liking." Interview by Christine Pillot. *Notre Librairie* (July–August 1990): 54–58.

————. "Werewere Liking: Créatrice, prolifique et novatrice." Interview by David Nadchi Tagne. *Notre Librairie* 99 (October–December 1989): 194–96.

Lionnet, Françoise. *Autobiographical Voices: Race, Gender, Self-portraiture.* Ithaca, N.Y.: Cornell University Press, 1989.

Lippert, Anne. "The Changing Role of Women as Viewed in the Literature of English Speaking and French Speaking West Africa." Ph.D. diss., Indiana University, 1971.

Lorde, Audre. *Sister Outsider.* Trumansburg, New York: Crossing Press, 1984.

Madubuike, Ihechukwu. *The Senegalese Novel: A Sociological Study of the Impact of the Politics of Assimilation.* Washington, D.C.: Three Continents Press, 1983.

Makouta Mboukou, Jean-Pierre. *Introduction à la littérature noire.* Yaoundé: CLE, 1970.

May, Georges. *L'Autobiographie.* Paris: Presses Universitaires de France, 1979.

Mbiti, John S. *African Religions and Philosophy.* Garden City, N.Y.: Anchor Books, Doubleday, 1970.

Mernissi, Fatim a. *Sexe, idéologie, Islam.* Condé-sur-Noireau: Tierce, 1983.

Midiohouan, Guy Ossito. *L'Idéologie dans la littérature négro-africaine d'expression française.* Paris: L'Harmattan, 1986.

Miller, Christopher. *Theories of Africans: Francophone Literature and Anthropology in Africa.* Chicago: University of Chicago Press, 1990.

Miller, Nancy K., ed. *The Poetics of Gender.* New York: Columbia University Press, 1986.

Mills, Sara. "Authentic Realism." In *Feminist Readings/ Feminists Reading,* edited by Sara Mills, Lynne Pearce, Sue Spaull, and Elaine Millard. London: Harvester Wheatsheaf, 1989.

Minh-ha, Trinh. *Woman, Native, Other: Writing Postcoloniality and Feminism.* Bloomington: Indiana University Press, 1989.

Mohanty, Chandra Talpade, Ann Russo, and Lourdes Torres, eds. *Third World Women and the Politics of Feminism.* Bloomington: Indiana University Press, 1991.

Mortimer, Mildred. *Journeys through the French African Novel.* Portsmouth, N.H.: Heinemann, 1990.

Mudimbe, Valentin. *The Invention of Africa.* Bloomington: Indiana University Press, 1988.

Mudimbe-Boyi, Elisabeth. "The Poetics of Exile and Errancy: Ken Bugul's *Le Baobab fou* and Simone Schwarz-Bart's *Ti Jean l'horizon.*" *Yale French Stud-*

ies: Post/Colonial Conditions: Exiles, Migrations, and Nomadisms 82, no. 2 (1993): 196–212.

Mwayila, Tshiyembe, ed. *Francophonie et géopolitique africaine.* Epinay-sous-Sénart: Editions OKEM, 1987.

N'Diaye, Catherine. *Gens de sable.* Paris: POL, 1984.

Ngara, Emmanuel. *Art and Ideology in the Novel.* London: Heinemann, 1985.

———. *Stylistic Criticism and the African Novel.* London: Heinemann, 1982.

Ngcobo, Lauretta. "African Motherhood—Myth and Reality." In *Criticism and Ideology. Second African Writers Conference: Stockholm* 1986, edited by Kirsten Holst Petersen, 141–54. Stockholm: Nordiska afrikainstituted, 1988.

———. "The African Woman Writer." In *A Double Colonization: Colonial and Post-Colonial Women's Writing,* edited by Kirsten Holst Petersen and Anna Rutherford. Mundelstrup, Denmark: Dangaroo Press, 1986.

Ngugi wa Thiong'o. *Decolonizing the Mind: The Politics of Language in African Literature.* London: James Currey; Portsmouth N.H.: Heinemann, 1989.

———. *Writers in Politics.* London: Heinemann, 1981.

Nicholson, Linda J., ed. *Feminism/Postmodernism.* London: Routledge, 1990.

Nkashama, Pius Ngandu. *Comprendre la Littérature africaine écrite.* Issy-les-Moulineaux: Edition Saint-Paul, 1979.

Nnaemeka, Obioma. "Mariama Bâ: Parallels, Convergence, and Interior Space." *Feminist Issues* 10, no. 1 (Spring 1990): 13–35.

Obbo, Christine. *African Women: Their Struggle for Economic Independence.* London: Zed Press, 1980.

Obiechina, Emmanuel. *Culture, Tradition, and Society in the West African Novel.* Cambridge: Cambridge University Press, 1975.

Ogundipe-Leslie, Molara. "African Literature, Feminism and Social Change." Interview by Irène Assiba d'Almeida. Forthcoming in *Matatu,* 1995.

———. "African Women, Culture and Another Development." *Journal of African Marxists* 5 (February 1984): 89, 35–36.

———. "The Female Writer and Her Commitment." In *Women in African Literature Today,* edited by Eldred D. Jones, Eustace Palmer, and Marjorie Jones, 5–13. London: James Currey, 1987.

———. "Not Spinning on the Axis of Maleness." In *Sisterhood is Global. The International Women's Movement Anthology,* edited by Robin Morgan, 498–504. New York: Anchor Books, Doubleday, 1984.

Ogunyemi, Chikwenye O. "Womanism: The Dynamics of Contemporary Black Female Novel in English." *Signs: Journal of Women in Culture and Society* 11, no. 1 (1985): 63–79.

Okonjo, Kamene. "Women's Political Participation in Nigeria." In *The Black Woman Cross-Culturally*, edited by Filomina Chioma Steady, 79–106. Cambridge, Mass: Schenkman Publishing, 1981.

Olney, James. *Autobiography: Essays Theoretical and Critical*. Princeton, N.J.: Princeton University Press, 1980.

Oyono, Ferdinand. *Houseboy*. Translated by John Reed. London: Heinemann, 1966. Originally published as *Une Vie de boy* (Paris: Juillard, 1960).

Parrinder, Geoffrey. *African Mythology*. 1967. Reprint. New York: Peter Bedrick Books, 1987.

Pascoe, Peggy. "Race, Gender, and Intercultural Relations: The Case of Interracial Marriage." *Frontiers: A Journal of Women's Studies* 12, no. 1 (1991): 5–18.

Rich, Adrienne. "Cartographies of Silence." In *The Dream of a Common Language*, 16–20. New York: W. W. Norton, 1978.

———. *Of Woman Born: Motherhood as Experience and Institution*. 1976. Reprint (10th anniversary ed.). New York: W. W. Norton, 1986.

Rimmon-Kenan, Shlomith. *Narrative Fiction: Contemporary Poetics*. London: Methuen, 1983.

Rosaldo, Michelle Zimbelist. "Women, Culture and Society: A Theoretical Overview." In *Women, Culture and Society*, edited by Michelle Zimbelist Rosaldo and Louise Lamphere, 17–42. Stanford, Calif.: Stanford University Press, 1976.

Savané, Marie Angélique. "Appel aux femmes du Sénégal." *Fippu, Journal de Yewwu Yewwi pour la libération des femmes* 1 (July 1987): 6–7.

———. "Elegance Amid the Phallocracy," translated by Anne-Christine d'Adesky. In *Sisterhood Is Global: The International Women's Movement Anthology*, edited by Robin Morgan, 593–99. Garden City, N.Y.: Anchor Books, 1984.

Schipper, Mineke. "Women and Literature in Africa." In *Unheard Words: Women and Literature in Africa, the Arab World, Asia the Caribbean and Latin America*, edited by Mineke Schipper, 22–58. London: Allison and Busby, 1984.

Senghor, Léopold Sédar. *Anthologie de la nouvelle poésie nègre et Malgache de langue française*. 1948; Paris: PUF, 1972.

Smith, Sidonie. *A Poetics of Women's Autobiography: Marginality and the Fictions of Self-Representation*. Bloomington: Indiana University Press, 1987.

Soyinka, Wole. "The Critic and Society: Barthes, Leftocracy and Other Mythologies." In *Black Literature and Literary Theory*, edited by Henry Louis Gates, Jr., 27–57. London: Methuen, 1984.

Spellman, Elizabeth V. *Inessential Woman: Problems of Exclusion in Feminist Thought.* Boston: Beacon Press, 1988.

Spivak, Gayatri C. "Can the Subaltern Speak?" In *Marxism and the Interpretation of Culture,* edited by Cary Nelson and Lawrence Grossberg, 271–313. Urbana: University of Illinois Press.

Stanton, Domna C., and Jeanine Parisier Plottel, eds. *The Female Autograph.* New York: New York Literary Forum, 1984.

Steady, Filomina Chioma. "African Feminism: A Worldview Perspective." In *Women in Africa and the Diaspora,* edited by Rosalyn Terborg-Penn, Sharon Harley, and Andrea Benton Rushing, 3–24. Washington, D.C.: Howard University Press, 1987.

Steady, Filomina Chioma, ed. *The Black Woman Cross-Culturally.* Cambridge, Mass.: Schenkman Publishing, 1981.

Stringer, Susan. "Innovation in Ken Bugul's *Le Baobab fou.*" *Cincinnati Romance Review* 10 (1991): 200–207.

Tesfagiorgis, Freida High W. "Afrofemcentrism and Its Fruition in the Art of Elizabeth Catlett and Faith Ringgold." In *The Expanding Discourse: Feminism and Art History,* edited by Norma Broude and Mary D. Garrard, 475–85. New York: IconEditions/HarperCollins, 1992. First published in *Sage: A Scholarly Journal on Black Women* 4, no. 1 (Spring 1987): 25–29.

Tétu, Michel. *La Francophonie: Histoire, problématique, perspectives.* Montréal: Guérin littérature, 1987.

Thiam, Awa. *La Parole aux négresses.* Paris: Denoel, 1978. Translated by Dorothy Blair as *Speak Out, Black Sisters: Feminism and Oppression in Black Africa.* London: Pluto Press, 1986.

Traoré, Sékou. *Questions Africaines: francophonie, langues africaines, prix littéraires, O.U.A.* Paris: L'Harmattan, 1989.

Wade-Gayles, Gloria. "The Truths of Our Mothers' Lives: Mother-Daughter Relationships in Black Women's Fiction." *Sage: A Scholarly Journal on Black Women* 1, no. 2 (Fall 1984): 8–12.

Wali, Obiajuma. "The Dead End of African Literature?" *Transitions* 10 (1963): 13–15.

Walker, Alice. *In Search of our Mother's Gardens: Womanist Prose.* San Diego, New York, London: Harcourt Brace Jovanovich, 1984.

———. *Warrior Marks: Female Mutilation and the Sexual Blinding of Women.* New York, San Diego, London: Harcourt Brace Jovanovich, 1993.

Wallace, Karen Smyley. "Women and Identity: A Black Francophone Female Perspective." *Sage: A Scholarly Journal on Black Women* 2, no. 1 (Spring 1985): 19–23.

Bibliography

Warhol, Robin R., and Diane Price Herndl, eds. *Feminisms: An Anthology of Literary Theory and Criticism.* New Brunswick, N.J.: Rutgers University Press, 1991.

Wilertyh, Evelyne. *Visages de la littérature féminine.* Liège: Pierre Mardaga, 1987.

Williams, Sherley Anne. "Some Implications of Womanist Theory" in *Reading Black, Reading Feminist: A Critical Anthology,* edited by Henry Louis Gates Jr., 68–75. New York: Penguin, 1990.

INDEX

Abortion: right to, 17; illegal, 159

Act: of telling, 72–74, 77–79; of writing, as appropriation, 9, 33, 34, 45, 173

Action: as part of speech, 3, 168; to take power, 6, 166; in feminist agenda, 16–19, 183n28; in traditional code of conduct, 132

Adulthood: passage into, 74–76, 79

Africa: as woman/mother, 8, 91, 116; traditional, 12, 28, 123, 124; invention of, 22; as diverse, 23, 125; names given in, 45; colonial, 55–57; and freedom of speech, 56; as womb, 91; contemporary, 124, 125, 144, 174; modern, 124, 140; problems in, 138; writers living in or out of, 170; demystified, 190n10

African humanism, 132, 134, 194n5

African literature: beginnings of, 3, 180n9; specificity of, 27; role of women in, 27, 30; political function of, 28; exclusion of women from, 30. *See also* Bâ, Mariama

African traditions: against girls' education, 5; and feminist aspirations, 13; and the West, 128; positive value of, 138, 174

Africans: women writers' awareness of being, ix; discrimination against, 57; colonial treatment of, 64, 105

African women: new literature by, ix, 181n10; self-definition of, x; void of literary expression form, 2; speaking up, 4; portrayal of, 4, 22; self-representation of, 8; and work, 11; represented by others, 22, 31; condition of, 29; battles with tradition, 43; new class of, 90; new generation of, 90

Agency, 103, 175

Al Saadawi: on women's silence, 1–2

Anzaldua, Gloria: on one's place within borders, 175, 176, 198n6

Art: literature as, 8–11, 23; for art's sake, 11, 29; in traditional Africa, 28, 123, 179n4; as mixture of form and content, 29; as transformation of experience, 71; role of, in cultural revival, 125

Autobiography: defined in African context, 25, 171; as *dé/couverte*, 33, 70; problematic of, 34–35, 186–187n2, 187n4, 189n23; function of, 46, 54, 62, 69; as history, 69, 189n21; as genre, 71, 124